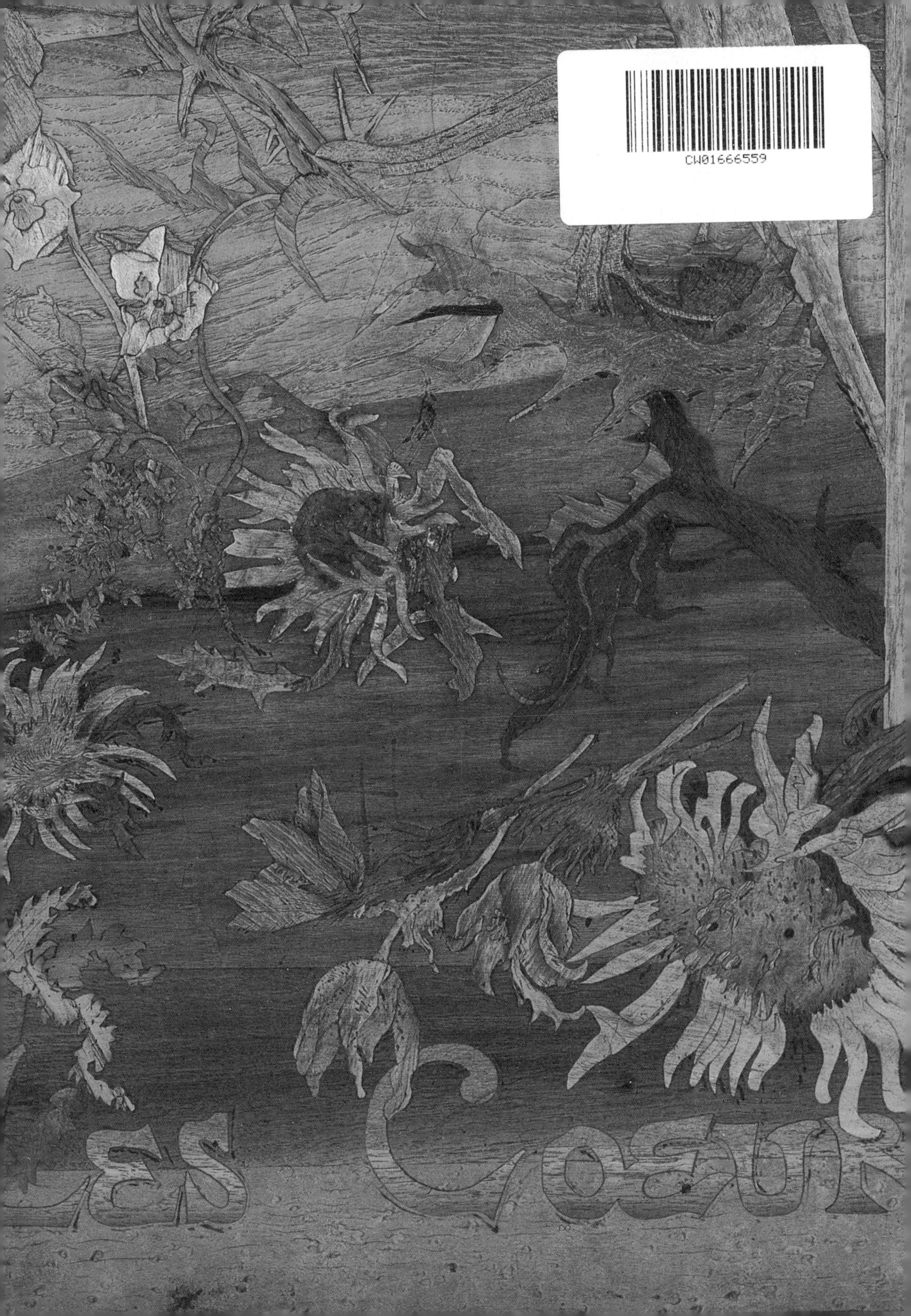

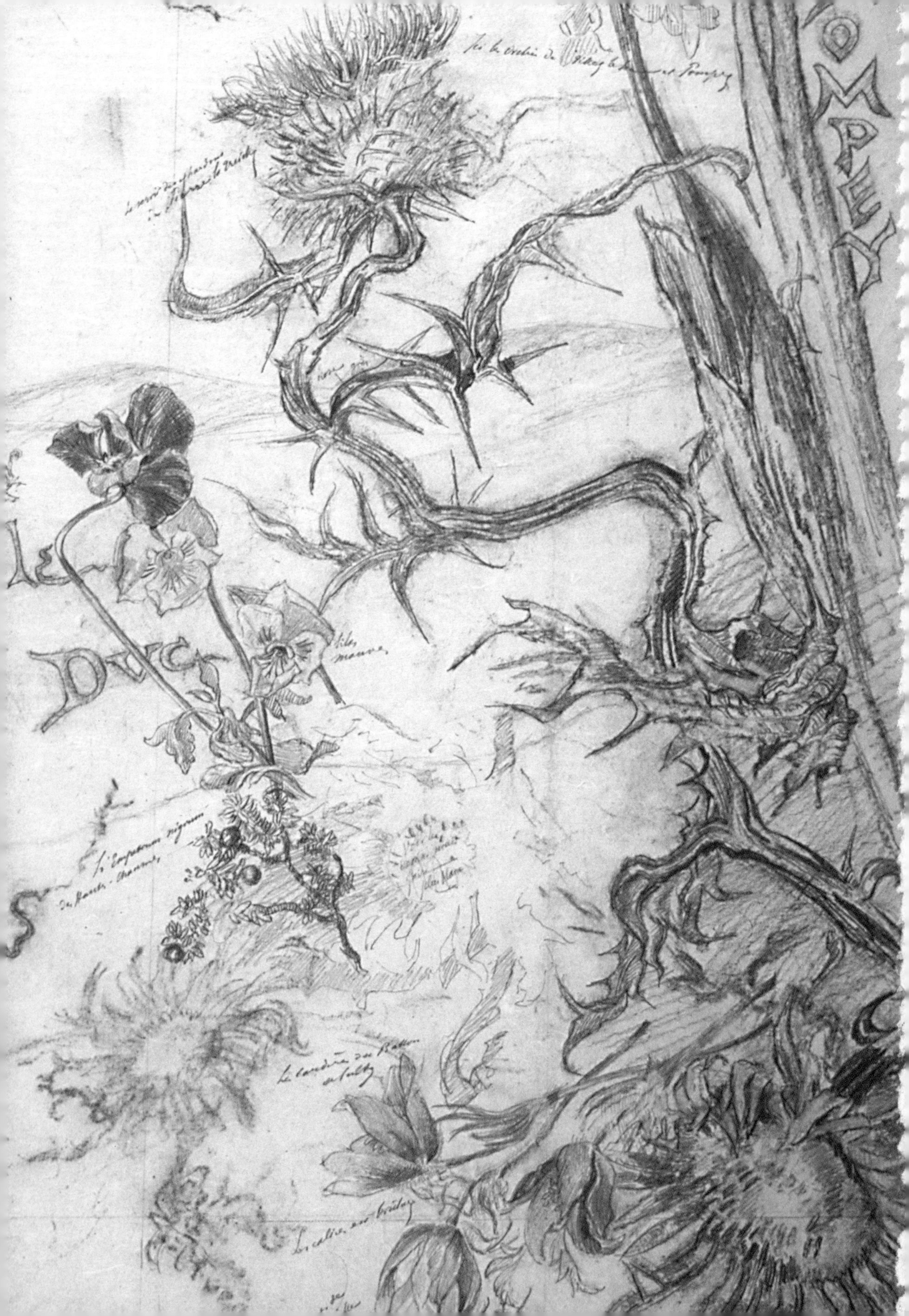

Le
Duc

HERMITAGE

ЭРМИТАЖ

HERMITAGE AMSTERDAM

Art Nouveau

DURING THE REIGN OF THE LAST TSARS

HERMITAGE AMSTERDAM

Art Nouveau

during the Reign of the Last Tsars

Lund Humphries
In association with the
Hermitage Amsterdam

HERMITAGE AMSTERDAM

The exhibition was made possible by:

FOUNDER: BankGiroLoterij

MAIN SPONSORS: FORTIS PHILIPS

SPONSORS: KPMG FUGRO Heineken International

INSURANCE: AON

SUBSIDISING BODIES:
State of the Netherlands
Province of North Holland
City of Amsterdam

WITH THANKS TO THE:
W.E. Jansen Fund

PARTNER OF
THE HERMITAGE FOR CHILDREN: VSBfonds

PARTNERS:

Internet / IBM Nederland
Media partner / Avro Kunst
Hotel partner / Eden Rembrandt Square Hotel
Travel partner / Voyage & Culture, Amsterdam
Courses / Vrije Academie voor
Kunsthistorisch Onderwijs, Amsterdam

I amsterdam.

CONTENTS

HERMITAGE AMSTERDAM

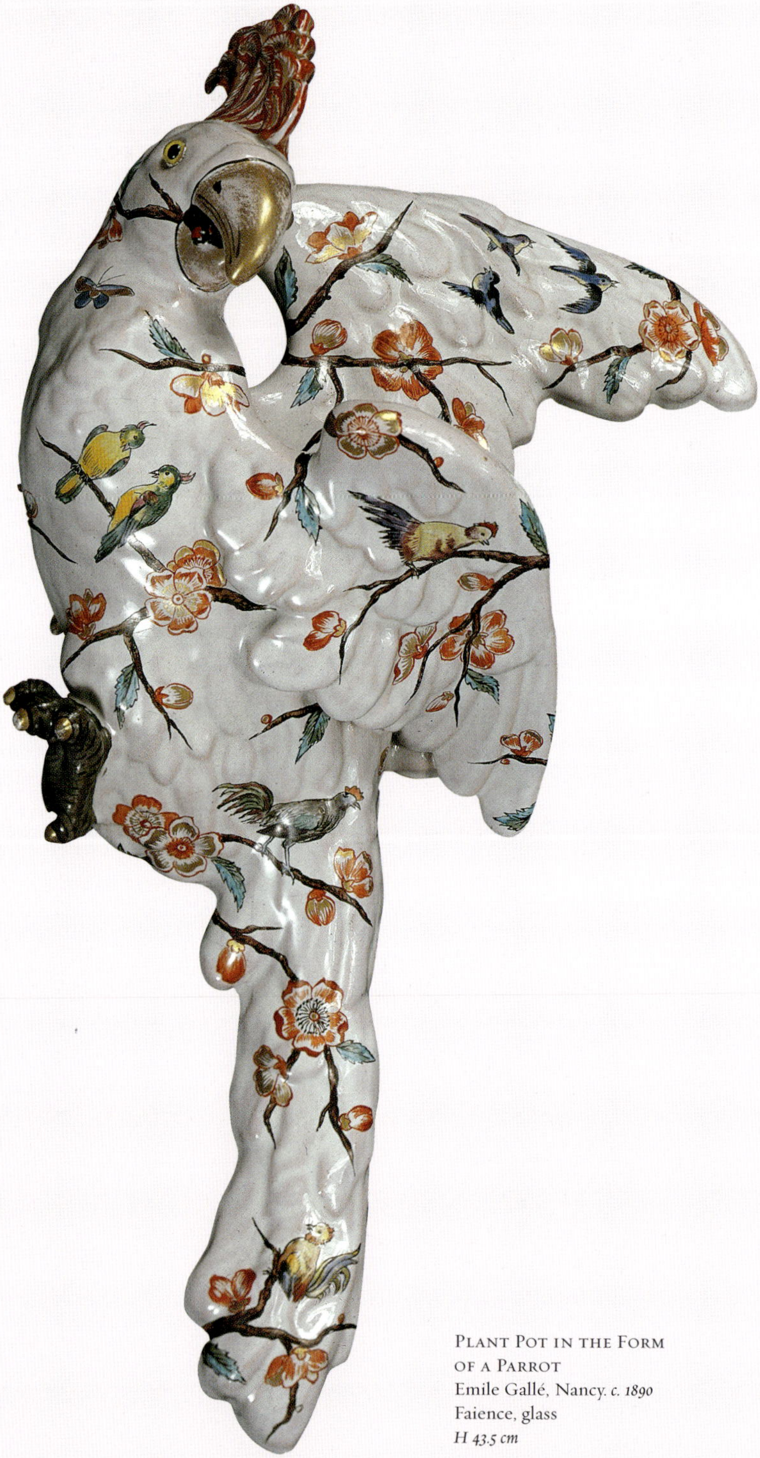

Plant Pot in the Form of a Parrot
Emile Gallé, Nancy. *c. 1890*
Faience, glass
H 43.5 cm

cat. no. 49

Orchids and Parrots

In Russia, Art Nouveau was the predecessor and prophet of revolution. Both social and artistic. It embodied refined beauty, the enthusiasm of the artist and a melancholy sense of the fragility of a beauty touched by corruption. Knowing the country's later history, we experience no difficulty reading this message within those monuments of Russian art and masterpieces by European masters of the 'modern' style in which our collection is so rich.

Art Nouveau did not truly fit into the imposing ceremony that unfolded within the imperial palaces. Yet it was very much suited to everyday life as lived by Russia's last rulers and the aristocracy. Works in Art Nouveau style fitted naturally into their comfortable private apartments. Whimsically curving lines were used for interiors and furnishings, charming visitors to country mansions and residences.

By contrast, to the inhabitants of France of the Third Republic, the style was a superb example of self-expression and pride, which was a determining factor when such objects were being selected as diplomatic gifts. The end of the 19th century was a time of rapid progress in Russo-French relations and diplomacy contributed to the concentration of masterpieces of European Art Nouveau in today's Hermitage. The marquetry table, *Flore de Lorraine.* Unique vases with orchids by Emile Gallé. The Sèvres sculptures *Dance with Scarves.* All set in the context of many other beautiful and fascinating pieces that have a story to tell of both art and politics.

Attracted by the new style, Russian artists went on to create their own embodiment of it. That version of Art Nouveau which grew out of the traditions of Fabergé was to become an international phenomenon. Russian furniture in the 'Modern' style was to be a unique expression of national tradition and mood.

One key artistic institution of the day was the Baron Stieglitz School of Technical Drawing. It trained Russian artists and designers, introducing them to the very latest achievements in the contemporary European Art Nouveau style. Gradually the School's study collection became a true museum collection. Thus paralleling the fate of Art Nouveau itself: so very recently it seemed to be the recent past, not history, and it is but a relatively short time since it assumed the respectability of a subject worthy of presentation in a museum context.

Today we have little difficulty in gaining a sense of the life that stands behind these objects from pre-war, pre-revolutionary Russia and Europe. The dresses of Charles Worth and the parrot of Emile Gallé speak to us directly, without the need for interpretation by art historian intermediaries.

Prof. dr. Mikhail B. Piotrovsky

Director, State Hermitage Museum, St Petersburg
President, Stichting Hermitage aan de Amstel

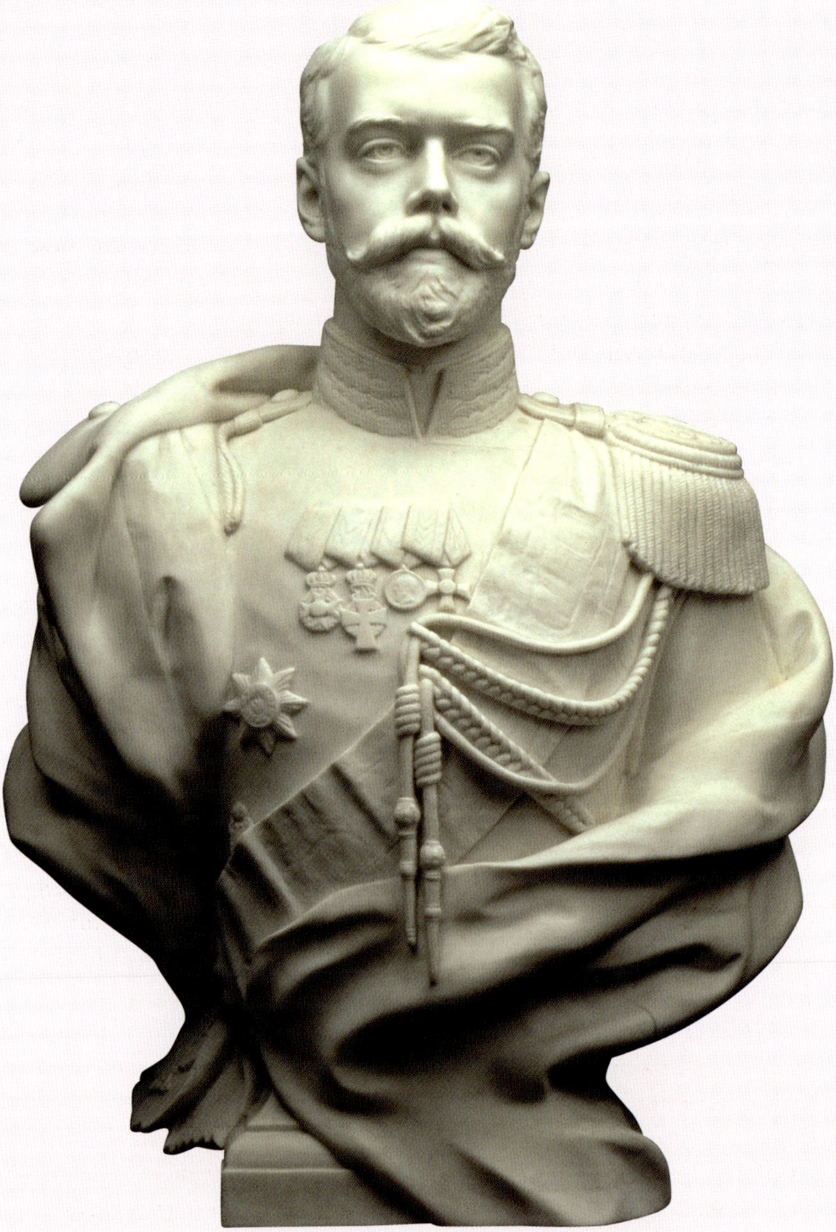

Bust Portrait of Emperor Nicholas II
Léopold Bernhard Bernstamm
(Léopold-Bernhard Leibber),
Sèvres Porcelain Manufactory, Paris. *1897*
Biscuit porcelain
H 46 cm

cat. no. 94

A new art

The exhibition *Art Nouveau under the last Tsars,* a joint presentation by the Hermitage Amsterdam and its parent museum in St Petersburg, displays the new kind of applied art which flourished at the end of the 19th century and the beginning of the 20th century. Art Nouveau was the name given to the French version of this 'new art', which was also known as *Jugendstil* in Germany and the *Wiener Sezession in* Vienna. All these forms of the new art derived from the need felt by a number of artists and architects to reassert the place of the crafts in industrial art and architecture.

The English Arts and Crafts movement played a significant role in this respect. The ideas of individuals such as William Morris (1834-1896) inspired new, clear forms of decoration and ornamentation in the applied arts and architecture, initially inspired by nature. The movement had a great influence on modern applied art, including Art Nouveau, throughout Europe. Art Nouveau was also based to a significant extent on natural forms, while influences from Persian, Japanese, Chinese and even ancient Egyptian art played a role as well.

Many Art Nouveau items in the Hermitage originally come from the region of Lorraine. These objects were presented to the Russian Tsars as diplomatic gifts by the French government, in the wake of the Franco-Prussian War of 1870-1871. After the war, a large area of Lorraine had been ceded to the Prussians, to the displeasure of the region's inhabitants. Feeling isolated, France looked around for a strong ally and found one in powerful Russia. In the years that followed the French government showered the Tsars with valuble gifts, made up of the finest examples of French applied art, made by the best artists, in the hypermodern Art Nouveau style. Currently on display in Amsterdam are a number of porcelain vases by the famous Sèvres porcelain factory, a great deal of glassware by Émile Gallé and the Daum brothers, a majestic table incorporating symbolism relating to the Lorraine and a book containing more than eighty drawings by artists of the region.

Russia also had its own Art Nouveau, or modern, style. Although this never became an official palace style, important firms such as the jeweller's house of Fabergé and the Meltzer furniture factory produced magnificent objects for the tsars. The exhibition also includes some of these pieces, many of which are little known in Western Europe.

My thanks go to Tamara Rappe, head of the Department of Western European Applied Art, and her colleagues in the Western European and Russian Departments at the Hermitage in St Petersburg. I also wish to thank Frans Leidelmeijer who contributed immensely to the realisation of this exhibition and catalogue. Finally I also whish to thank the Hermitage Amsterdam's regular sponsors, who have, once again, made a splendid exhibition possible.

Ernst W. Veen
Director, Hermitage Amsterdam

HERMITAGE AMSTERDAM

'Emile Gallé et les ouvriers et collaborateurs ont enfermé ce page dans la table offerte par la Lorraine au Peuple Russe, et qu'ils ont confectionnée dans un sentiment de fraternité et de patriotique espérance; ils espèrent que leur ouvrage de bois et de bronze sera moins durable que l'amitié et la grandeur des deux Peuples, la Russie et la France'

Emile Gallé and his workers and colleagues have enclosed this page in the table presented by Lorraine to the Russian People and which they have created in a sentiment of fraternity and patriotic hope; they hope that their work in wood and bronze shall be less long-lived than the friendship and greatness of the two Peoples, Russia and France.

Text by Émile Gallé on a sheet of paper found in the table Flore de Lorraine, cat 153
Nancy, 1893

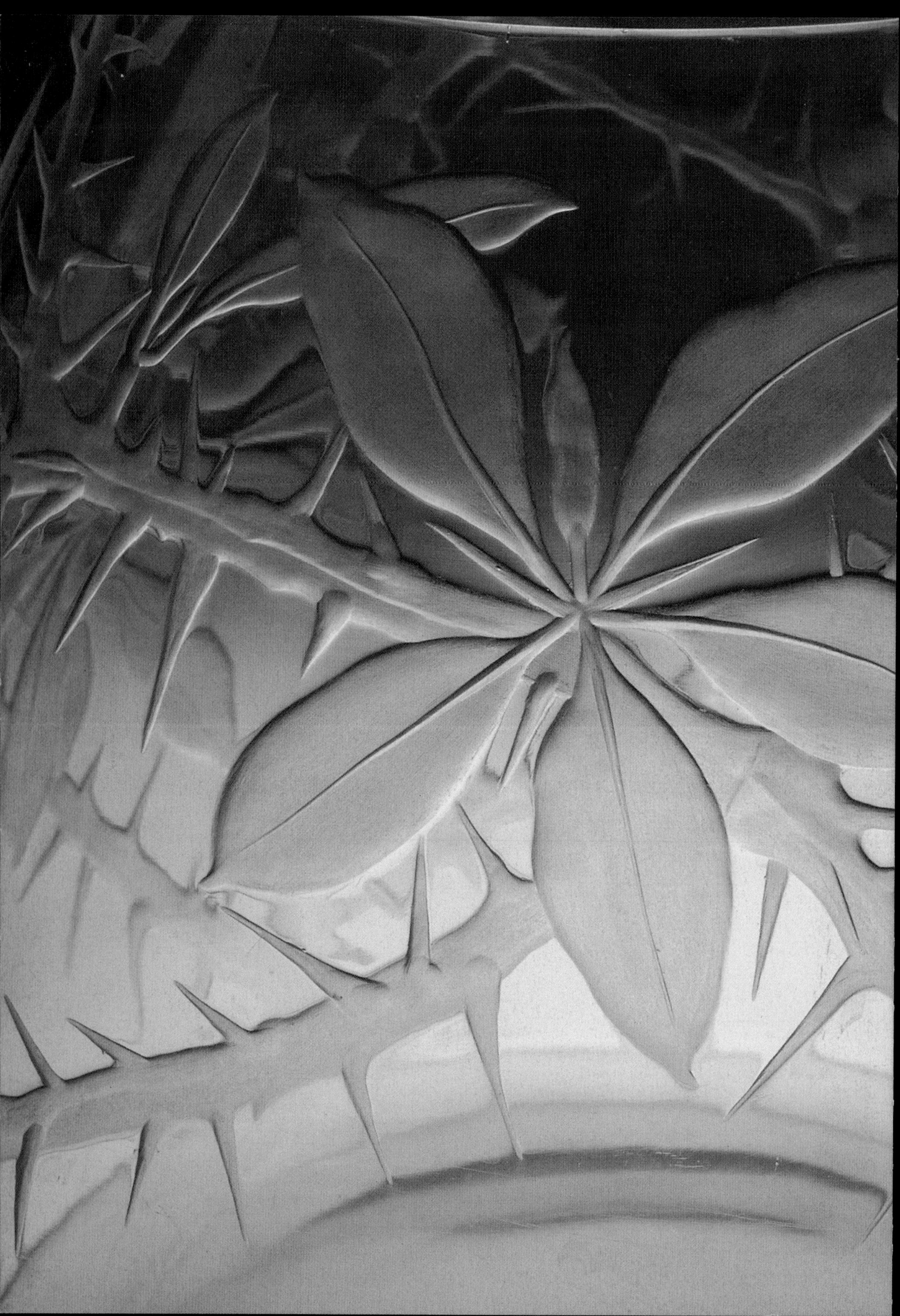

Frans Leidelmeijer

Art nouveau, a new style for a new time

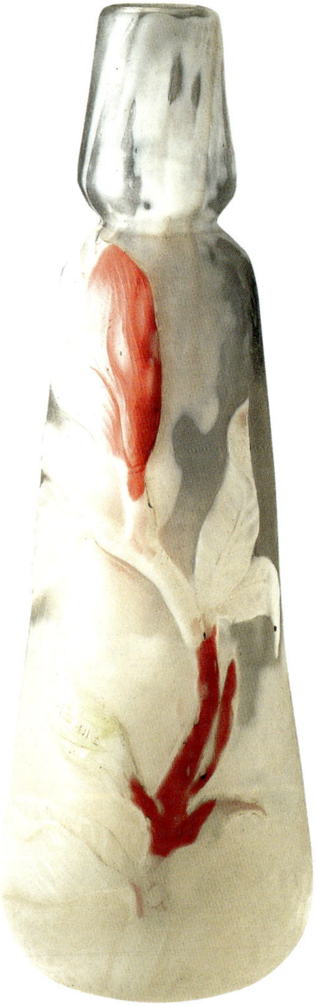

(previous page)
CAT. NO. 83
DETAIL OF EUPHORBIA VASE
Craftsman Grigory Omorokov, Imperial Porcelain and Glass Manufactory, St Petersburg.
Design by Rudolph Wilde. *1908*
Crystal

(left) CAT. NO. 38
VASE WITH MAGNOLIAS
Emile Gallé, Nancy. *c. 1900*
Three-layer glass with intarsia
H 27.3 cm

From 1890 onwards a new style appeared in architecture and the applied arts in Europe and North America. In international circles the French term *Art Nouveau* was used to designate this style, although it also became known by the German name *Jugendstil*. In Austria the new style was called the *Wiener Sezession* ('Viennese Secession'), in Spain *Modernismo,* in Italy *Stile Liberty,* in Russia *Stil Moderne* and in the Netherlands *Nieuwe Kunst.*

Despite these diverse names and the varying manifestations of Art Nouveau in different countries, there are a number of common factors: the role played by the natural world and major historical styles as sources of inspiration, the integration of folk art, symbolism and a fascination for non-Western cultures, most notably those of Japan, China, Persia and, in the Netherlands, Indonesia. Another characteristic of Art Nouveau is the use of forms and ornaments that are often stylised and distorted.

PRIOR HISTORY

In the period before Art Nouveau evolved, there was a stylistic vacuum in Europe and North America: the last major 19th-century styles to emerge had been the Empire and Biedermeier styles. This vacuum prompted artists to revive older styles, from Classical Antiquity, the Middle Ages, the Renaissance and the reigns of Louis XIV, XV and XVI. This phenomenon is known as Historicism. A combination of historical styles is known as eclecticism.

During the 19th century the guild system was also abandoned and the production of utilitarian objects and implements shifted from workshops to factories, thereby severing the traditional link between art and craft. Many factories were built, a consequence of the industrial revolution which had begun in England in the late 18th century and subsequently spread to the rest of the western world during the course of the century that followed.

The revival of historical styles in art circles and the change in production methods were responsible for a degree of decline in architecture and the applied arts. This decline was also fostered by the patrons of architecture and art, a broad, rising class of *nouveaux riches* who had made their fortunes in industry and thus replaced the aristocracy as consumers of art, for they aspired to display their newly acquired wealthy by copying the style of their aristocratic predecessors – badly.

A positive consequence of economic development was construction on a large scale. Industrialisation brought many changes, creating a demand for new kinds of buildings and encouraging the construction of Neo-Baroque stations, Neo-Classical museums and Neo-Roman prisons.

The urge to modernise

During the second half of the 19th century the calls to develop a contemporary design style became increasingly strident, prompted, in part, by the excesses of rampant Historicism. Examples of historicising architecture include, in the Netherlands, De Haar Castle in Haarzuilens, rebuilt in 1890, and Zocher's Stock Exchange Building, constructed in 1845, and, in Germany, King Ludwig's Schloss Neuschwanstein, near Hohenschwangau in Bavaria, erected between 1869 and 1891. After many years of vilification, 19th-century Historicism has now been granted its rightful place in art history.

An important event, which ushered in a new period of development in the applied arts, was the Great Exhibition of 1851, the first such international exhibition of the industrial age. Britain, the first industrial superpower, organised the event which was held in the ultra-modern Crystal Palace in London, a revolutionary building constructed of modern materials, cast iron and glass, and designed by an engineer, Joseph Paxton (1803-65).

The exhibition presented products from nearly every country in the world, gathered together for the first time in one venue. Alongside a substantial collection of European furniture from the 13th century onwards, there were also ethnographic artefacts from Africa and Asia. Comparison between contemporary Western products, which were generally profusely decorated, and items from earlier periods and other cultures favoured the latter in many instances. The artistic quality of these objects, plus the fact that they clearly reflected a specific period and culture, made a deep impression on visitors, who also became aware that simple objects could have their own artistic value, provided these objects were pleasing in form and proportions.

The Great Exhibition fostered a critical attitude towards the situation then existing in the art world. In England and France this led to public debates and measures intended to promote improvements in the applied arts.

The English writer, art critic and philosopher John Ruskin (1819-1900) and his disciple William Morris (1834-96), a writer and

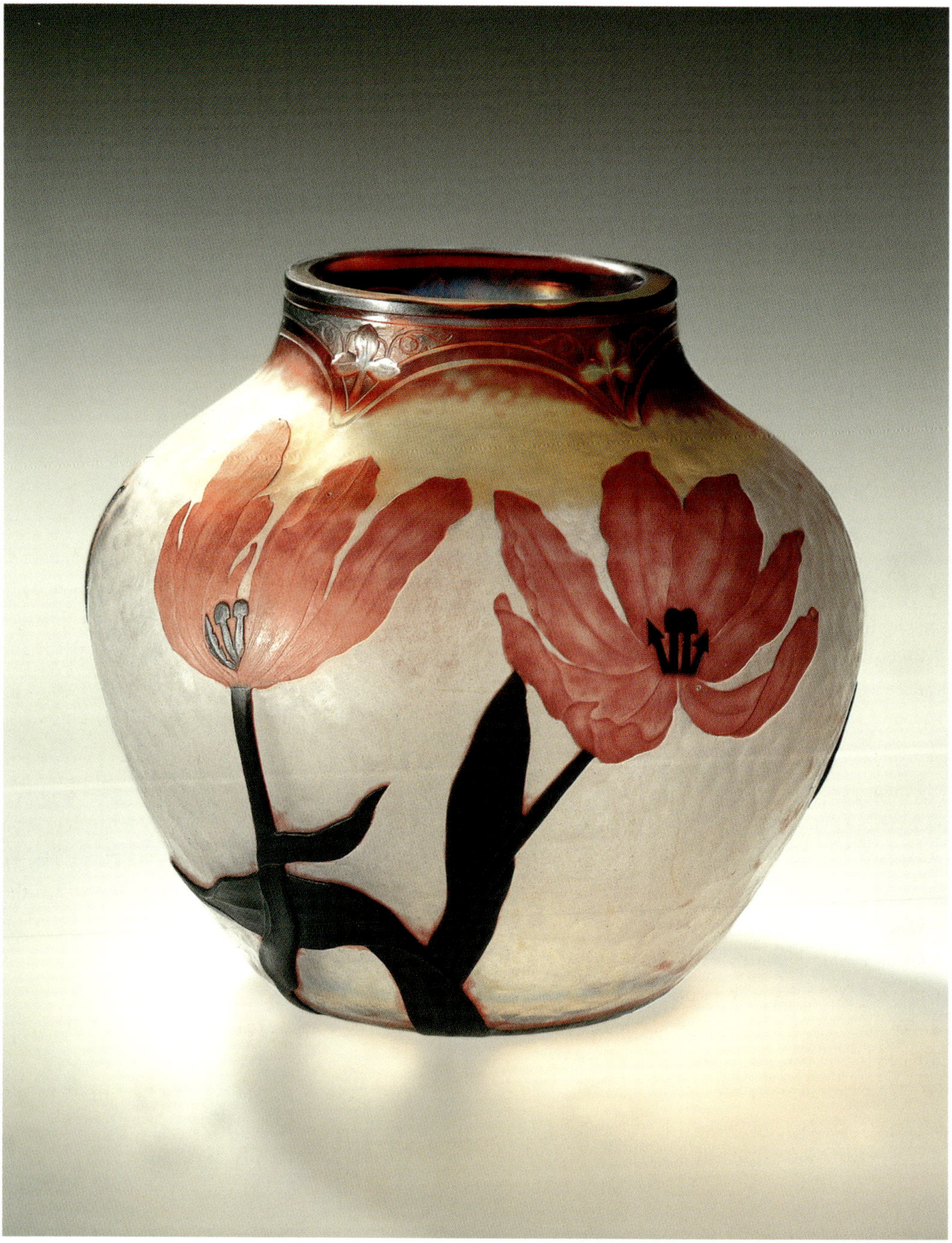

Vase with Tulips
Manufactory Daum Frères, Nancy. *1895*
Five-layer glass
H 16 cm

cat. no. 50

designer, loathed machinery and machine production, which they regarded as responsible for the decline in the applied arts. Ruskin also advocated equal status for the applied arts and fine art, as well as a return to craft production. Another of his ambitions was to restore the collaboration between artists and craftsmen.

Ruskin acted on his convictions. In 1854, for example, he joined forces with the Pre-Raphaelite artists Dante Gabriel Rossetti (1828-82), Ford Madox Brown (1821-93) and Edward Coley Burne-Jones (1833-98) to found the Working Man's Guild. This was a workplace where artists could practise various craft disciplines, as in the Middle Ages. The Pre-Raphaelites were a group of artists who painted in the style of the early Italian Renaissance. Their work often featured a particular type of long-haired woman with a mystical aura and a cool sexuality. Elizabeth Siddal (1829-62), Rossetti's wife, was the prototype for this woman. The 'Pre-Raphaelite woman' was the forerunner of the 'Art Nouveau woman', who is often encountered in the work of Art Nouveau artists in the period around 1900, both in painting and the applied arts. The Pre-Raphaelite painters were also active in the applied arts, for they decorated furniture and designed tapestries. They thus made an important contribution to the English Arts and Crafts movement, which was founded by William Morris.

Morris also established a cooperative workplace, firstly at his home, The Red House in Kent, and later the renowned firm of Morris & Co. in London. His socialist ideas made him unwilling to paint pictures, as he considered that to be an elitist activity. Although Morris believed that everyone should be able to acquire handcrafted pieces, such as tapestries, stained glass windows, wallpaper and furniture, much to his disappointment the objects made in his workplace could only be afforded by a small elite, owing to the use of expensive materials and the labour-intensive character of craft production.

Morris' ideas and work would exert a considerable influence on Art Nouveau architects and artists. Idealistic workplaces, founded in the spirit of the Arts and Crafts movement, would appear throughout Europe.

The German architect and art theoretician Gottfried Semper (1803-79) also worked in London, where he had made a modest contribution to the organisation of the 1851 Great Exhibition and fitted out several national pavilions. Semper had pronounced views on design and the applied arts, attaching value, for example, to making simple and effective objects available to a wider public. Like John Ruskin, Semper opposed the separation of fine art and applied art. His art theories influenced Hendrik Pieter Berlage (1856-1934), generally regarded as the father of modern architecture in the Netherlands, for Berlage studied at Zurich Polytechnicum, where instruction was based on Semper's ideas.

Semper's theories received their first practical application in 1857, when the English authorities commissioned the reorganisation of applied art education at the South Kensington Museum (now the Victoria and Albert Museum). Several schools and a library were attached to this museum, where the permanent display of objects from earlier periods was intended to serve as a source of inspiration for students in the development of a new style. This approach would be copied in a number of countries, including

Austria (Vienna, 1864), Russia (Moscow, 1864, and St Petersburg, 1876) and Germany (Berlin, 1867). In 1877 a Museum of Applied Art was established in the Netherlands, in Haarlem, followed several years later by another museum in Amsterdam. Two art training courses were opened at the Rijksmuseum, during its construction, the underlying premise being that it was impossible to develop a good modern style without good art education.

In France it was the Neo-Gothic architect Eugène Viollet-le-Duc (1814-79) who promulgated the most important theories. He maintained that structure was everything: forms should logically flow from this structure, to which decoration should be subordinated. In 1863 l'Union Centrale des Beaux Arts Appliqués à l'Industrie and various Musées des Arts Décoratifs were founded in France. Viollet-le-Duc's rational style of architecture was a major influence on the Dutch architect Pierre Cuypers (1827-1921), designer of the Rijksmuseum and Amsterdam Central Station.

Around 1890, once all these theories had been developed by architects and designers and the new art training courses had proved their value, the first signs of a new contemporary style began to emerge. This new style would chiefly develop in the major cities of Europe and North America, reaching its apotheosis at the 1900 Exposition Universelle in Paris, where almost every country had a pavilion displaying its own contribution to Art Nouveau.

Brussels

Although the quest for a modern style of architecture and design began in England with the Arts and Crafts movement, the first results were achieved on the European mainland. In Brussels the first Art Nouveau building was created by Victor Horta (1861-1947), an admirer of Viollet-le-Duc's work. Belgian Art Nouveau is characterised by a dynamically undulating line, also known as the 'whiplash line'. The architect Henry van de Velde should also be mentioned in connection with Belgian Art Nouveau architecture.

When Horta and Van de Velde built houses they also designed the fittings and contents, from doorbells to teaspoons. The lady of the house even received a 'makeover', in the form of Van de Velde's 'Reform dress', a generously cut gown of supple fabric which did not require the wearing of a constricting corset, an otherwise standard undergarment for women in the period.

From its inception Belgian Art Nouveau influenced many European architects and designers. The popular whiplash line appeared all over Europe and Brussels became known as the capital of Art Nouveau.

Paris

The name Art Nouveau derives from a shop in Paris, Galerie de l'Art Nouveau, which opened its doors in 1895. The owner, Siegfried Bing (1838-1905), came from a family of Hamburg porcelain dealers. Although he initially sold Japanese art, which was highly popular in this period, and even travelled to Japan to purchase his merchandise, he soon gave young Western designers an opportunity to show their work in his gallery. Bing stocked an international range of items, including furniture by Henry van de Velde, glassware by Tiffany, pieces by the furniture designers Georges de Feure (1868-1928) and Lucien Gaillard (1861-1933), and jewellery by René Lalique (1860-1945). Alongside these Art Nouveau items, he also dealt in paintings and sculptures.

Another notable figure in French Art Nouveau was the architect Hector Guimard (1867-1942), who was initially influenced by the work of Victor Horta. His famous metro entrances, flanked by organic flowers surrealistically rising from the pavement, still adorn the streets of Paris. As French Art Nouveau incorporates many stylised flower motifs, it is also known as floral Art Nouveau.

Nancy

Nancy, capital of the province of Alsace-Lorraine, was another important centre of floral Art Nouveau. It was the home of the École de Nancy, whose undisputed leader and theoretician was the virtuoso glass artist Emile Gallé (1846-1904). Vases of layered glass, with floral decorations cut through the layers, are characteristic Gallé pieces, inspired by 18th-century Chinese glassware. Gallé also designed Art Nouveau furniture with marquetry or inlay, in a style influenced by Rococo and Japanese art. Until 1900 he designed ceramics as well, in a historicising style (cat. 49).

From 1890 the French government presented unique objects by Gallé as diplomatic gifts to foreign heads of states. In 1896, for example, Tsar Nicholas II and his wife Alexandra Fyodorovna received an exceptional pair of Gallé vases from the French president (cat. nos. 26-27).

The École de Nancy also included the glass-making company run by the brothers Auguste (1853-1909) and Antonin Daum (1864-1930). The Daums worked in a style similar to Gallé's, although the vases created by Auguste, the designer, were often more elegant in form. Like Gallé they also produced objects made of layered glass with etched and enamelled decorations. One of their specialities was the *'martelé'*, or hammered, effect (cat. 50); another, objects in pâte-de-verre (coloured glass paste), after designs by Almaric Walter. The designer Louis Majorelle, also a prominent member of the École de Nancy, produced elegant furniture, decorated with stylised maquetry motifs derived from nature.

Glasgow

Scotland was the home of the Glasgow Four, who comprised Charles Rennie Mackintosh (1868-1928), Herbert MacNair (1868-1955) and their wives, the sisters Frances (1873-1921) and Margaret MacDonald (1865-1933). The architect and designer Mackintosh was their leader. His architecture was robust and clean in form, recalling that of ancient Scottish castles; the interiors he designed for his buildings were singularly light in colour. Mackintosh's furniture was slim and angular; his chairs, made of oak, sometimes painted white or black, often incorporated conspicuously high backs, while upholstery featured stencilled roses or slim, elongated female figures. These decorations were made by Mackintosh's wife Margaret, and influenced in style by the English draughtsman and illustrator Aubrey Vincent Beardsley (1872-98).

Vienna

In Vienna the Wiener Sezession was founded in 1897 by Josef Hoffmann (1870-1956), Kolo Moser (1868-1918) and Josef Maria Olbrich (1867-1908). Sezession means 'secession' or 'formal separation'. These artists had 'seceded' from the conservative society of

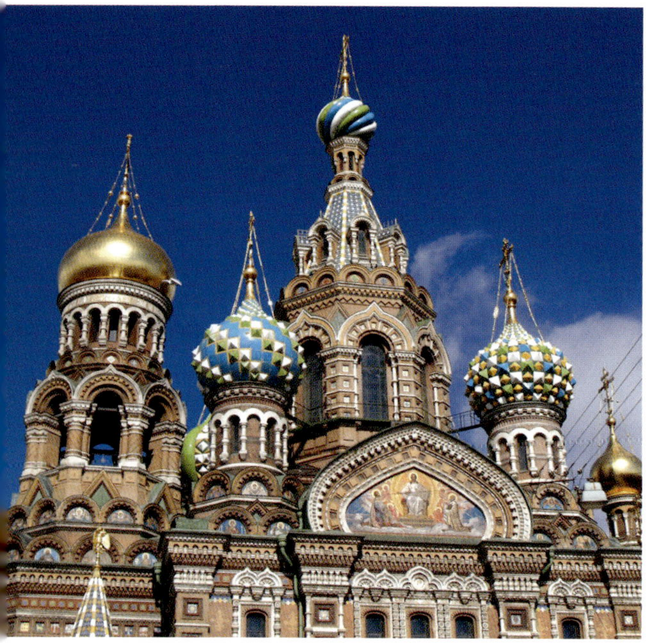

artists Das Künstlerhaus. Their exhibition building, designed by Olbrich is still regarded as one of the jewels of Jugendstil architecture. Although the members of the Sezession, especially Josef Hoffmann, initially worked in a style similar to that of Belgian Art Nouveau, around 1900 they were influenced by Austrian Biedermeier to produce tauter, cleaner lines.

In 1903 the Sezession's members founded the *Wiener Werkstätte,* modelled on English guilds. Various forms of applied art were practised in these workshops, which initially produced clean, geometrical designs. Wiener Werkstätte artists greatly admired the Scottish architect and designer Charles Rennie Mackintosh, and expressed this admiration in angular forms and the use of black and white. Wiener Werkstätte geometrical design is often regarded as one of the predecessors of Art Deco. Circa 1910, however, the workshops' designs became more Baroque in appearance.

Munich

In Munich *Jugend,* the journal devoted to modern art and design, was published for the first time in 1896. This periodical gave its name to the new style which became known as Jugendstil. To a large extent Munich Jugendstil was based on the Belgian whiplash line, with conspicuous influence from the English Arts and Crafts movement. Important designers were Peter Behrens (1868-1940), Richard Riemerschmied (1868-1957), Bernhard Pankok (1872-1943) and August Endell (1871-1925).

Darmstadt

In Darmstadt, capital of the Grand Duchy of Hesse-Darmstadt, an artists' colony was founded in 1899 under the patronage of Grand Duke Ludwig of Hesse, grandson of Queen Victoria of England and brother of the last Tsarina of Russia, Alexandra Fyodorovna. English and Scottish Art Nouveau was a considerable influence on the colony's style which was clean and geometrical. Josef Olbrich, Peter Behrens and Hans Christiansen (1866-1945) built large houses for themselves, with harmonising, unified interiors, on the Mathildenhöhe. The colony's exhibition building was designed by Olbrich.

Amsterdam

The Beurs van Berlage (1903), or Berlage's Stock Exchange Building, in Amsterdam, is generally regarded as the beginning of modern architecture in the Netherlands. Berlage was indebted for this design to the work of his colleagues K.P.C. de Bazel (1869-1923) and H. Walenkamp (1871-1933) from the years 1895-97. Both De Bazel and Walenkamp were members of the influential association of architects Architectura et Amicitia; they were also confirmed theosophists and worked in accordance with mathematical design methods derived from theosophy. Theosophy is sometimes described as a comprehensive, universal philosophy, based on the scientific and spiritual evolution of nature, and embracing the fields of science, philosophy and religion. Rudolf Steiner (1861-1925) was initially a member of the Theosophical Society, before he left in 1912 to formulate his own ideas which became known as anthroposophy.

When Berlage designed the Amsterdam Stock Exchange Building he employed the Egyptian Triangle, a design system akin to the theosophical system, which is why the building is so taut and angular in form. Dutch architectural traditions, the influence exerted by socialism and Berlage's repudiation of the Belgian whiplash line ensured that Belgian Art Nouveau did not find a following in Amsterdam. Hence there are few buildings in this style to be seen in the Dutch capital.

In 1900 Berlage, the furniture designer Jac. van den Bosch and the businessman W. Hoeker founded 't Binnenhuis, a sales outlet where like-minded designers could sell their work. The furniture and other pieces were pure in form and mostly incorporated geometrical decoration. Their angular shapes were the product of the theosophy-based design methods promoted by applied arts courses. The Binnenhuisstijl remained highly influential until 1910.

From 1898 Van Wisselingh, a renowned firm of art dealers on the Rokin in Amsterdam which sold paintings by artists of the Barbizon and Hague Schools, supplied wealthy clients with entire interiors designed by Theo Nieuwenhuis (1866-1951), Gerrit

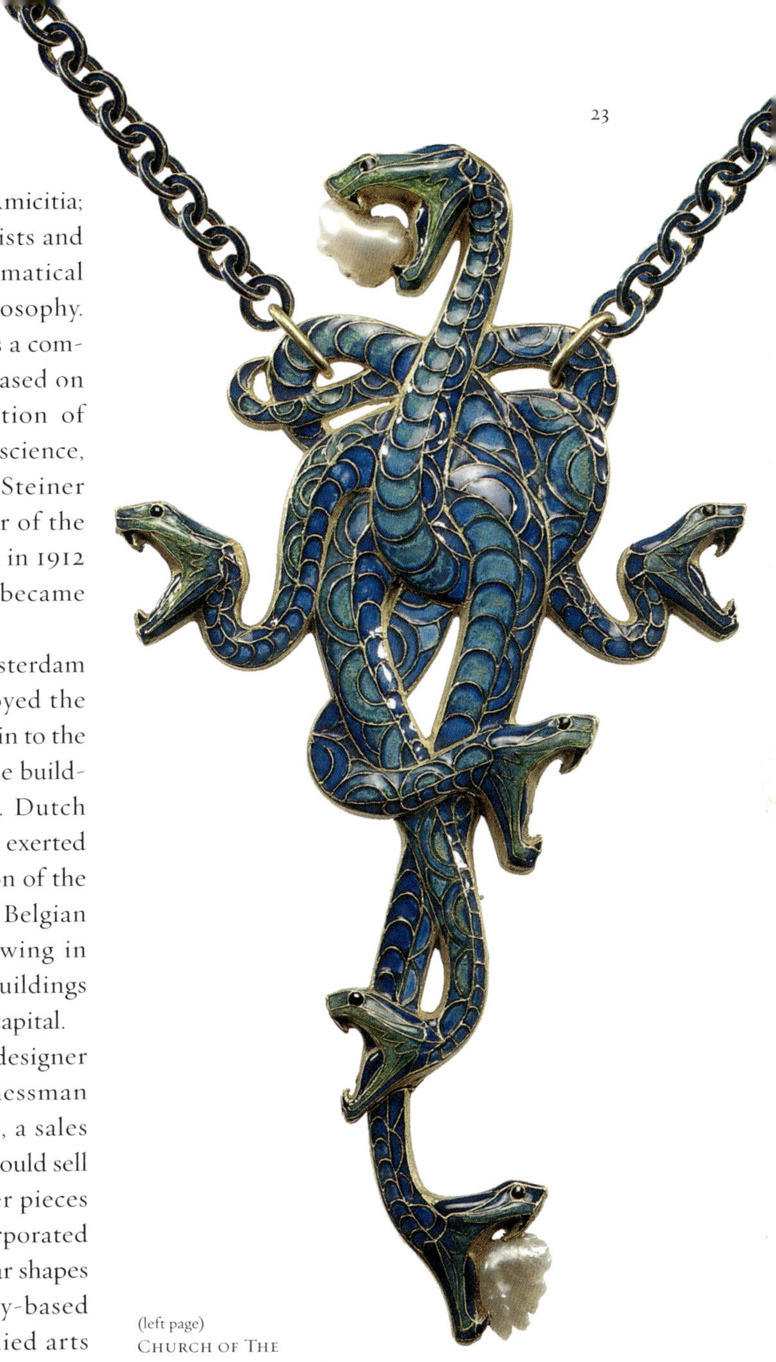

(left page)
Church of The Saviour on spilled Blood, Tserkov Voskreseniya,
St Petersburg, *1883-1907*
Photo: Vincent Boele, *2007*

(above) CAT. NO. 125
Pendant with a Ball of Snakes
René-Jules Lalique, Paris. *1901*
Gold, pearl, enamel
H 11 cm

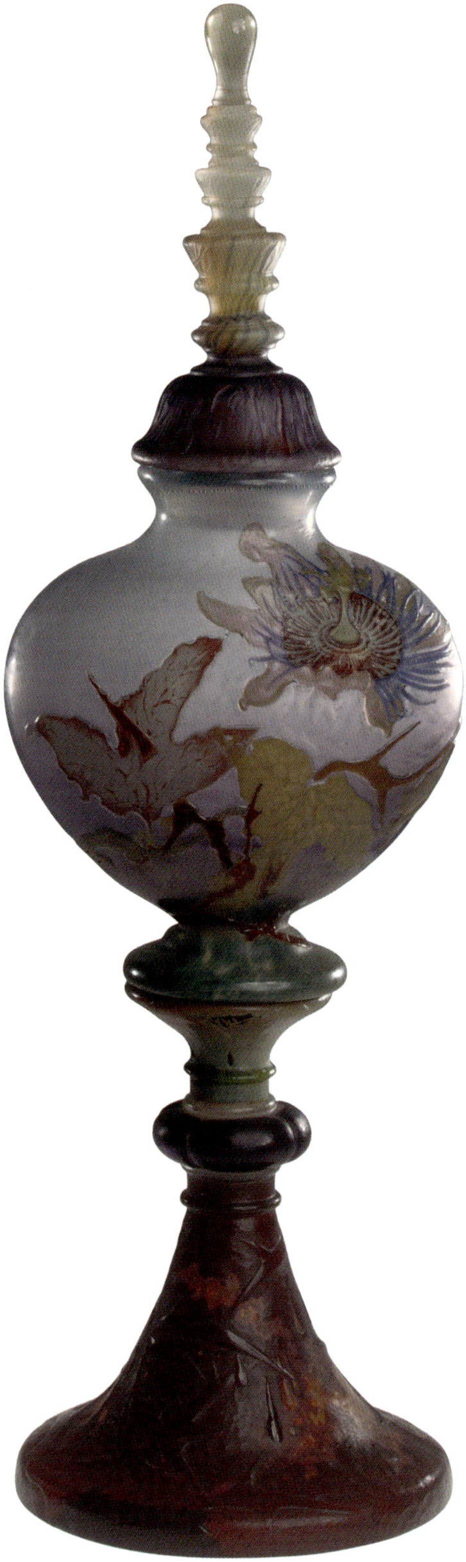

Willem Dijsselhof (1866-1924) and Carel Adolph Lion Cachet (1864-1945). These interiors were made of expensive tropical woods, often decorated with sophisticated carvings.

The firm had its own furniture studio, coppersmith's workshop and batik department. Batik was widely used in Nieuwe Kunst (the Dutch Art Nouveau) for screens, upholstery, wall coverings and book bindings. This originally Javanese technique would become an integral part of the Nieuwe Kunst and thus a characteristic of the Dutch modern style.

The Hague

Berlage and his associates founded 't Binnenhuis in response to the opening, in 1898, of Arts and Crafts, a firm of modern art dealers in The Hague. The firm, which sold Belgian Art Nouveau, including furniture by Dutch designers, modelled itself on the Paris Galerie de l'Art Nouveau. Arts and Crafts was established by a group of artists centred around the design duo Chris Wegerif and his wife, Agathe. Johan Thorn Prikker (1868-1932), the Symbolist painter, was artistic director of the firm for its first two years. His friend, the Belgian designer Henry van de Velde, had encouraged him to start designing applied art. After Thorn Prikker left Arts and

Vase *Passiflora*
Emile Gallé, Nancy. *c. 1889*
Body: five-layer glass.
Foot: two-layer glass, metal foil
H 63.5 cm

cat. no. 25

Crafts, the firm sold furniture designed by the Wegerifs, in a style similar to that of the Wiener Sezession.

The renowned Rozenburg ceramic factory also put the city of The Hague firmly on the 'Art Nouveau map', producing eggshell porcelain, cast in bizarre forms and painted with sophisticated flora and fauna motifs.

Russia

At the beginning of the 19th century Russia was predominantly an agrarian country with a class-ridden society. The major cities of St Petersburg and Moscow accommodated a flourishing cultural life in which European fashions were closely followed. Large land owners had serfs to work their huge estates. The immense country had a poor infrastructure, which adversely affected the outcome of the Crimean War (1853-56), for Russia was defeated as a result of the failure of new troops and supplies to reach the battle front when required.

After the war new roads and canals were constructed, and a railway network established. This allowed the country's natural resources to be effectively exploited and thus stimulated the advent of industrialisation, as in the rest of Europe. In 1861 Tsar Alexander II abolished serfdom. In 1881, however, this reforming monarch was killed in a bomb

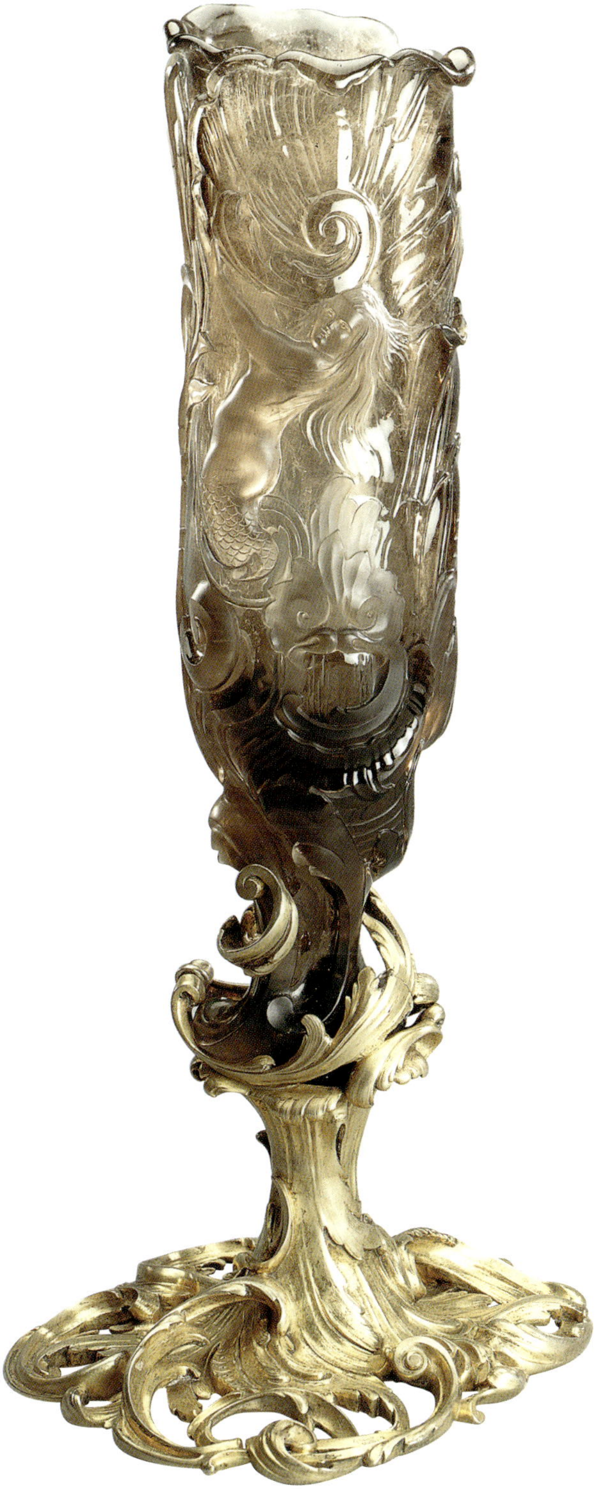

Vase
Peterhof Lapidary Factory, St Petersburg. *1898*
Craftsman: Yuly Rapoport, Mounted by firm of Carl Fabergé, St Petersburg
Vase: smoky quartz. Mount: silver
H 37 cm

CAT. NO. 128

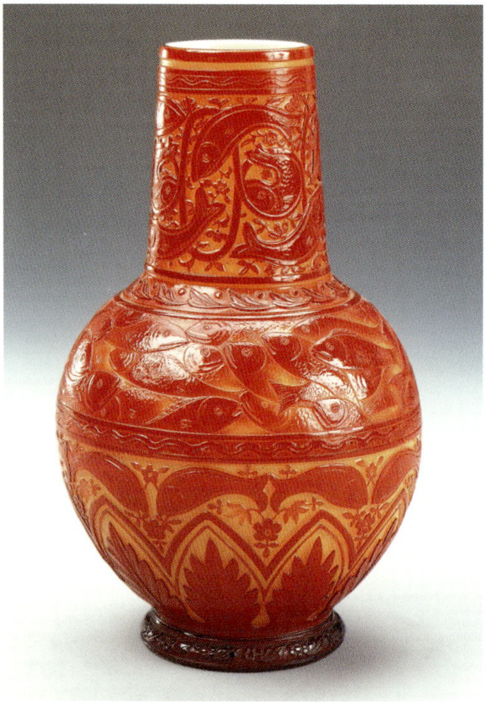

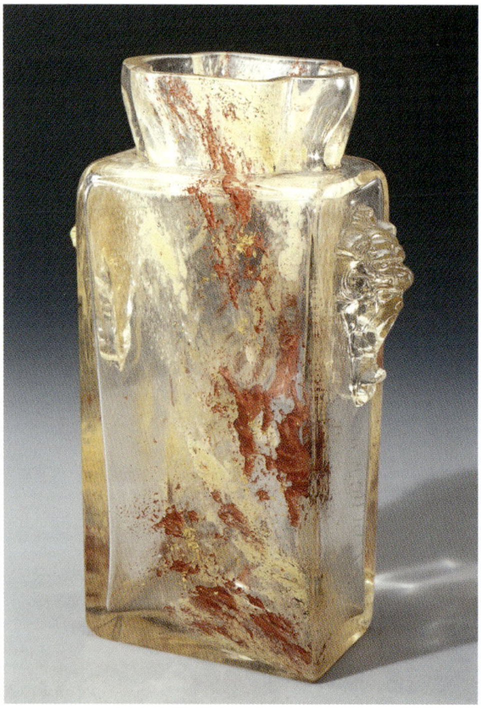

attack. The Church of the Saviour on Spilled Blood, which his successor Alexander III had built as a monument on the site of the attack, is a good example of historicising Russian architecture. It was constructed between 1883 and 1907 by the architects Alfred Parland and Ivan Makarov.

The growth of industrialisation created a huge demand for labour. Former serfs moved en masse to the big cities where many of them were able to make their fortune. They became the new rich and took the place of the old aristocracy who saw their wealth shrink as a result of losing cheap serf labour to work their land. Moscow became the centre of the textile industry and the hub of the railway network. People moved to Moscow from all over Russia, turning the city into a melting pot of diverse cultures.

The process of modernising the fine and applied arts began during the 1880s, with the formation of a splinter group of artists and critics who rejected the nationalistic and academic style. This group comprised Alexander Benois (1870-1960), Sergey Diaghilev (1872-1929), Valentin Serov (1865-1911), Konstantin Korovin (1861-1939) and Léon Bakst (1866-1924). Several of them would later play an important role in the Ballets

(above) CAT. NO. 17
Vase with Decoration in Chinese Style
Thomas Webb and Sons factory,
Stourbridge. *c. 1889*
Three-layer glass
H 18.5 cm

(below) CAT. NO. 11
Vase
Appert Frères, Clichy. *1886-89*
Model by Ernst-Baptiste Léveillé, Paris
Two-layered glass, gold foil
H 26.7 cm

Russes. With the financial help of two patrons of Russian art, the railway magnate Savva Mamontov and Princess Maria Tenisheva, they founded the art journal *Mir Iskusstva* ('The World of Art'), with Diaghilev as editor-in-chief. The World of Art group also created theatrical productions and organised exhibitions of fine art and applied art, to which they invited foreign artists as well.

Mamontov and Princess Tenisheva had established two artists' colonies on their estates close to Moscow, Abramtsevo and Talashkino. Here various artists produced innovative applied art, with medieval Russian art and architecture and folk art serving as their inspiration. During their time at these colonies Victor Vasnetsov (1848-1926), Mikhail Vrubel (1856-1910) and Elena Polenova (1850-98) designed furniture, ceramics, wood carvings, stained glass and textiles. Peasants were employed to make the objects, using traditional craft skills. On his Abramtsevo estate, Mamontov also erected a simple church in Neo-Russian style, resembling the medieval churches of Novgorod.

At the 1900 Exposition Universelle in Paris, where European countries displayed their Art Nouveau for the first time, the Russian contribution consisted of work produced by artists at the two colonies. The pavilions in *teremok* style, inspired by medieval buildings with copious amounts of carved wood, were fitted with furniture and objects made in Abramtsevo and Talashkino. This style, based on a combination of vernacular and modernity, drew a great deal of international attention, particularly from countries with an arts and crafts tradition.

As elsewhere in Europe in the period around 1900, the new Russian middle classes in the big cities demanded homes with interiors in the new style. A new phenomenon in this period were the art journals, such as *The Studio, l'Art décoratif* and *Der Architekt,* which published the latest foreign developments in the field of architecture and interior art.

These publications introduced Russians to international Art Nouveau. The first Russian journal to pay attention to this style was *Stroitel* ('The Builder'), which published an article, in 1899, about the Art Nouveau architecture and interiors designed by Otto Wagner, Victor Horta, Joseph Olbrich and Hector Guimard.

Other Russian publications quickly followed this example, discussing the work of Emile Gallé, Tiffany, René Lalique and Lucien Gaillard. Their comments were generally positive, although they did warn against mindless imitation.

Authoritative critics such as Pavel Makarov and Voldichin regarded the modern style as one of the many modernising processes of the age, which they believed would bring both social and cultural benefits to the new middle classes and higher ranks of society.

Alongside the architecture and applied art in Neo-Russian style produced in the workshops of Abramtsevo and Talashkino, a movement also developed which combined the influences of of international Art Nouveau with Russian elements. Its works were displayed at the 'Architecture and Artistic Applied Art' exhibition, held in Moscow from 1902 to 1903, which presented furniture by the Russian architects Fyodor Shekhtel, Konstantin Korovin, William Walcott and Ivan Fomin, combined in rooms with furniture by Mackintosh and Olbrich.

The exhibition was well received in leading publications. Ivan Fomin's work in par-

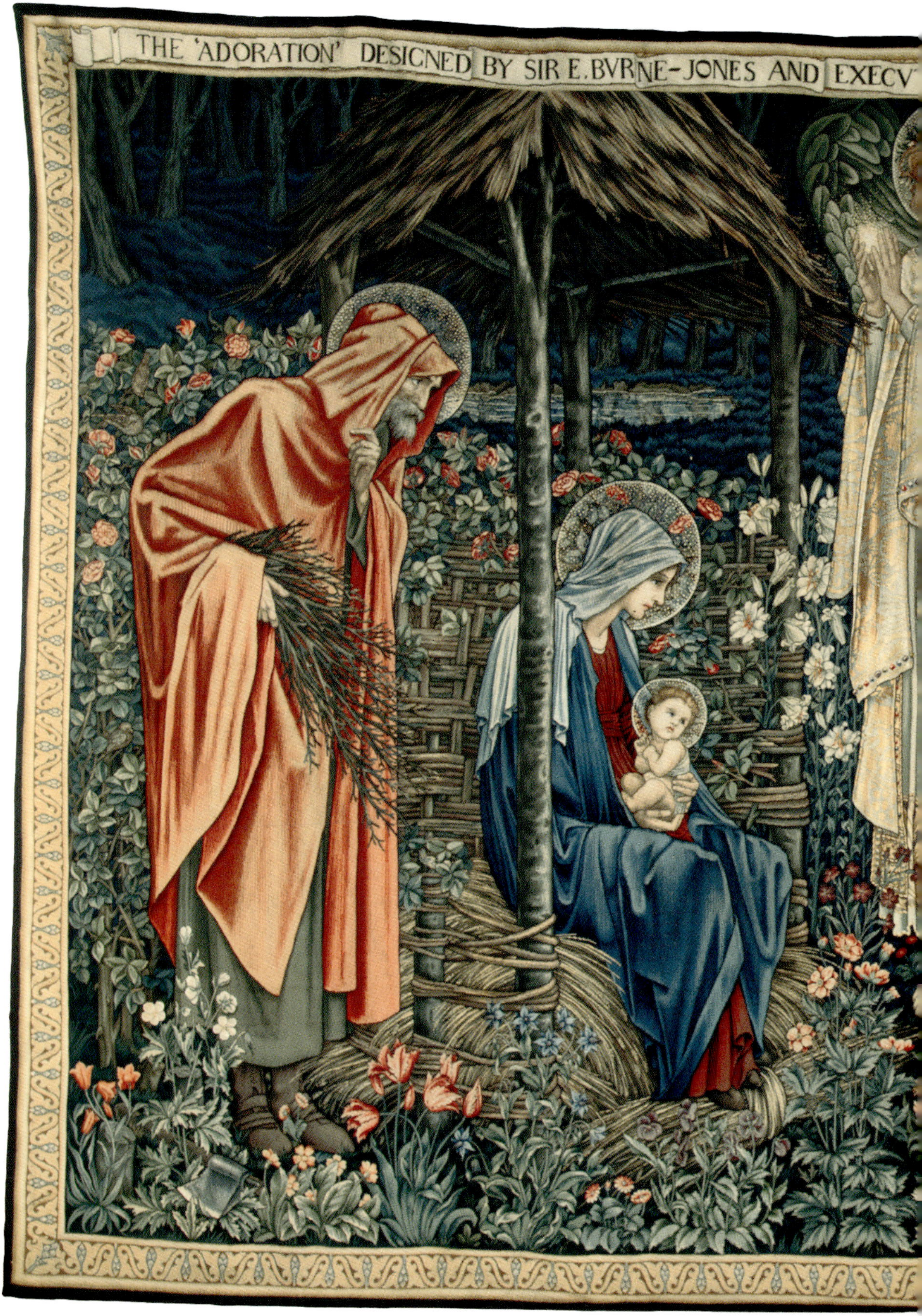
THE 'ADORATION' DESIGNED BY SIR E. BVRNE-JONES AND EXECV

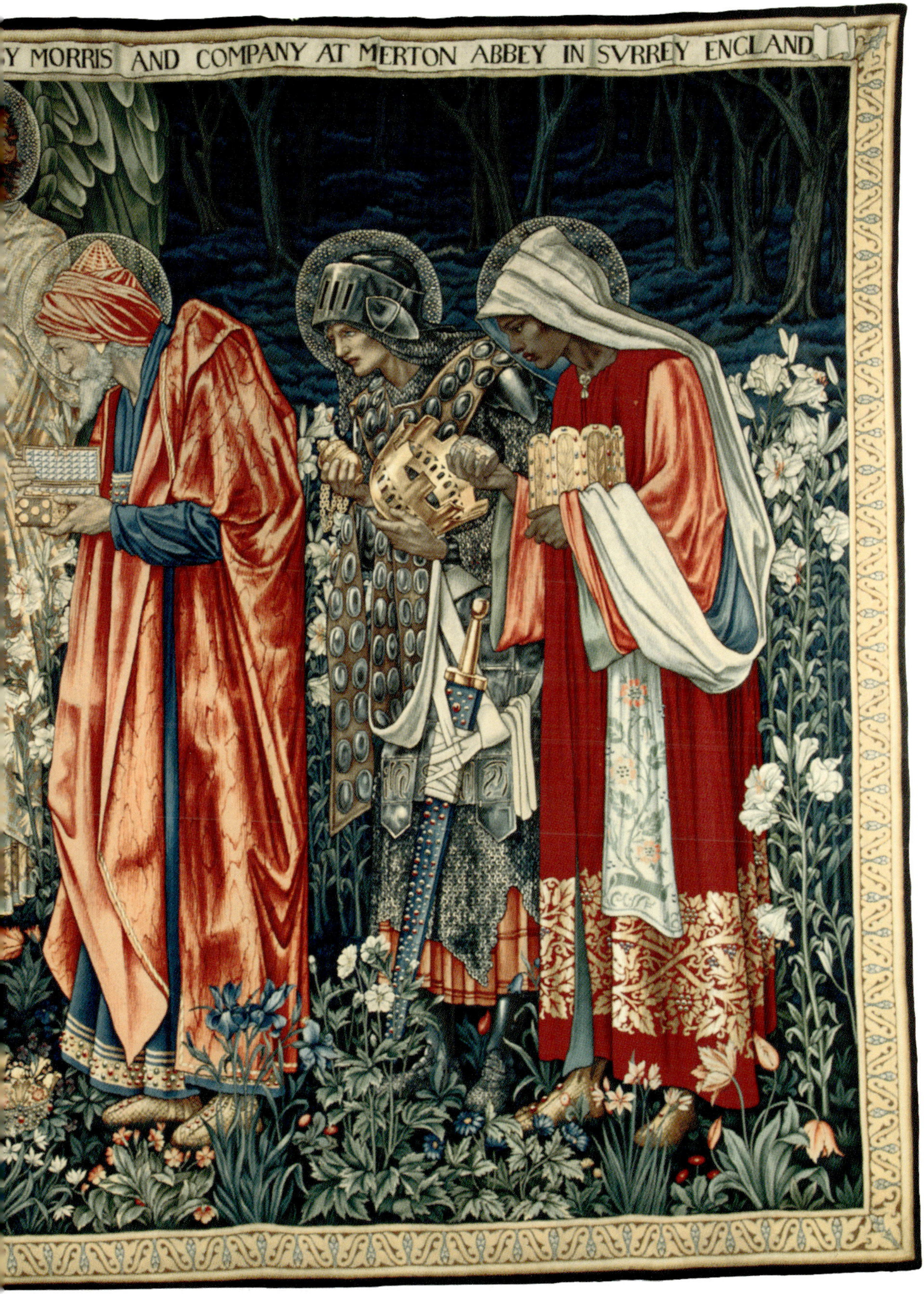
Y MORRIS AND COMPANY AT MERTON ABBEY IN SVRREY ENGLAND

ticular was praised by the critic at the art journal *Mír Iskusstva,* Sergey Diaghilev, who thought that Fomin's modern designs showed that he retained a respect for the influence of Russian culture.

The exhibition was immediately followed by another in St Petersburg, organised in 1904 by a group of artists and designers under the auspices of *Mír Iskusstva* and entitled 'Contemporary art'. This exhibition displayed rooms and furniture by Russian designers whose principal inspiration was the work of foreign designers. Although the exhibition was well received by public and press, some critical notes were sounded: Diaghilev, for example, found the room in Neo-Russian style by Konstantin Korovin somewhat theatrical and thought the design made no connection between the space and the interior.

The Russian modern style was thus dual in character. On the one hand it focused on international Art Nouveau, on the other it derived inspiration from traditional Russian national motifs.

St Petersburg

In St Petersburg, where artists and designers were less inspired by traditional Russian folk art, it was the architect Roman Meltzer who received many commissions to build imperial houses and apartments for the upper classes. His style chiefly derived from international Art Nouveau, such as the Wiener Sezession and British and Finnish Arts and Crafts, and thus represented a synthesis of luxury and rusticism. In the interior of his own home, however, Meltzer did incorporate motifs from Russian folk art.

Although Meltzer's clients wanted their homes funished in a modern style, they also needed these to be functional, and functionality was not necessarily a feature of Neo-Russian designs.

(previous spread) CAT. NO. 138
Tapestry: *The Adoration of the Magi*
William Morris & Co., Merton Abbey, Surrey. *1902*
Cartoon by Edward Burne-Jones. *1890*
Wool
255 x 379 cm

(right) CAT. NO. 83
Euphorbia Vase
Craftsman Grigory Omorokov, Imperial Porcelain and Glass Manufactory, St Petersburg.
Design by R. Wilde. *1908*
Crystal
H 17 cm

The world-famous firm of Carl Fabergé, which was based in St Petersburg with a branch in Moscow, produced small decorative items (objets de vertu), such as cigarette cases, snuffboxes and photo frames. These were mostly made of silver and gold, set with precious and semi-precious stones, and were of exceptional quality. The firm received commissions from the imperial family for private pieces and also items for diplomatic gifts. At Easter Tsar Nicholas II presented Fabergé eggs set with precious stones to his family. The firm's branch in Moscow made pieces in a style that reflected the Neo-Russian movement.

The Imperial Porcelain Manufactory in St Petersburg, founded in 1744, was owned by the Crown and worked exclusively for the imperial court. Alexander III's marriage to Princess Dagmar of Denmark, the future Tsarina Maria Fyodorovna, sparked his enthu-

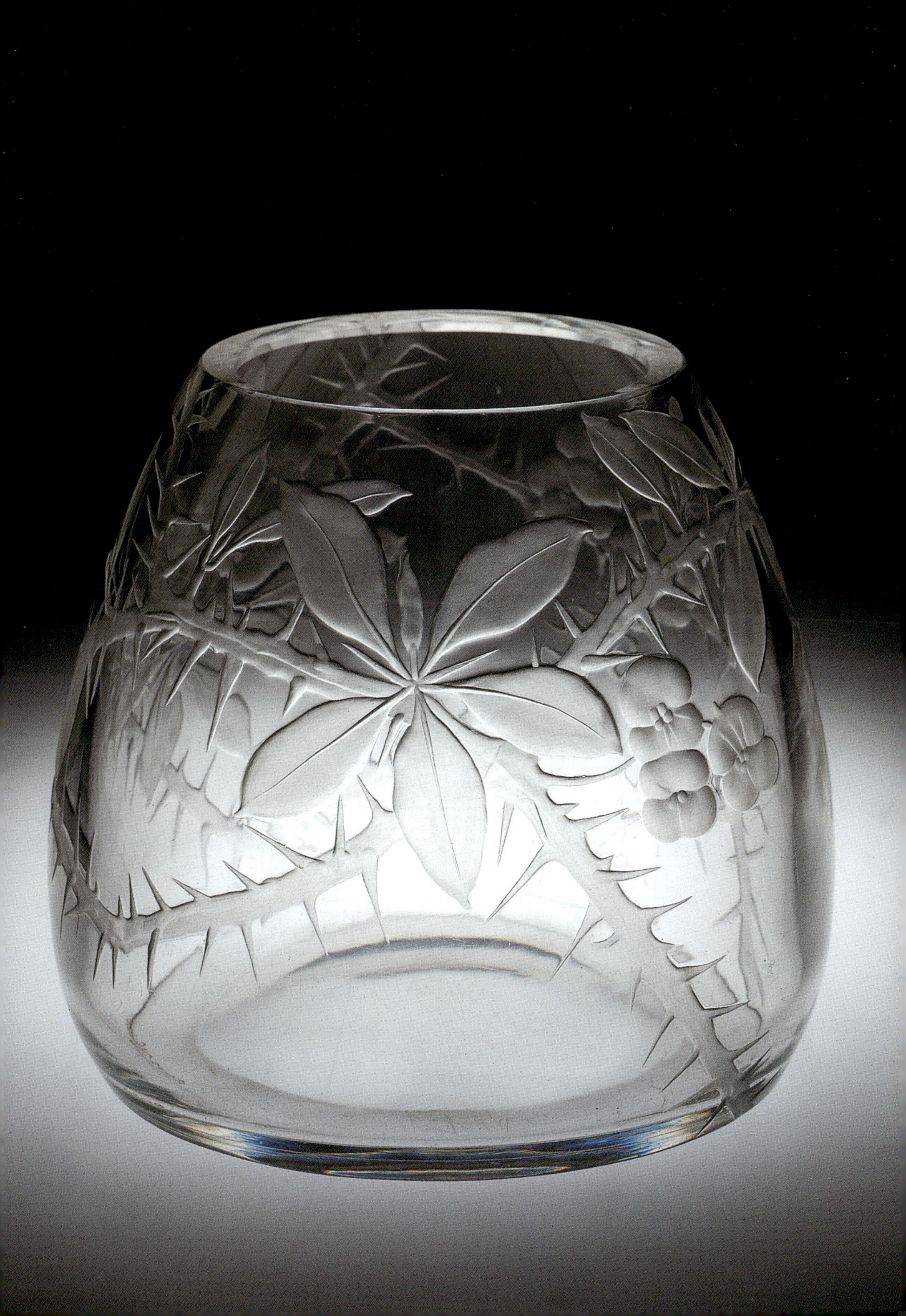

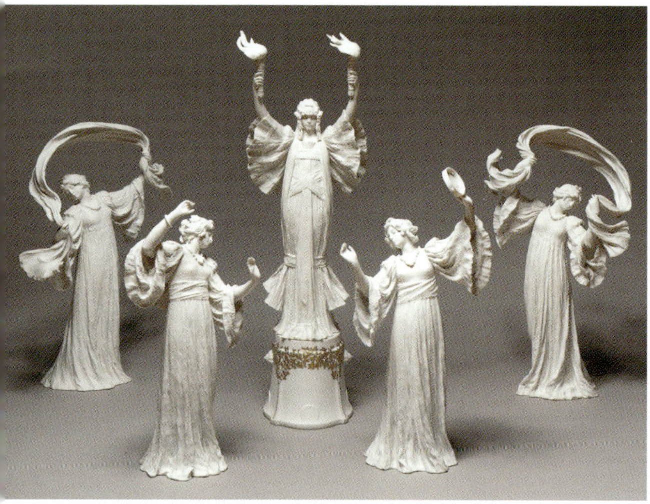

siam for the Art Nouveau decorations on ceramics produced by the Royal Porcelain Factory in Copenhagen. The imperial couple were particularly fond of the factory's Japanese-inspired underglaze decorations. From 1892 the Imperial Porcelain Manufactory also its decorators adopted these devices, having been taught these by the Danish painter Carl Frederik Liisberg.

In 1890 the Imperial Russian Glass Manufactory, established in the 18th century, merged with the Imperial Porcelain Manufactory. In 1900 Baron Nicholas de Wolff became director of the two firms. Encouraged by Maria Fyodorovna, he ensured that both establishments employed Art Nouveau decors. The type of glass produced by the Russian factory displays great affinity with the work of Emile Gallé and the Daum brothers of Nancy. Glassware by the Ecole de Nancy may thus have constituted a direct source of inspiration, although it is equally possible that work by the Swedish Reymre and Kosta glass factories, which made the same kind of glass, may have played a role.

The forms produced at the Russian factory are often simple, to showcase the flora and fauna decors cut into the layered glass. In the west work from the Imperial Glass Manufactories is rarely found and thus virtually unknown.

It is not known whether the last Tsar and Tsarina of Russia took an active role in developing and promoting the modern style, along the lines of that played by the Tsarina's brother, Grand Duke Ludwig in Darmstad with regard to Jugendstil.

The exhibition includes a pâte-de-verre (glass paste) mask of a woman, by the French glass artist Henri Cros, who breathed new life into this Ancient Egyptian technique in the late 19th century. The mask comes from the private collection of Tsarina Alexandra Fyodorovna, who seems to have been extremely fond of the piece. During visits to her family in Darmstadt she also appears to have brought back Gallé vases which she displayed in her private rooms.

Towards the end of the first decade of the 20th century, the modern style seems to have became widespread in Russia, and many architects reverted to working in a Neo-Classical style. This is a tendency also encountered in the rest of Europe.

In 1909, however, the founders of the influential journal *Mír Iskusstva,* caused a sensation in Paris with their innovative approach to ballet and opera, Les Ballets Russes. The cultural elite of Paris were astounded by the costumes and sets, designed by Léon Bakst and others, which featured exotic motifs and bright, glowing colours derived from Russian folk art. Soon afterwards, these motifs and colours found their way into the fashion designs of Paul Poiret and the interiors produced by Atelier Martine, thus forming one of the sources of inspiration for the new style to emerge from Art Nouveau, Art Deco.

Moscow

The Pertsov apartment complex in Moscow, built in the years 1905-7, is a good example of a modernised take on tradition, designed by a fine artist, Sergey Malyutin, a leading member of the Talashkino group.

The design of the building, like the interior, is based on Old Russian architecture and decorative motifs, which have been incorporated in the carved woodwork, the wall paintings and the handcrafted furniture. Such elements are not always very practical in the appartment complex's generally small rooms.

The house commissioned in Moscow by the wealthy merchant Stepan Ryabushinsky is an excellent example of the type of modern style which was mainly inspired by international Art Nouveau, yet incorporated subtle references to Russian folk art. This was built in 1900-2 by the most talented architect of the modern style, Fyodor Shekhtel (1859-1926).

The Ryabushinsky House is a *Gesamtkunstwerk* with a clean exterior enlivened by a mosaic frieze of irises. The richly-fitted interior forms a unity, incorporating a range of materials such as ceramics, wood, stained glass and metals. The most striking element is the staircase in the centre of the house, onto which every room opens. This organically formed staircase is made of highly polished concrete, in which marble and granite dust have been mixed. Although its undulating lines derive from international Art Nouveau, its massive character is typically Russian. The interior of the house reveals that Shekhtel was familiar with the work of the most important foreign architects and designers, such as Mackintosh, Olbrich, Gaillard, Majorelle, Endell and Tiffany.

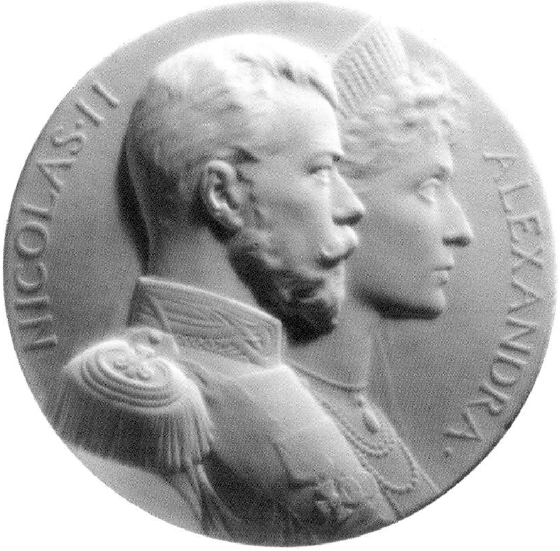

(left page) CAT. NOS. 96-99
Pieces from the Dance with Scarves
(Le Jeu de l'Echarpe)
Sculptor Agathon Léonard van Weydeveldt,
Sèvres Porcelain Manufactory. *1900*
Biscuit porcelain
H 45 to 73 cm

(above) CAT. NO. 95
Medallion with Paired Portrait of
Nicholas II and Alexandra Fyodorovna
Sculptor Jules-Clément Chaplain,
Sèvres Porcelain Manufactory, Paris. *1896*
Biscuit porcelain
Diameter 9 cm

(overleaf) CAT. NO. 155/52
Allegory in Honour of
the Franco-Russian Alliance
Alphonse Monchablon, *1893*
Watercolour on paper
H 21 cm

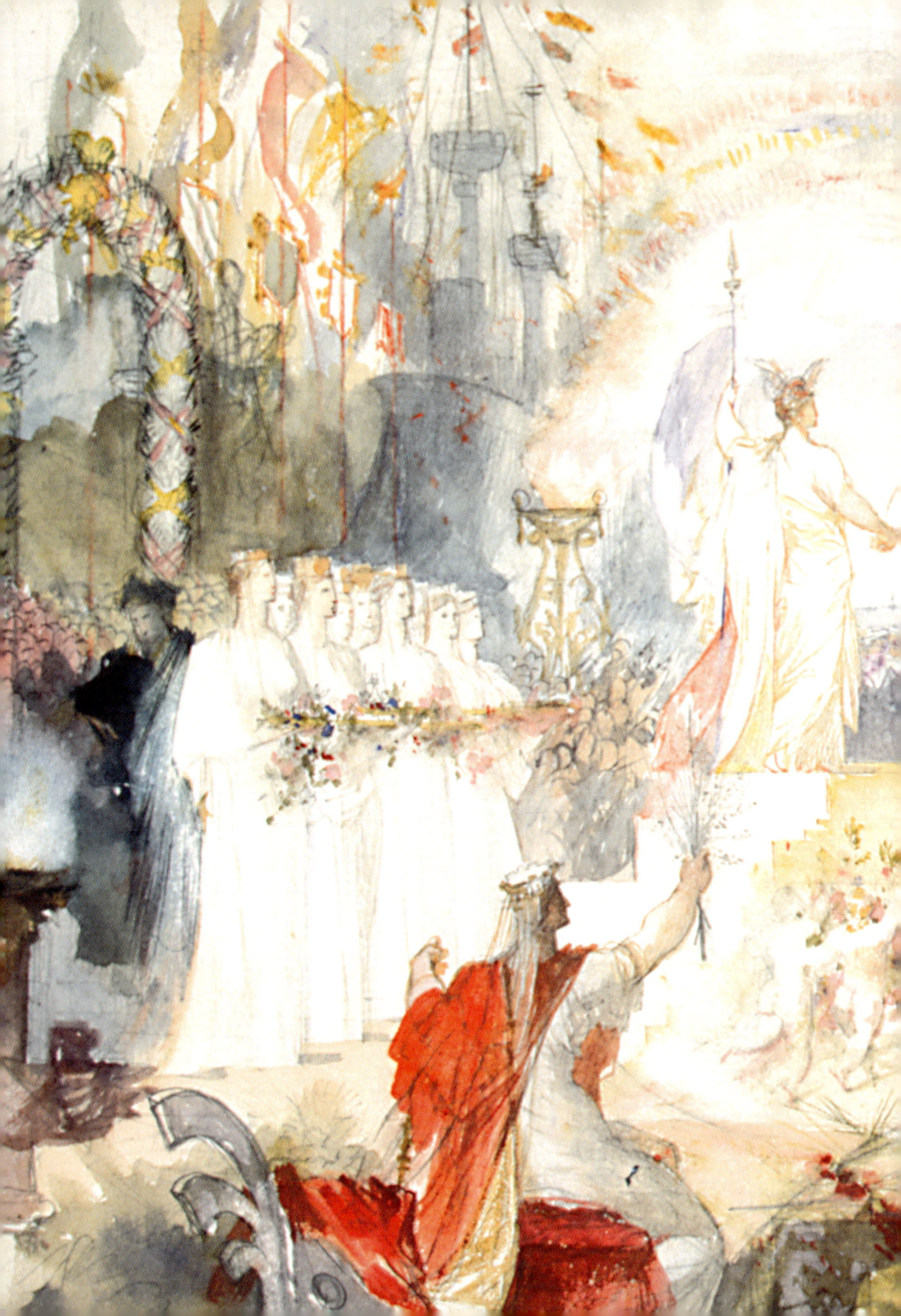

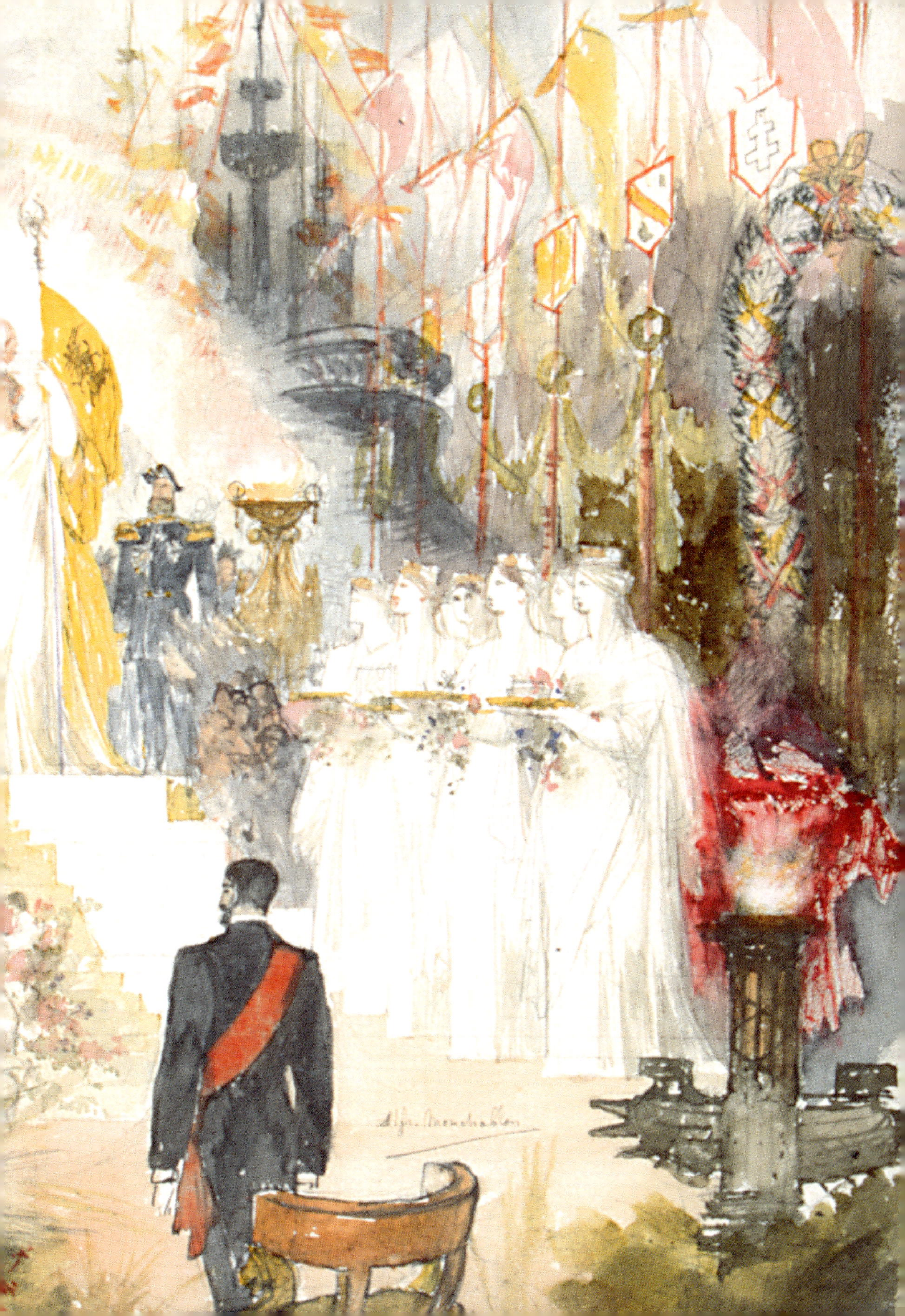

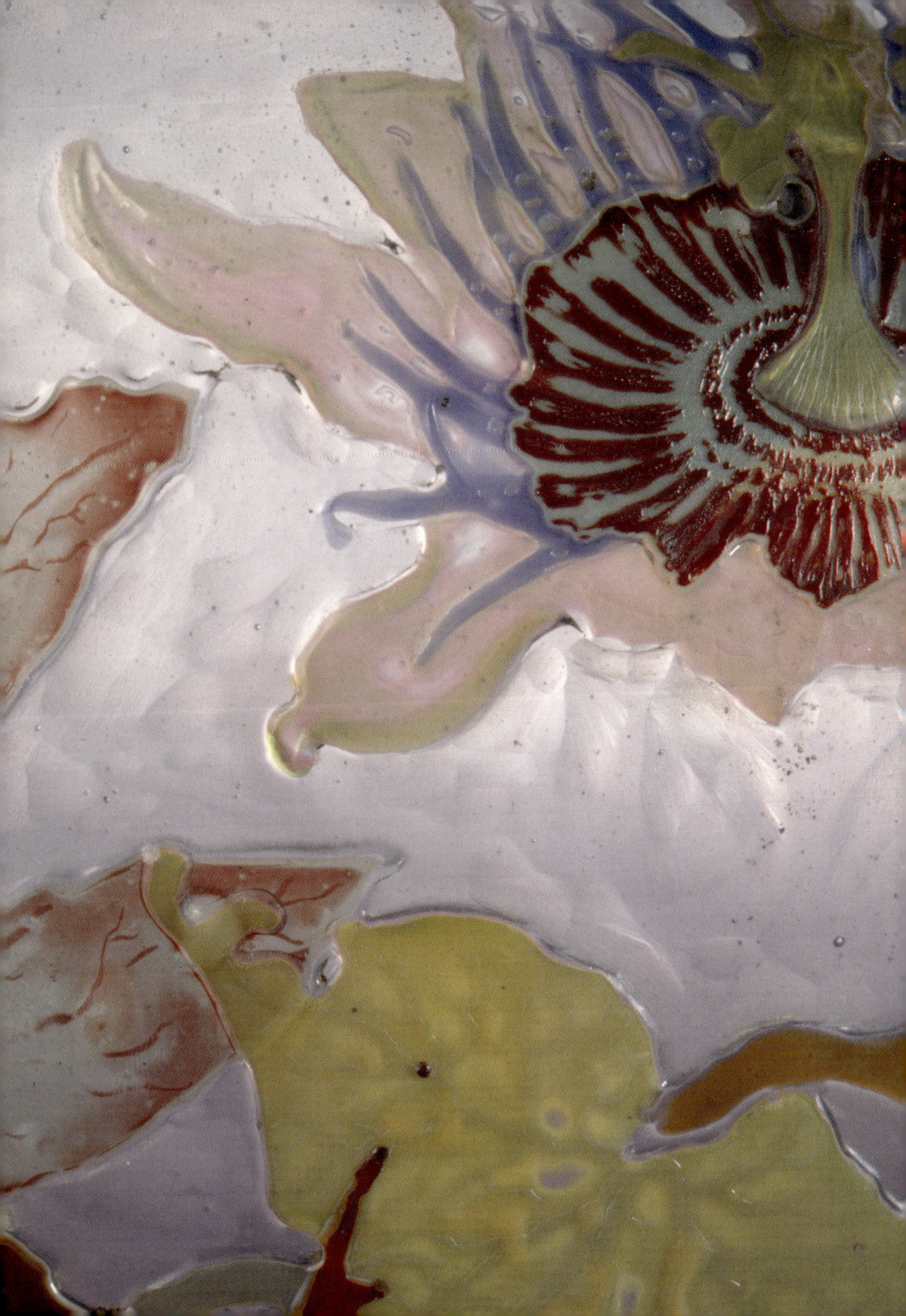

Tamara Rappe

Art and Diplomacy in the Reign of Alexander III and Nicholas II

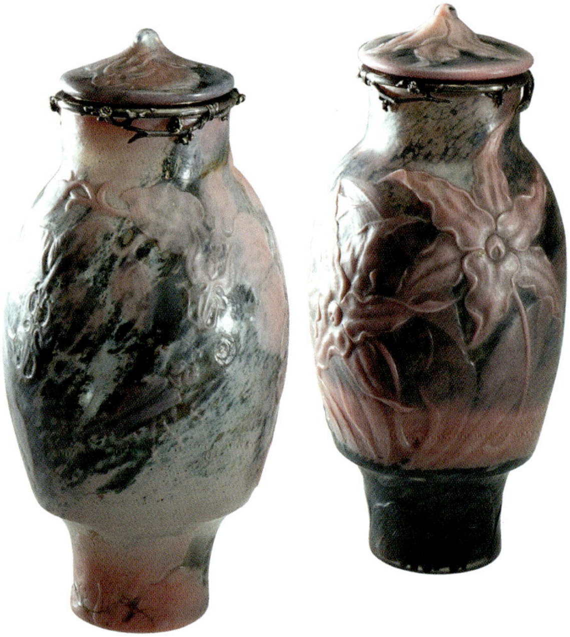

(previous page) CAT. NO. 25
Detail vase *Passiflora*
Emile Gallé, Nancy. *c. 1889*
Five-layer glass.

(left) CAT. NO. 26-27
Two lidded Vases with an Orchid
Vase: Emile Gallé, Nancy. *1889-90*.
Setting: Bapst & Falise, Paris
Vase: two-layer glass. Setting: silver
H (with lid) 28 cm

(right page) CAT. NO. 73
Female Mask
Henri Cros, France. *c. 1896*
Glass (pâte-de-verre)
H 23 cm

It is possible, through the Hermitage's collection of Western European Art Nouveau (called 'Stil Moderne' in Russian), to trace many specific features of the style's birth and development. That collection took shape around the turn of the 19th and 20th centuries, a time of great changes in Russia, and it is linked above all with the names of two Tsars, Alexander III (1881-94) and his son, the last Russian Emperor, Nicholas II (1894[1]-1917).

Unlike its predecessors, it should be stated, Art Nouveau was not a court style. The ceremonial halls of Russian palaces built in the Baroque and Neoclassical ages were not suited to house beneath their vaults objects of such mobile, winding forms, products of a new age. Yet the imperial family could not be behind the times and so it was that Nicholas II's wife, Empress Alexandra Fyodorovna, acquired vases by Gallé while the widow of Alexander II, Dowager Empress Maria Fyodorovna, by birth a Danish Princess, purchased objects made in the 'new style' from the Royal Manufactory in Copenhagen.[2] Art Nouveau's more intimate approach was not in keeping with the Winter Palace's rich decoration and the style was thus reflected to the greatest degree in the imperial family's country residences around St Petersburg, for instance in the Alexander Palace at Tsarskoe Selo, or the Cottage at Peterhof, from whence many objects entered the Hermitage collection after the Revolution.

The first masterpieces of French applied art in this style, made by leading craftsmen and in the best centres of production, made their appearance in the Winter Palace as early as the late 19th and early 20th centuries, arriving as diplomatic gifts to Russian emperors. Among them is the table *Lotharingian Flora* (Flore de Lorraine), presented by the French government to Alexander II during a visit by Russian sailors to Toulon in 1893, a visit undertaken on the eve of conclusion of an alliance between France and Russia.[3] Lorraine's fate depended on this alliance and the region therefore had a particular interest in Russian goodwill. Perhaps this explains why Lorraine was given the honour of producing a gift for the Russian court. The result was a marquetry table produced by Emile Gallé in collaboration with masters of the School of Nancy. *Lotharingian Flora* presents an allegorical tale of the region's battle to free itself from German domination. Made of walnut and adorned with marquetry of different kinds of wood, the table contains a plethora of symbolic elements: the sunflowers and forget-me-nots of the stand, the inscription on the edge, 'Pervincio' (the Latin name for bindweed, which means 'to bind together tightly'), the depiction of a Gallic oak and a Russian pine. More symbols are crammed onto the table top: to right are the arms of Lorraine, a cross with lilies on the ends, entwined with honeysuckle (symbol of a warm alliance) and tongues of flame; to right is a spider and its web, allegorical depiction of the German domination, the incrusted drops of glass representing tears. Perhaps the symbolism is a little naïve – the towns of Lorraine are represented by flowers, with lunaire or lunaria for Luneville, charme or hornbeam for Charmes-la-Côte, or the flowers and plants that symbolise the towns in the coat-of-arms, with a thistle for Nancy. In the left corner we see the dawn, as three birds of the night fly into the distance. Below is the inscription: 'preserve the hearts that you have won' (Gardez les coeurs qu'avez gagnés). During restoration of the table a note was discovered inside listing the names of all those masters who took part in its creation. The object superbly combines features characteristic of the transitional phase of Gallé's work, from Historicism to Art Nouveau, and this prestigious gift played a significant role in his

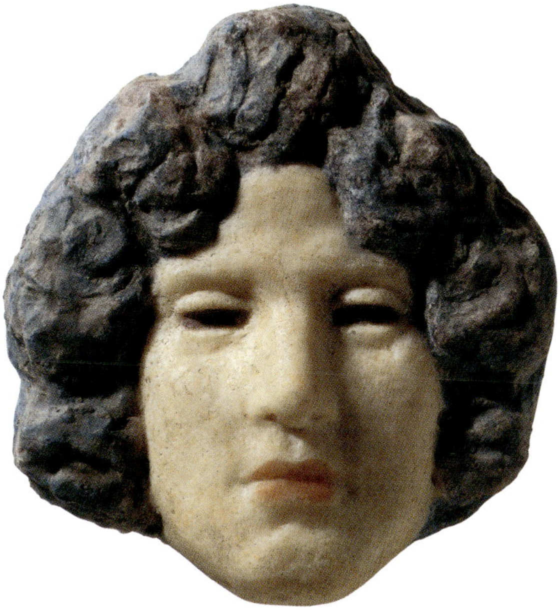

1. In 1894 Alexander III died to be replaced by his son Nicholas, who was to be crowned only in 1896.
2. *Nikolay i Aleksandra. Dvor poslednikh russkikh imperatorov. Konets XIX – nachalo XX v.* [Nicholas and Alexandra. The Court of the Last Russian Emperors. Late 19th – Early 20th Century], exh. cat., Hermitage Museum, St Petersburg, 1994, p. 302.
3. T. V. Rappe, 'Pamyatniki russko-frantsuzkikh svyazey poslednego desyatiletiya XIX veka' [Monuments of Russo-French Relations in the Last Decade of the 19th Century], *Soobshcheniya Gosudarstvennogo Ermitazha* [Proceedings of the State Hermitage], issue LV, 1991, pp. 18-24.

establishment as a craftsman. On 8 May 1894 the Russian ambassador in Paris Baron de Mohrenheim officially expressed his thanks of His Majesty of Lorraine and soon after an alliance was concluded against Germany that included both Russia and France. Thus could a piece of furniture help shape politics.

Accompanying the table was *The Golden Book* (Le Livre d'Or), containing more than 80 drawings by artists of Lorraine within a superb leather binding. Once the object of so much attention in the medieval and Renaissance eras, binding came once more within the orbit of craftsmen at the turn of the 19th and 20th centuries and *The Golden Book* is among the most outstanding examples of this art form. Taking part in creating its binding were celebrated artists of the time, René Wiener and Victoir Prouvé, members of Nancy's Alliance provinciale des industries d'art. On the title page is an allegorical image in which Lorraine stretches forth the hand of friendship to Russia, surrounded by numerous symbols, among them the thistle (favourite of all flowers in the Art Nouveau style), olive branches and crosses of Lorraine.

Several of the drawings in the book show works of applied art, being designs for other gifts made to the Russian sailors: a punch bowl by Camille Martin adorned with thistles, and glasses by Auguste Daum showing crosses of Lorraine and stylised eagles intended as gifts to the officers (cat. 28). Glasses made to this design are now to be found in the Musée d'Orsay in Paris. One such glass was recently acquired by the Tsarskoe Selo Museum Reserve in Pushkin.

From the fact that objects created by masters of the School of Nancy were chosen for presentation as diplomatic gifts we can be sure both of their high quality and that those masters enjoyed the recognition of their contemporaries.

Also linked with Gallé and the School of Nancy are two unique vases in the Hermitage with depictions of orchids. These were presented to another Russian Tsar, Nicholas II, during a visit to France in 1896. Engraved upon the vases are lines of poetry by Emile Hinzelin. Made in the 1890s, the vases were not made specifically for the Russian Tsar. They superbly reflect features of the new style both in the ornament – particularly the silver mounts (only partially preserved) – and in the pinkish-lilac glass with its etching and carving. This technique was perfected by Gallé and made his works famous during this period. Two kinds of orchid – a flower that became almost the symbol of fin de siècle art – are used in the decoration, confirming the suggestion of Elena Anisimova that these vases form an illustration to Gallé's scientific interest in the evolution of different specimens of orchid, which he studied throughout his life.[4] It seems unlikely that the Russian Emperor would be presented with these vases if their meaning truly lay in 'the charm of death', which forms the essence of Hinzelin's poem.

Paris celebrated a 'Russian week' from 5 to 10 (17 to 22) October 1896. In the presence of the Emperor Nicholas II the foundation stone was laid of the Alexander III Bridge – a gift from the Russian state to the French capital. In the Hermitage is the small steel hammer with an ivory handle that was used by Nicholas during the opening ceremony.[5] Through this visit in 1896 many gifts presented to the imperial couple entered the Winter Palace, most of them the work of France's leading masters. Amongst them is a silver figure personifying Peace by Lucien Falise, whose name was well known in both France and Russia. Of greatest value, however, are the objects given to Nicholas II and Alexandra Fyodorovna during their visit to the Sèvres Porcelain Manufactory, thanks to which we have a vivid example of how older production centres were reacting to Art Nouveau style.[6] Above all, we should note two large vases with the arms of the Russian Empire after models by Albert Ernest Carrier-Belleuse (cat. 92-93). Although they were created by one of the leading Art Nouveau masters, their form and decoration is traditional. Another vase, known as the Nîmes Vase, is adorned using a technique much favoured in Art Nouveau, pâte-sur-pâte (cat. 100). Another piece, a mask in glass paste by Henri Cros, is of interest not for any great artistic value but because of the material, which Cros introduced to Art Nouveau glass (cat. 73). The gifts also included several biscuit porcelain figures of Nicholas II's predecessors on the throne of Russia, of Catherine II, Paul I and Alexander I, and a biscuit porcelain plaque with a portrait of the reigning Tsar and Tsaritsa and an inscription commemorating their visit to the Manufactory on 8 (20) October 1896 (cat. 134).

Numerous ceremonies were held during the visit of 1896, some of them recorded in a vast canvas by Georges Becker, showing the meeting of the two heads of state, Nicholas II and Felix Faure, in Paris. Special medals were struck in honour of this historic event and a huge body of souvenirs produced, among

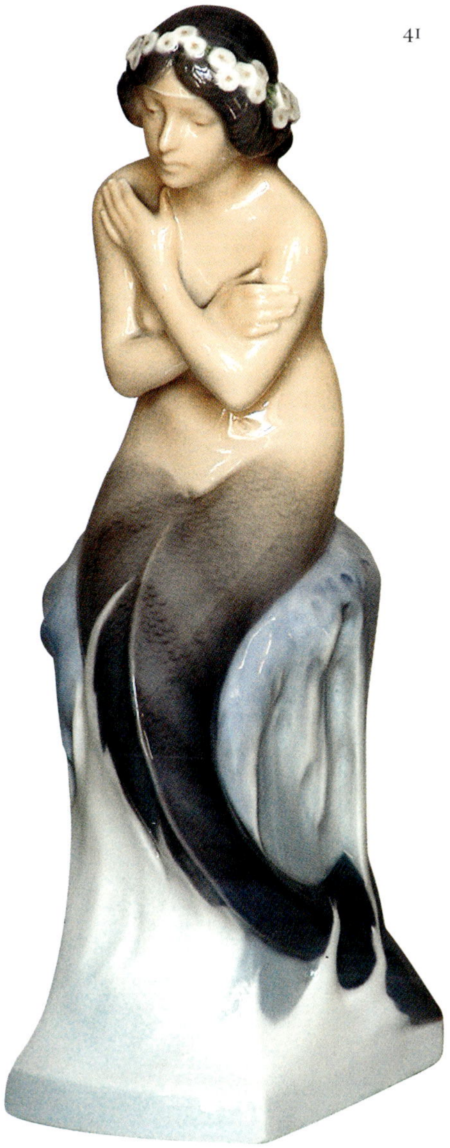

FIGURE OF A MERMAID
Model by Christian Thomsen, Royal Porcelain Manufactory, Copenhagen. *1911*
Porcelain
H 25 cm

CAT. NO. 103

4. *EMIL' GALLE I BRAT'YA DOM. "LOTARINGSKIE ORKHIDEI..."* [EMILE GALLÉ AND THE BROTHERS DAUM. "LOTHARINGIAN ORCHIDS"], EXH. CAT., HERMITAGE MUSEUM, ST PETERSBURG, 1999, P. 40.
5. *NIKOLAY I ALEKSANDRA...*, P. 250.
6. N. I. KAZAKEVICH, *ZAPADNOEVROPEYSKIY FARFOR V ERMITAZHE. ISTORIYA SOBRANIYA* [WESTERN EUROPEAN PORCELAIN IN THE HERMITAGE. THE HISTORY OF THE COLLECTION], ST PETERSBURG, 2003, PP. 225-27.

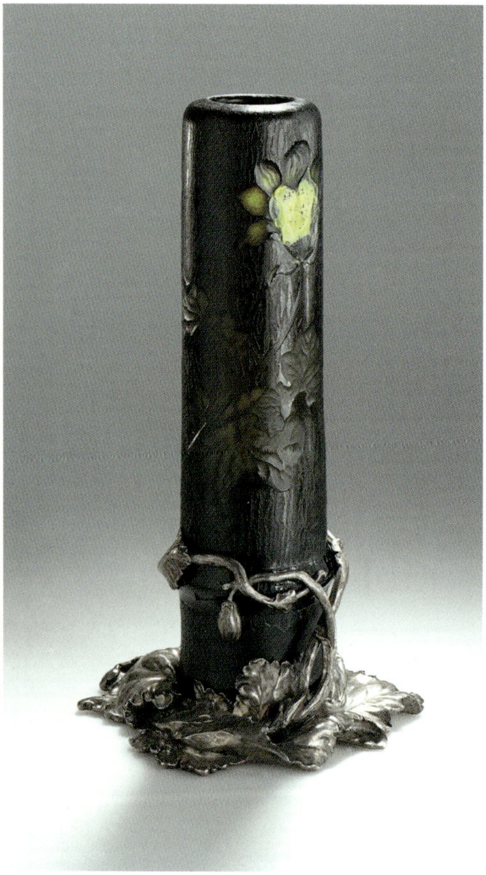

(above) CAT. NO. 31
VASE WITH DAHLIAS
Vase: Emile Gallé, Nancy. *1898*. Setting: Yury Rapoport, firm of Carl Fabergé
Vase: three-layer glass with intarsia. Mount: silver
H (with setting) 25.8 cm

(below) CAT. NO. 153
TABLE *FLORE DE LORRAINE*
Workshop of Emile Gallé, Nancy. *1893*
Design by Emile Gallé and L. Hestaux
Walnut, marquetry of different kinds of wood and glass, metal
H 97 x W 207 x D 77 cm

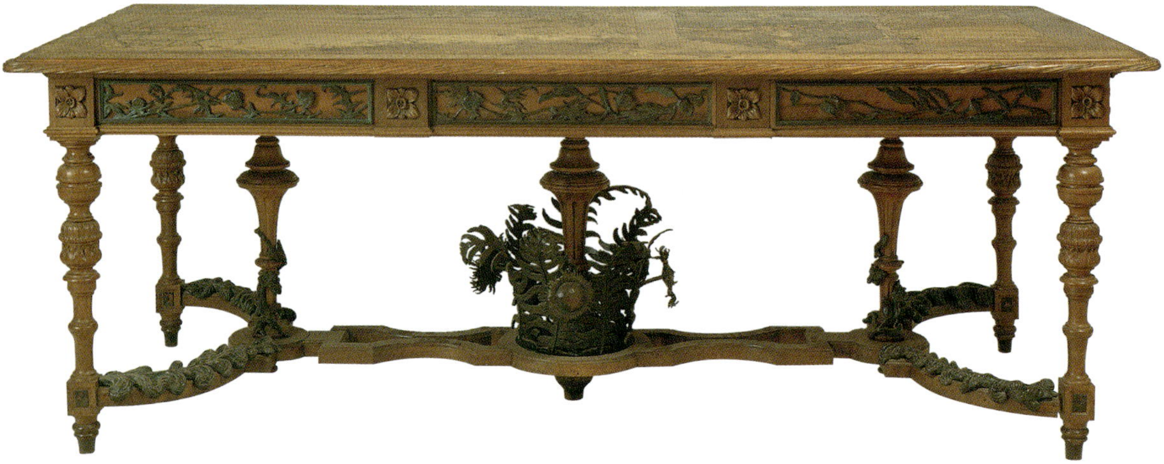

them small crosses, handkerchiefs, badges and commemorative medals for members of the delegation. These small objects, lacking any particular artistic interest, are nonetheless excellent examples of French mass output in the late 19th century. Some of those souvenirs are to be found today in the Hermitage collection.

During a later visit to Paris in 1901, Nicholas II received another gift from the French government, this time a table decoration, *Dance with Scarves,* by Agathon Léonard van Weydeveldt.[7] This superbly elegant work enables us to judge just how much the products of the celebrated Sèvres Manufactory had altered. Created for the Exposition Universelle in Paris in 1900, the table service consists of fifteen figures, each in a different pose, that form a musical rhythm of flowing lines in a manner typical of Art Nouveau.

Nor did the Art Nouveau style pass by the Gobelins Tapestry Manufactory, as we can see from a series of tapestries showing *The Seasons* presented to Nicholas II in 1914 during a visit to St Petersburg by the French President, Raymond Poincaré.[8] Author of the cartoons for these tapestries was a celebrated master of poster design, Jules Cheret. His female figures personifying the four seasons recall his graphic images: while the background is only summarily indicated, it is the expressive line of the figure that forms the key artistic element in each image.

Through diplomatic visits, therefore, at the turn of the century the Hermitage collection gained important works from France. Particularly notable amongst these were items by Emile Gallé. (The very fact that his works were included amongst gifts to the Emperor indicates the status he enjoyed.) On 24 May 1902 the magazine *L'Illustration* published twelve glass objects created by Gallé and presented to Russia during a visit by the President of France, Emile Loubet.[9] Amongst these is the *Passiflora* vase (cat. 25), with depictions of the sabre laid by Loubet upon the tomb of Alexander III. That sabre, adorned with an olive branch, was the work of Lucien Falise, and running along the ribbon that winds around the blade are the words 'Je me souviens de mon alliance' [I remember my allegiance]. Thus, each in their own way, French gifts of applied art contained hidden or overt symbolic references to the French people's desire for alliance with Russia.

In addition to those items that were presented as gifts, Art Nouveau objects were specially commissioned in Russia for the adornment of various imperial residences. From the palace of Grand Duke Vladimir, for instance, the Hermitage gained a cupboard bearing the mark of the French trading house L'Escalier de Cristal,[10] clearly revealing the influence exerted by Japanese art on Art Nouveau during the last quarter of the 19th century. Oriental motifs are reflected in the object's form – recalling a pagoda – and in its decoration, with bronze fittings in the form of dragons and figures in Oriental attire, while the central door includes an inset

7. Ya. E. Vilensky, '"Tanets s sharfami" v Ermitazhe' ["The Dance with Scarves" in the Hermitage], *Na rubezhe vekov... Iskusstvo epokhi moderna* [At the Turn of the Centuries. Art of the Age of Art Nouveau], St Petersburg, 2006, pp. 129-35.
8. *Ibid.*, pp. 69-70.
9. *L'Illustration*, 24 mai 1902, No. 3091.
10. T. V. Rappe, 'Novoe o frantsuzskoy firme XIX veka Eskal'ye de kristal' [New Information about the French 19th-century Firm Escalier de cristal], *Prikladnoe iskusstvo Zapadnoy Evropey i Rossii* [Western European Applied Art in Russia], Leningrad, 1983, pp. 119-27.

watercolour by the artist George Clairin showing a woman in a kimono. This cupboard was designed by Edouard Lièvre, the design acquired by L'Escalier de Cristal. It was one of six cupboards sent to Russia, as we know from inscriptions on drawings in an album of designs by the firm, kindly shown to us by M. Philippe Thiébaut. The album includes numerous objects sent to Russia by Escalier de Cristal for the imperial family and for other Russian clients. Russian archives provide further evidence of contacts with the French trading house in the form of invoices and accounts.[11]

It is thus clear that Emile Gallé and many other Art Nouveau masters were known and admired at the Russian imperial court.

Art Nouveau in the Hermitage in the Last Quarter of the 19th – Early 20th Century

In addition to these masterpieces that arrived via the imperial family or as diplomatic gifts, the Hermitage collection includes the works of masters of the turn of the 19th and 20th centuries that came through other channels. Most of them derive from a museum set up in St Petersburg in 1881, attached to the School of Technical Drawing created with funding from the patron Baron Alexander Stieglitz. Indeed, the foundation of such a museum was characteristic of the last quarter of the 19th century. Museums of applied art were being established in Britain and Germany and Russia was not behind in setting up its own such institution. Very soon the Stieglitz Museum had become the most important collection of applied art in Russia. Its collections were formed through the efforts of the director, Maximilian Messmacher, and its Honorary Patron, Alexander Polovtsov, the Emperor's Secretary of State, Secretary of the State Council, manufacturer and politician. It was Polovtsov and Messmacher who ran the acquisitions policy and much depended on their taste and competency in matters of art. Items were purchased at auction in Paris, Vienna, Berlin and Munich. Polovtsov's memoirs frequently record his search for objects to be purchased for the Stieglitz Museum during his foreign travels.[12] Simultaneously, Polovtsov was assembling his own collection, later to be sold in part to the Museum by himself and his relatives.

Russia's leading museum of the applied and decorative arts was bound to react to contemporary fashion. Works from the second half of the 19th and early 20th century, not at that time prized by collectors, were

(right) CAT. NO. 139
Tapestry *L'Hiver. Les Houx*
[Winter. Holly]
Design by Jules Chéret
Manufacture Nationale des Gobelins, Paris. Woven by Ch. Thuaire, L. Claude. *1911–13*
Wool, silk
270 x 170 cm

(overleaf) CAT. NO. 143
The Arrival of Tsar Nicholas II in Paris, October 1896
Georges Becker. *1896-97*
Oil on canvas
180 x 200 cm

11. Russian State Historical Archive, Fund 255, *opis'* 3, *delo* 89, f. 167; Fund 521, *opis'* 1, *delo* 89, etc.
12. *Dnevnik Gosudarstvennogo sekretarya A. A. Polovtsova* [Diary of Secretary of State A. A. Polovtsov], Moscow, 1966, vol. 1, p. 441.

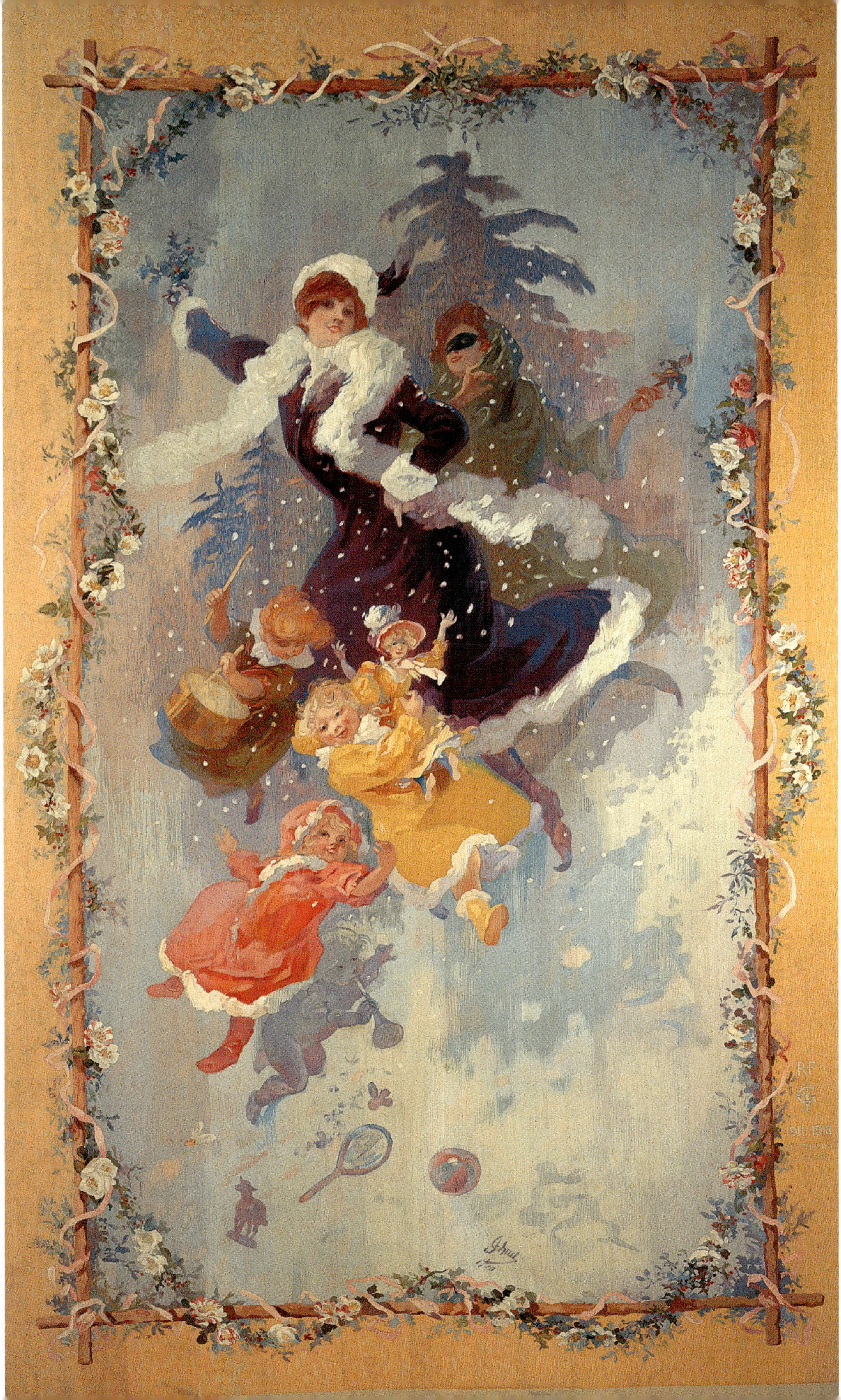
RF
1911 1913

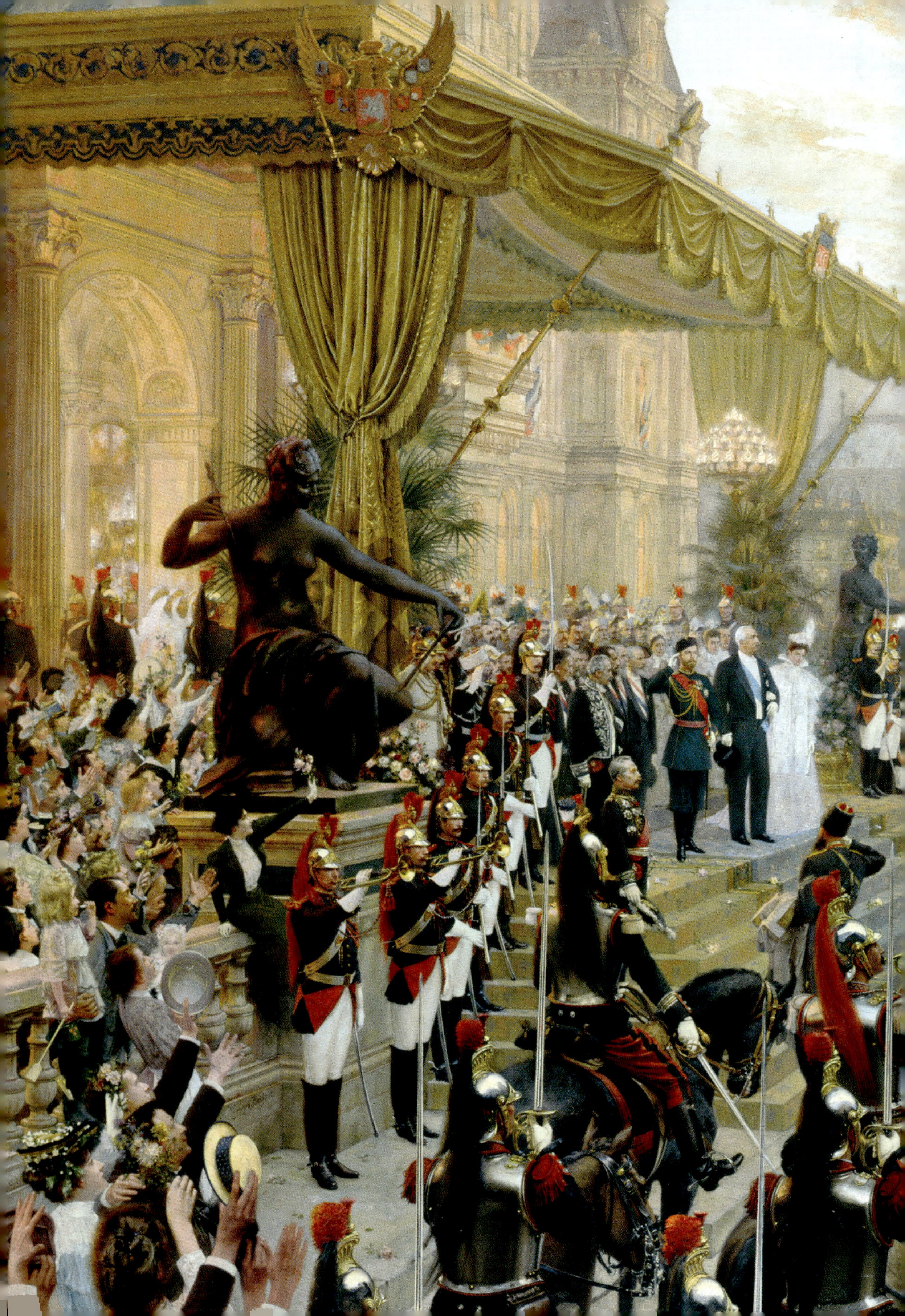

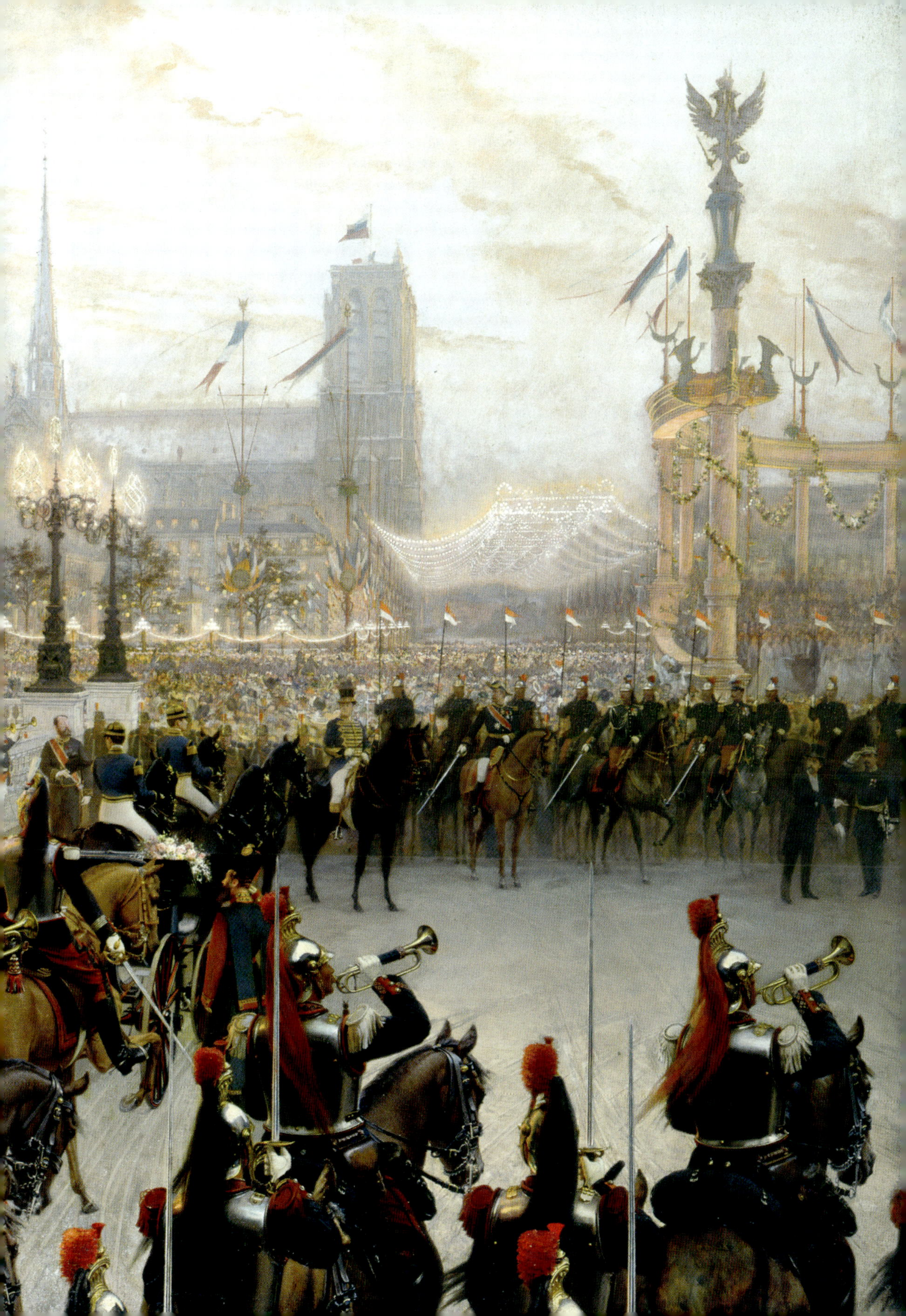

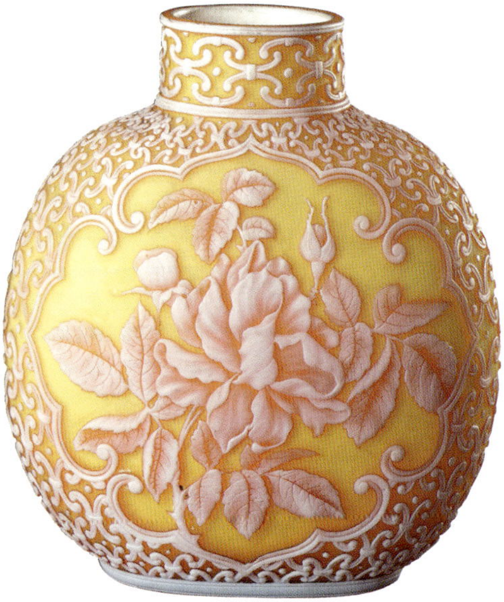

(above) CAT. NO. 16
Vase with a Rose
Thomas Webb and Sons factory, Stourbridge. *c. 1889*
Four-layer glass
H 15 cm

(right page) CAT. NO. 35
Vase with Symbols of Night
Emile Gallé, Nancy. *1900*
Two-layer glass
H 30.5 cm

acquired by the Stieglitz Museum with the aim of creating a full artistic and historical picture of the development of the arts in Europe. The Museum was particularly interested in glass, ceramics and jewellery and we gain some idea of the collectors' taste from those contemporary masters whose work was chosen for acquisition. In the end, the body of Art Nouveau works that arrived in the Hermitage from the Stieglitz Museum reflected all the main trends in the development of the applied arts during that period, forming the core of the Hermitage's collection of late 19th and early 20th-century works.

From 1851 the best examples of all the industrial arts were shown at regular International Exhibitions. One aspect of the Stieglitz Museum's activities was the purchase of objects directly from such exhibitions.

In 1878, Nadezhda Polovtsova, wife of Alexander Polovtsov and adopted daughter of Baron Stieglitz, acquired from the Exposition Universelle in Paris a collection of contemporary European glass which she then presented to the Stieglitz Museum.[13] It included the products of British firms employing a newly fashionable method of creating an iridescent surface, world-famous Bohemian items, glass pieces from the Italian firm of Salviati & Co. and the French firm of Joseph Brocard, as well as items by the celebrated masters J. & L. Lobmeyer.

Attention was once more directed towards glass makers at the Universal Exhibition of 1889. Through Alexander Polovtsov, the Museum acquired layered glass by the English firm of Thomas Webb, several items by the celebrated Emile Gallé representing the School of Nancy (including a vase with a dragonfly and a toad – symbolic contrast of the forces of good and evil) and glass by Ernst Leveillé, an artist working in Paris. These purchases were complemented by a gift of English and French items from Nadezhda Polovtsova.

Attention was drawn at the 1900 Paris Exposition Universelle by products from a ceramics workshop at Rookwood. This celebrated American ceramic ware was covered with coloured glazes and received a Grand Prix in Paris. Today the Hermitage has several vases by Anna Valentien, Sally Toohie and John Wareham, celebrated masters at Rookwood. Other acquisitions included European ceramics by Taxile Doat, who worked at the Sèvres Manufactory.

Another particular aspect of the Museum's activities lay in the purchase of applied art from leading contemporary masters, the selection of such items reflecting the interests of the Stieglitz Museum's agents in coloured enamel and all kinds of glassware. From the celebrated French jewellery firm Bapst & Falise they acquired, in the year it closed (1892), a copper dish in the Art Nouveau style covered with painted enamels depicting daffodils, tulips and the four seasons. From another French jeweller, Georges Jean, who specialised in transparent enamels, the Museum purchased in 1900 a small plate bearing his signature and a small copper vase with animals enamelled by the Paris master Paul Louchet. In September of that year three glass vases with depictions of chrysanthemums, begonias and symbols of the night were purchased in the shops of Emile Gallé for 1,500 francs. In 1901, the Stieglitz Museum added to its collection several glass pieces and a cylindrical copper box covered in enamel, straight from the workshop of Louis Comfort Tiffany. That same year, the attention of the Museum's agents was drawn to leather bindings being produced at the Oxford University Press: decorated leather bindings were a particularly popular aspect of Art Nouveau style. A year later, purchases were made from

13. T. V. Rappe, 'Istoriya formirovaniya kollektsii evropeyskogo moderna v Ermitazhe' [History of the Formation of the Hermitage Collection of European Art Nouveau], *Na rubezhe vekov... Iskusstvo epokhi moderna* [At the Turn of the Centuries. Art of the Age of Art Nouveau], St Petersburg, 2006, pp. 23, 25.

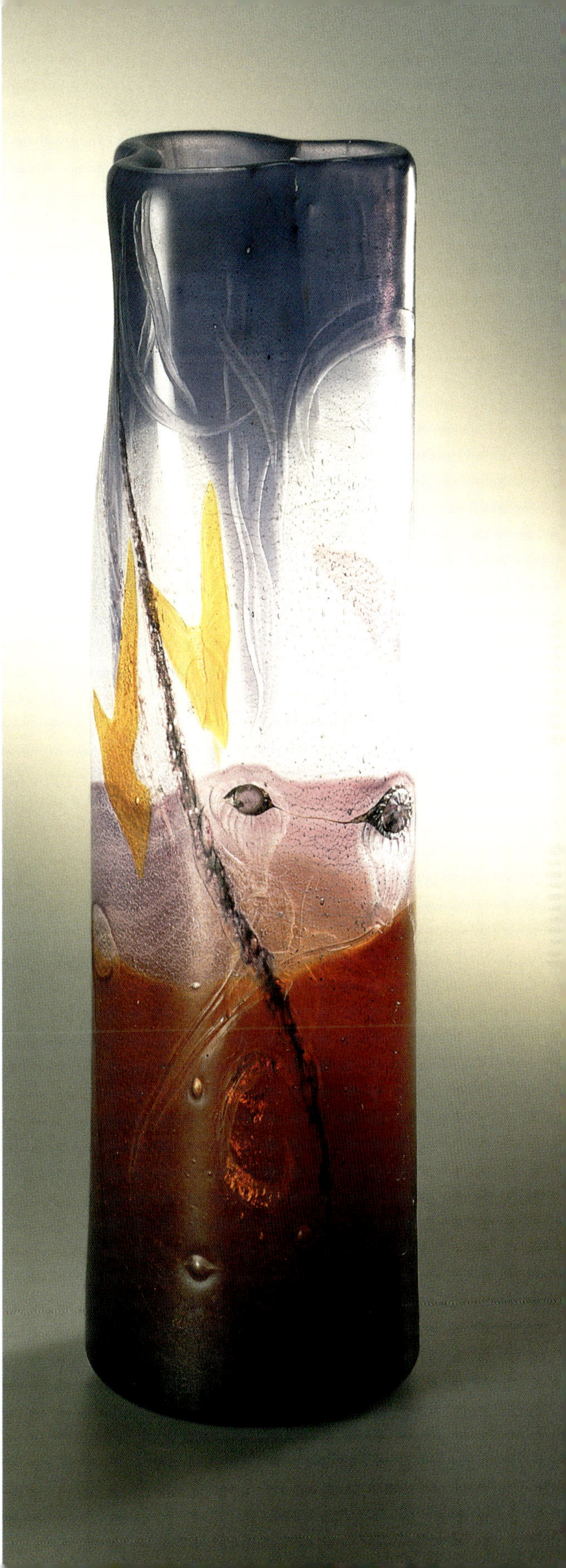

the workshop of leading jeweller René Lalique: a pendant, a pendant brooch, a buckle, comb and winebowl all in the Art Nouveau style. In 1906 two plates and two vases on stone mass, using the pâte-sur-pâte technique, were acquired from ceramicist Marta Raphael, once again the choice of objects being quite deliberate: Raphael had graduated from the Stieglitz School of Technical Drawing, although her career took shape abroad, in Germany, Bohemia and in Vienna. In each of those lands Art Nouveau had its own very specific features, all of which can clearly be seen in her works.

The Stieglitz School had long-established links with the Bing shop, celebrated in the age of Art Nouveau, acquiring there mainly Oriental pieces. A few individual European items were, however, purchased through the shop: in 1901 the Museum acquired ceramic and ivory pieces and a stained glass panel with magnolias by Tiffany. Stained glass was, indeed, another typically Art Nouveau form, widespread in France – particularly in the School of Nancy – but also in the rest of Europe and America. Tiffany used transparent, milk and matt glass, tinted various colours, to create quite extraordinary designs.

With the Russian Revolution of 1917, a new and fascinating phase began in the history of the Stieglitz Museum. Works from many nationalised collections flowed into the Stieglitz Museum which was, by decree of the Soviet Government, transformed into The First Branch of the Hermitage Museum. In 1924 it was closed and its collections were in part transferred to the Hermitage itself. Amongst the private collections which brought the Museum works of applied art were those of the Princes Gorchakov, the Counts Shuvalov and Vorontsov-Dashkov and the Dukes of Leuchtenberg, as well as non-nobles such as Arkady Rudanovsky. These, however, mainly contained works of the 18th and 19th centuries, with almost no Art Nouveau pieces. There are but a few items worthy of notice: a table by Gallé with dragonfly legs that came from the Gorchakov collection, or a fan from the Vorontsov-Dashkov house, while the Yusupov collection produced a number of dresses from the Paris house of Worth and several Art Nouveau pieces of jewellery.

It was thanks to the Stieglitz Museum that the Hermitage gained a superb collection of Art Nouveau reflecting all the main trends in the development of the applied arts during that period.

That collection is not a static one: additions are made regularly. Many pieces have arrived in recent decades through the Hermitage Purchasing Commission, using money provided by the state specifically for this purpose. In the 1950s and 1960s items by celebrated European masters of the late 19th and early 20th century that once adorned the homes of St Petersburg's inhabitants might often be encountered on the Russian antiques market. It was from this source that the Hermitage gained its main collection of works by Gallé and the Daum brothers, more than 70 pieces in all, and during this period many items from the Royal Copenhagen Manufactory were acquired. There were acquisitions in these years of glass by Lalique, porcelain from the Swedish Rörstrand manufactory, a vase in stone mass from the Doulton factory at Burslem in England and many others. Such products were not highly prized in the middle of the 20th century and could easily be acquired through the Hermitage Purchasing Commission and from Leningrad's sole

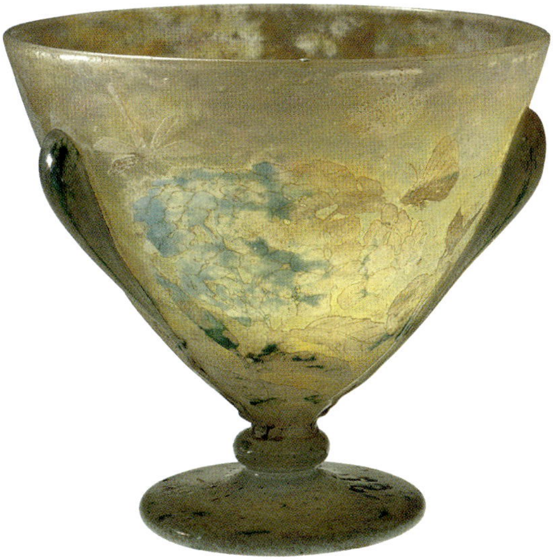

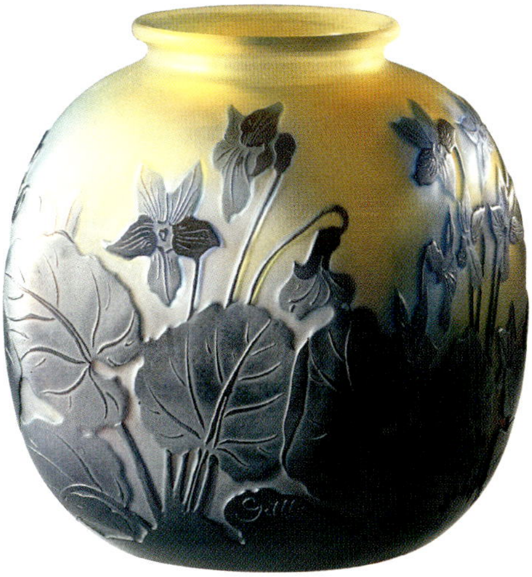

remaining antique shop. In the 1970s the Museum acquired a number of unique pieces, such as a desk designed by Henry van de Velde. A table of this kind was first produced for a study in Munich and the design was then repeated on numerous occasions, the Hermitage example being one of a number of variations. It is decorated with copper and carving in the form of a flattened frog on the doors and is the only piece in the Hermitage designed by Van de Velde. Nonetheless, it is sufficient to demonstrate this artist's role in the development of Art Nouveau.

Today items produced at the turn of the 19th and 20th centuries only rarely become available, although occasionally pieces are placed before the Purchasing Commission that are valuable in filling gaps in the Art Nouveau collection. Very recently a ceramic parrot was acquired, an early and characteristic work by Gallé (cat. 49). Only a knowledge of Gallé's work enables one to comprehend the significance of this piece in our understanding of his career. Another purchase was of a unique tray with painted enamels in the Oriental manner, also by Gallé, illustrating the influence of Oriental art on the French craftsman.

Through a combination of different circumstances, therefore, the Hermitage today has a unique collection of works by European masters that makes it possible to present not all but certainly many aspects of Art Nouveau and its formation in Western Europe.

(left) CAT. NO. 63
VASE WITH HYDRANGEAS,
BUTTERFLIES AND DRAGONFLIES
Manufactory Daum Frères,
Nancy. *c. 1910*
Three-layered glass
H 14.4 cm

(right) CAT. NO. 48
VASE WITH VIOLETS
Manufactory of Emile Gallé,
Nancy. *1930s*
Three-layer glass
H 11 cm

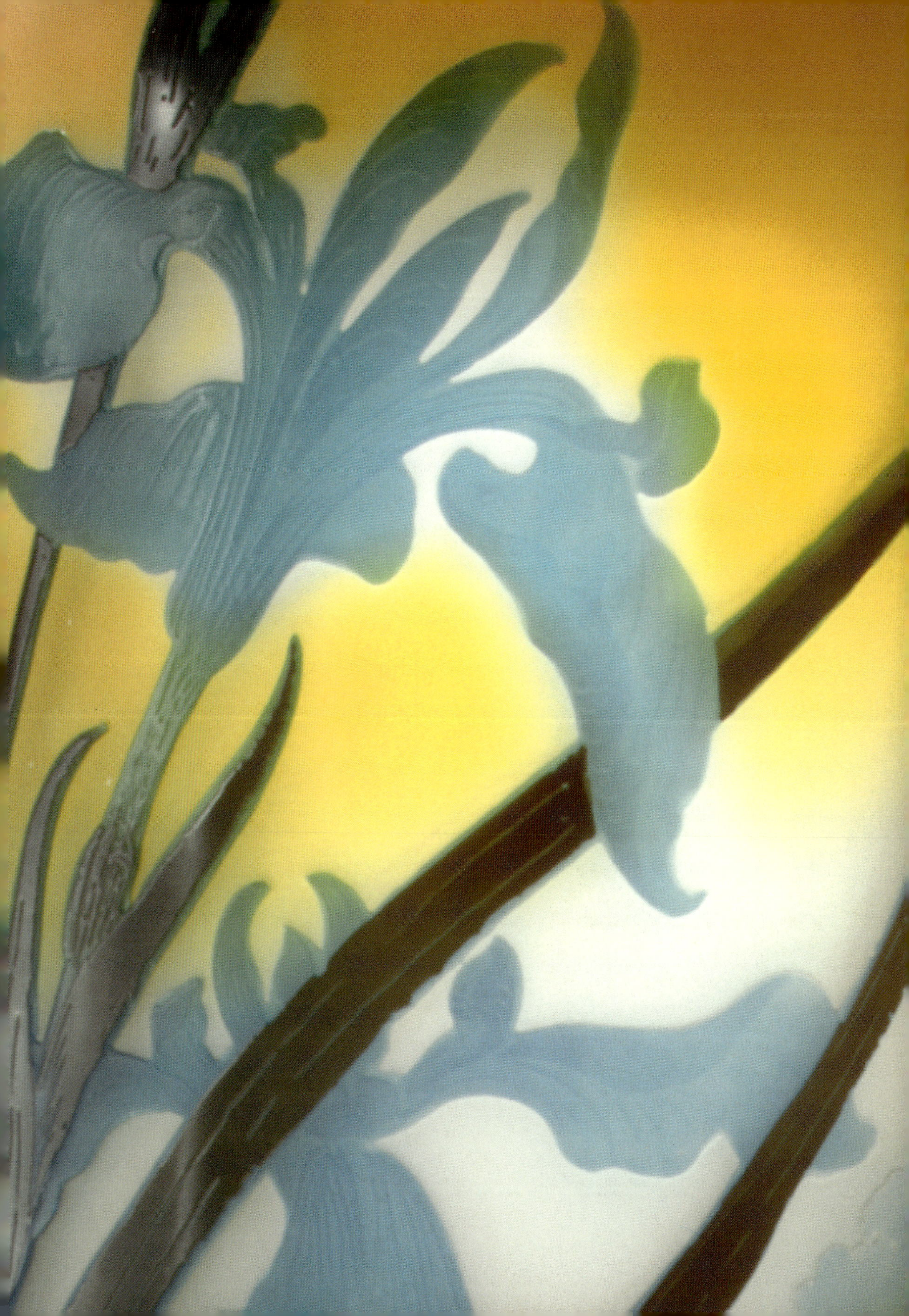

Elena Anisimova

European Artistic Glass of the Age of Art Nouveau

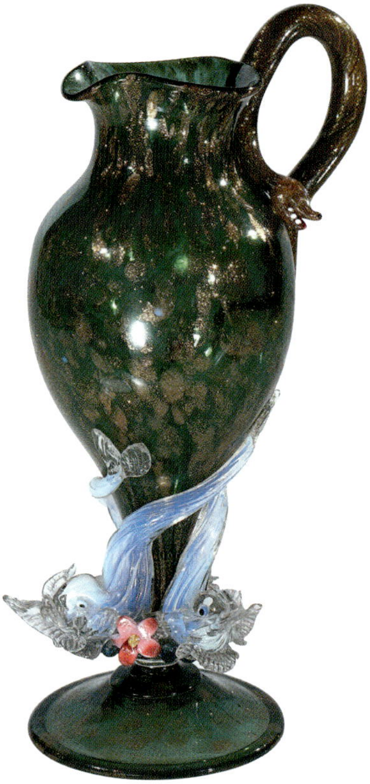

(previous page) CAT. NO. 39
VASE WITH A LANDSCAPE WITH A LAKE
Manufactory of Emile Gallé, Nancy. *c. 1904*
Four-layer glass

(left) CAT. NO. 1
JUG WITH A SNAKE-SHAPED HANDLE
Salviati Dottore Antonio, Venice. *c. 1878*
Glass
H 26.5 cm

(right page, left) CAT. NO. 8
VASE IN THE FORM OF A MOSQUE LAMP
Philippe-Joseph Brocard, Paris. *1878*
Glass, painted enamel
H 14.6 cm

(right page, right) CAT. NO. 14
VASE WITH A THISTLE STEM
Thomas Webb and Sons factory, Stourbridge. *c. 1889*
Glass
H 22.6 cm

In Europe the flourishing of artistic glass production coincided with the dominance of Art Nouveau. Extensive use was made of this fragile material in architecture and in the decoration of interiors at the turn of the 19th and 20th centuries. '... the house with all its relevant adornments and arrangements is a finish work of applied art, its true expression', wrote William Morris.[1] One such adornment was glass applied art. There was a general renaissance of the art of stained glass, used to adorn not only mansions by leading architects of the style such as Victor Horta and Henry van de Velde, but also public buildings and even the entrance halls of apartment blocks. The range of objects available in glass, obligatory element in the decoration of any interior with pretentions to style during this period, grew considerably. Manufactories and artistic workshops produced glass tableware and vases of all kinds, lamps, perfume bottles and even small sculptures.

Taking advantage of the material's rich potential, major craftsmen such as Emile Gallé, Louis Comfort Tiffany and René Lalique were able to develop their own individual approach to working with glass. The signatures they placed on their works are evidence of the importance of each piece that emerged from the workshops. It was during this period, indeed, that trademarks began to be placed widely not only on individual handmade pieces but, due to growing competition, on all kinds of manufactured products.

Industrial progress did not free glassmakers from the need to master all aspects of the craft, but it did extend the material's poten-

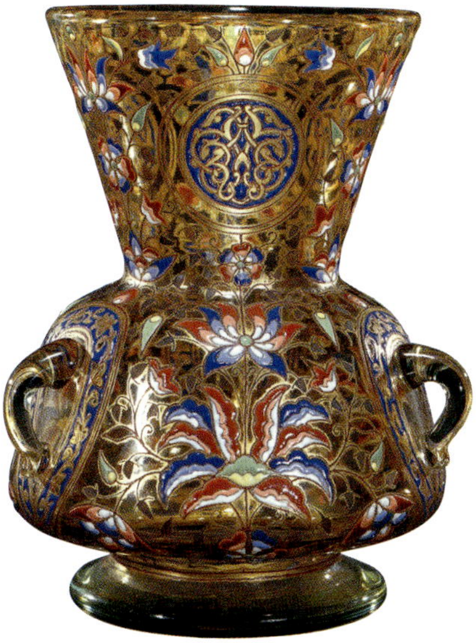

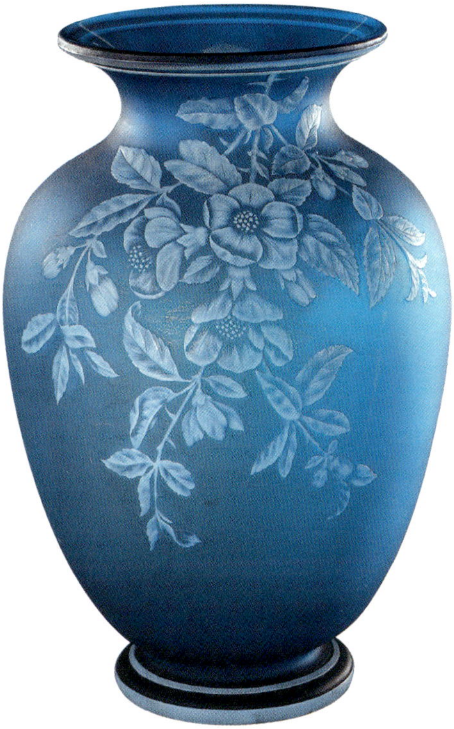

tial, allowing for experimentation with all kinds of technical advances and for creation of a richer range of colours.

Glass in the Mid-19th Century

In speaking of a renaissance of European glass in the 19th century we must look back to a key event, the first ever international exhibition, the Great Exhibition held in London in 1851. This marked the start of a search for a new expressive language in all spheres of the applied arts, blossoming towards the end of the 19th century in Art Nouveau. Crystal Palace – then the largest ever construction of glass and metal, created by Joseph Paxton for the Great Exhibition – demonstrated the possibilities open to architecture of the future. It was the first construction to use such huge panes of window glass, a daring innovation, and extensive use of glass was later to be one of the defining features of Art Nouveau.

For several decades following the Great Exhibition of 1851, attention was concentrated on reviving – using new technical advances – the existing methods for producing and working glass. Enamelling, applying gilding between layers of glass, carving into multi-layer glass – these were but a few of the traditional methods of decoration demonstrated at the next international exhibition, the Exposition Universelle held in Paris in 1878.

1. Cited from the Russian translation in V. V. Vanslov, 'Morris ob Arkitekture i sinteze iskusstv' [Morris on Architecture and the Synthesis of the Arts], in the anthology: *Estetika Morrisa i sovremennost'* [Morris's Aesthetics and the Modern Age], Moscow, 1987, p. 94.

Amongst the manufactories presenting their works in glass at the exhibition, greatest recognition was won by traditional European glassmaking centres, leaders for several centuries in this form of the decorative and applied arts: by Venice and the central European lands of Germany, Austria and Bohemia.

By the second half of the 19th century, the dominant company in Venice was Salviati & Co.,[2] its products looking to models of the golden age of Italian glassmaking in the 16th and 17th centuries. Salviati craftsmen combined different techniques used at various stages in the history of Venetian glassmaking. Their works from this period, in the Historicist style, tend to be brightly coloured, combining colourless and coloured glass and making extensive use of gold and copper foil.

Central European manufactories presented works in Renaissance style at the 1878 Exposition Universelle, as well as vessels repeating the forms and decoration of 14th-century Syrian pieces. They adorned their products with engraving and painted enamels.

In the 1870s Britain joined the ranks of leading glass producers. Thanks to the activities of John Northwood I and the firm of Thomas Webb & Sons[3], multi-layer glass became fashionable. The technique of carving into contrasting coloured two-layer glass, recalling the engraving of layered cameos, was known in Ancient Rome. The first work to be produced in the modern form of this technique was a copy, made by John Northwood in 1876, of the celebrated 1st-century AD Portland Vase:[4] there was no coincidence in the fact that the English craftsman was using a Classical prototype.

The Paris exhibition of 1878 presented the results of many experiments in the making of glass conducted during the 1860s and 1870s. It demonstrated both the extensive possibilities already open to glass production and the variety of dominant artistic styles. It was to be the starting point for a search for new expressive means, allowing for maximum exploitation of this fragile and plastic material around the turn of the 19th and 20th centuries.

New Centres for Glass Production

Towards the end of the 19th century we see a change in the leading glass producers, with the masters of France and the United States of America now enjoying greatest fame. In both lands there was a lack of clear national traditions that allowed for considerable freedom in seeking a new language, combined with an advanced technical base that made possible considerable experimentation with many methods of working glass.

Vase with a Toad and a Dragonfly
Emile Gallé, Nancy. *1888*
Two-layered glass
H 16.1 cm

cat. no. 22

2. Salviati & Co., founded on the island of Murano in 1860 by Antonio Salviati (1816-90). It produced artistic glass and mosaics.
3. Thomas Webb & Sons, one of the leading English glass manufactories in the second half of the 19th century. It began production of objects from multi-layered so-called 'cameo' glass in 1876.
4. The Portland Vase, an example of Roman cameo-glass. Dated by scholars at the British Museum, where the vase is now located, to the 1st century AD.

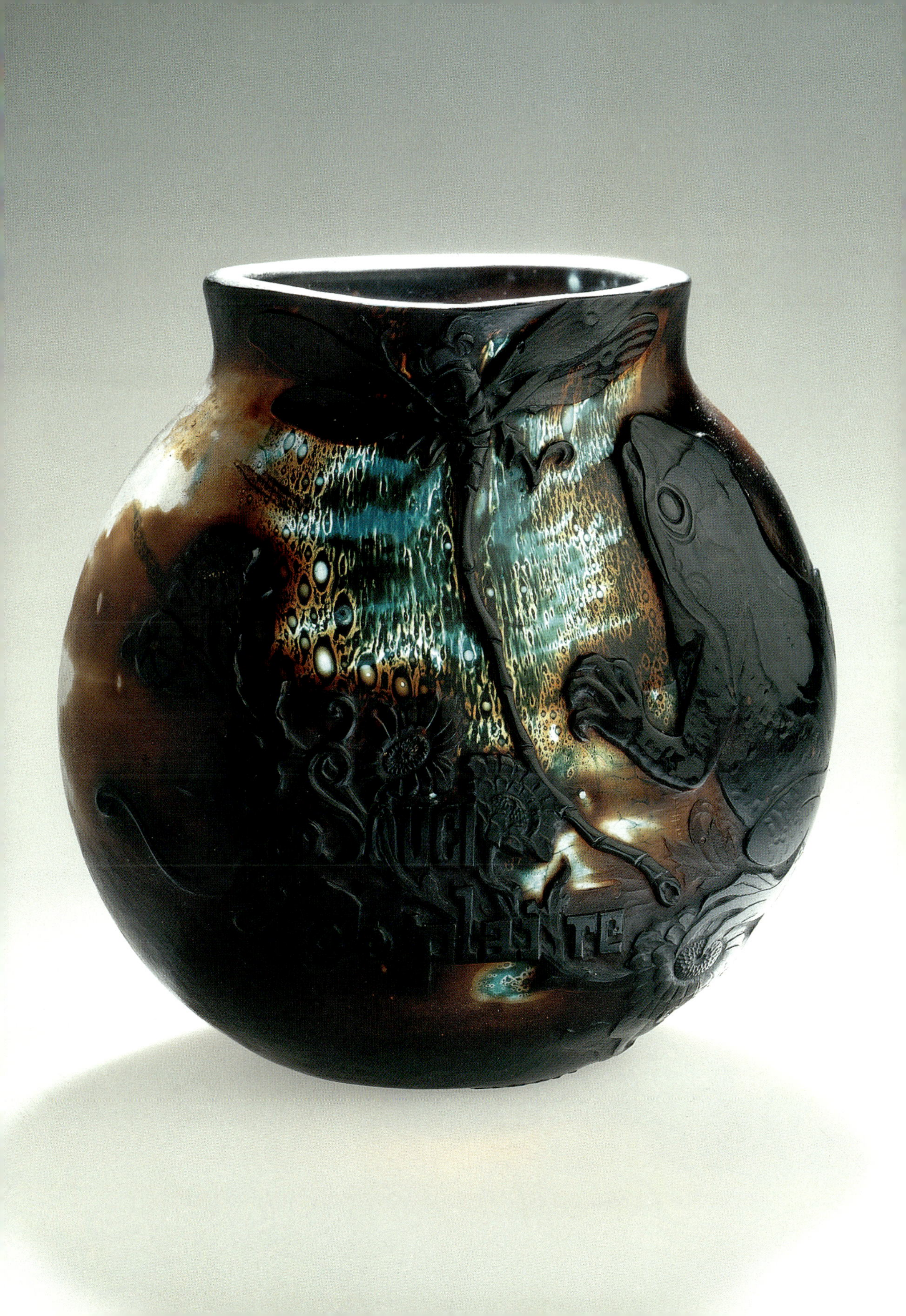

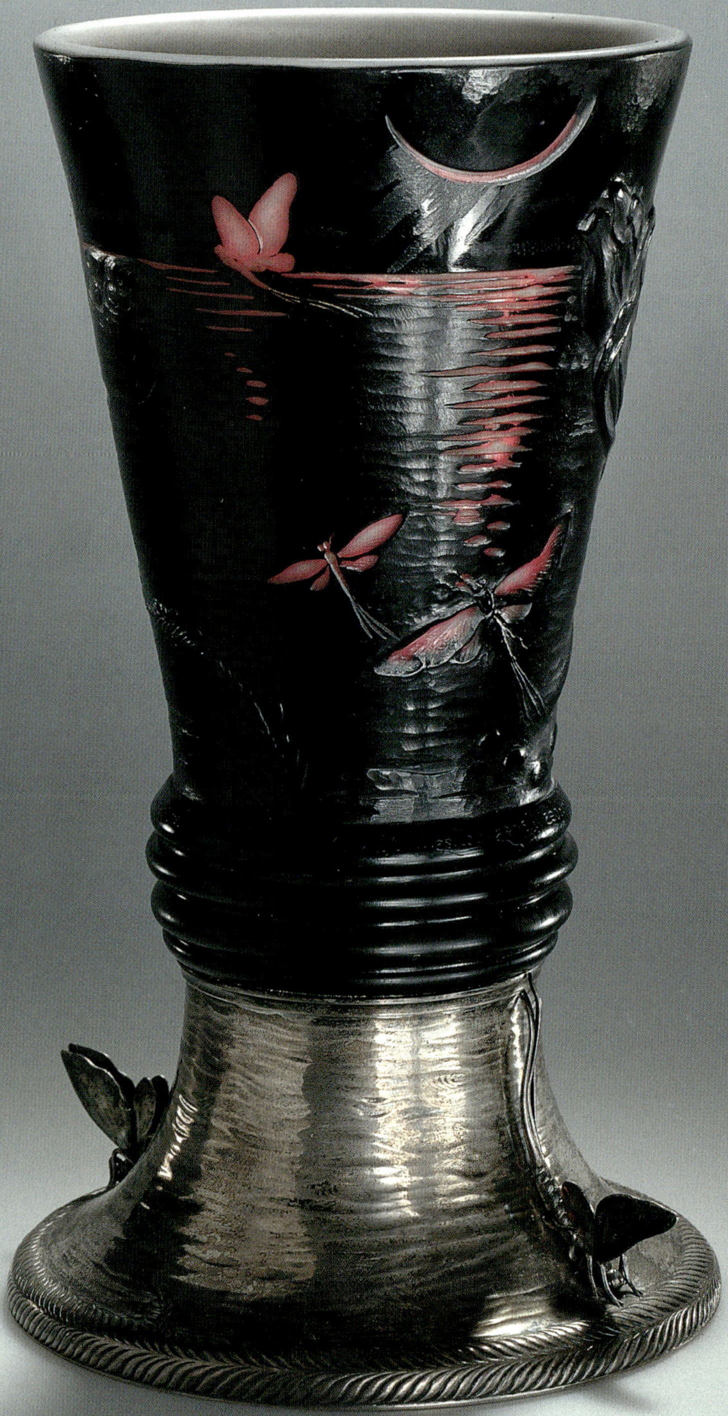

France was to be the founder of the new style in European glassmaking. During the 1870s, French glass was dominated – as was typical of applied art of the time – by a mixture of restrospective styles from different ages. One contemporary wrote: 'Entering at that time an elegant Paris salon, one risked finding oneself in some cosmopolitan bazaar in which all epochs, from Amenophis to Louis XVI, and all nations from China to India, were gathered together.'[5]

One of the first artists to reject traditional decorative principles in working glass in the 1870s was the Paris master François-Eugène Rousseau (1827-91), who created vases from transparent colourless or tinted glass in his studio. He achieved the decorative effect of many of his works solely through the introduction of dots or spots of metal oxides into the mass of freely arranged colour, through the frosting of the surface or the creation of craquelure effects. In his skill in emphasising the beauty of the material itself, Rousseau revealed his interest in Oriental culture. The influence of Oriental art was most strikingly manifested in his works using two-layered carved glass that recall in technical terms the vessels made by 18th-century Chinese craftsmen.

Vase with Water Anemones
and Dragonflies in Flight
Vase: Emile Gallé, Nancy. *1892*
Setting: Yury Rapoport, firm of Carl Fabergé
Vase: four-layer glass. Mount: silver
H (with setting) 20.5 cm

CAT. NO. 29

In the middle of the 1880s Rousseau began to collaborate with his pupil, Ernest-Baptiste Léveillé (1841-1913) whose independent works revealed a loyalty to the aesthetic principles and technological devices of his teacher.

The work of the two masters was recognised by contemporaries in a series of awards at Expositions Universelles in Paris in 1878 and 1889. It was not they, however, who were to be the founders of the new style.

Emile Gallé and Nancy

At the end of the 19th century, the centre of French glass production was to be Nancy, in Lorraine, a region celebrated for centuries as a centre of glassmaking. As a result of the Franco-Prussian War of 1870-71 and the annexation of Alsace and part of Lorraine by Germany, Nancy was temporarily the capital of this French province. Many talented artists flowed in from the occupied territories and events so tragic for France and, particularly, for Lorraine were to lead to a rise in national consciousness and patriotism. The heraldic symbols of Lorraine and Nancy, frequently placed on works by masters of the region, reflect this interest in local history.

Closely linked with Nancy is the master who was to exert a decisive influence on the development of Art Nouveau glass, Emile Gallé (1848-1904). Gallé came from a family of glassmakers and received a superb and varied education. He drew well, studied botany, literature, philosophy and politics, interests that were to be reflected in his creations.

5. 'Wenn man jetzt einen eleganten Pariser Salon betritt, so läuft man Gefahr, in einen kosmopolitischen Bazar zu greaten, wo alle Jahrhunderte, von dem des Amenophis bis zu dem Ludwig XVI., und alle Nationen, von China bis Italien, sich Stelldichein gegeben', E. Levasseur, 1903; Cited in Susanne Netzer, *Glas der Moderne. 1880-1930*, Berlin, 1994, p. 9.

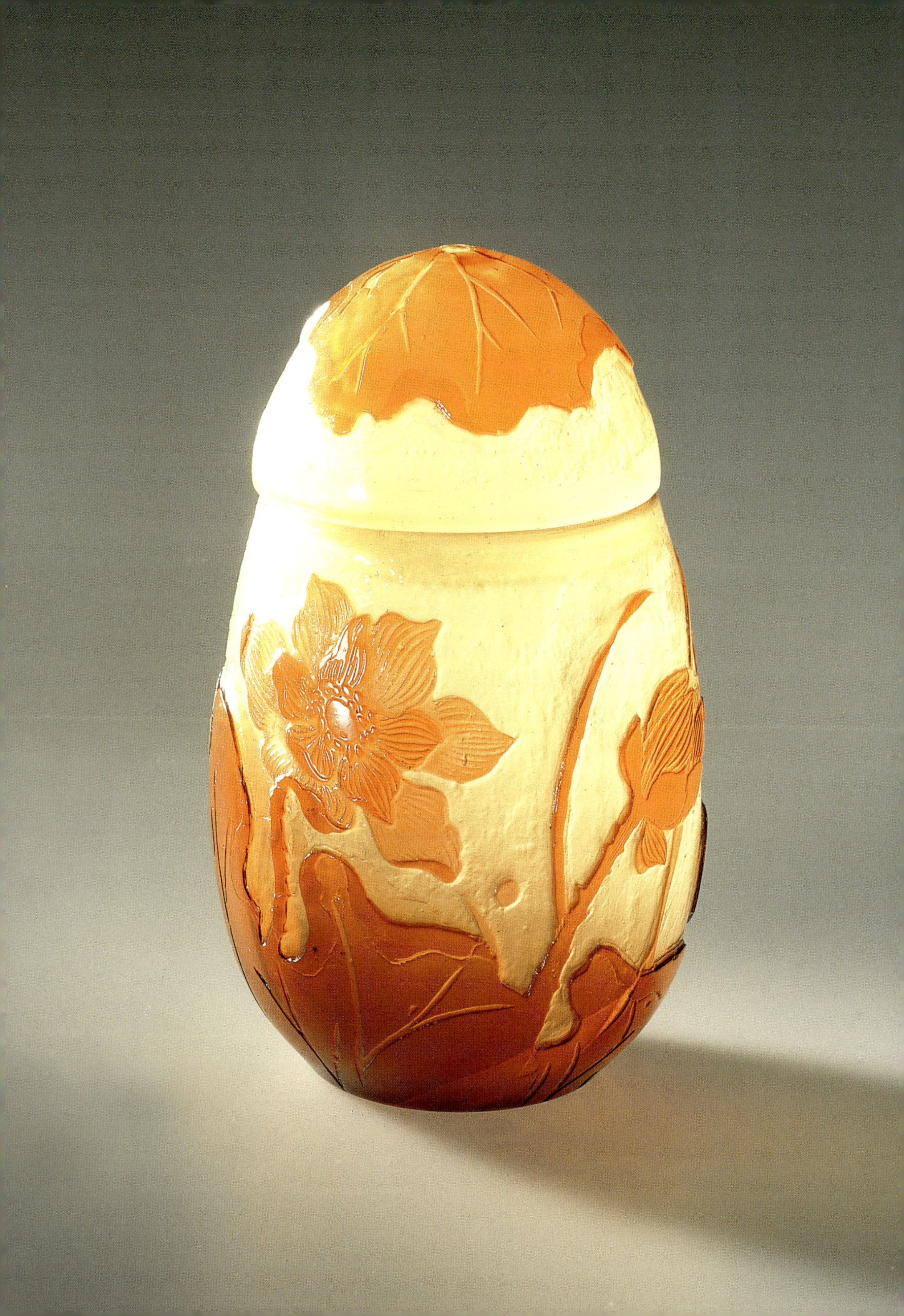

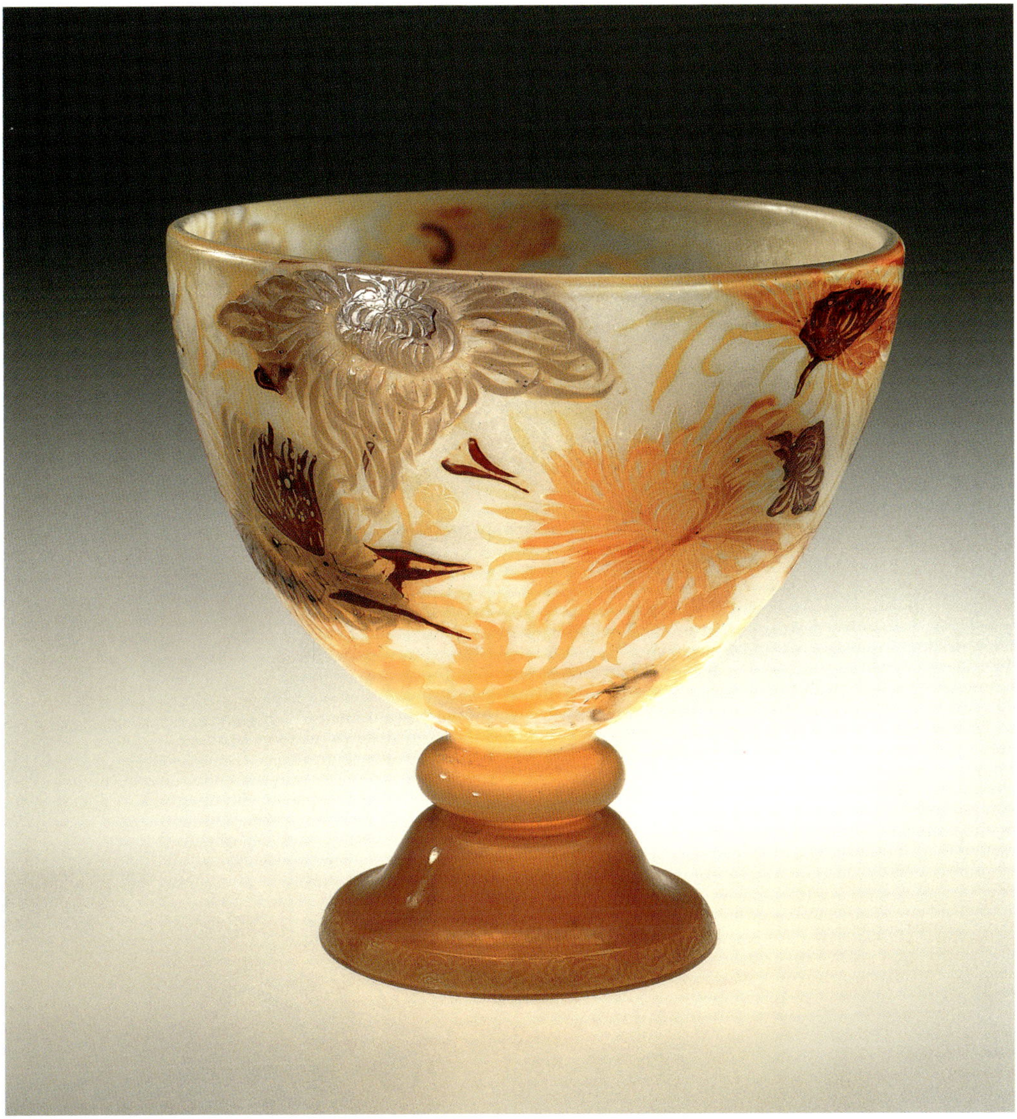

(left)
Lidded Vase with Lotus
Emile Gallé. Nancy. *1897*
Two-layer glass
H (with lid) 11.5 cm

CAT. NO. 30

(above)
Vase with Chysanthemum
Emile Gallé, Nancy. *1900*
Four-layer glass
H 26 cm

CAT. NO. 33

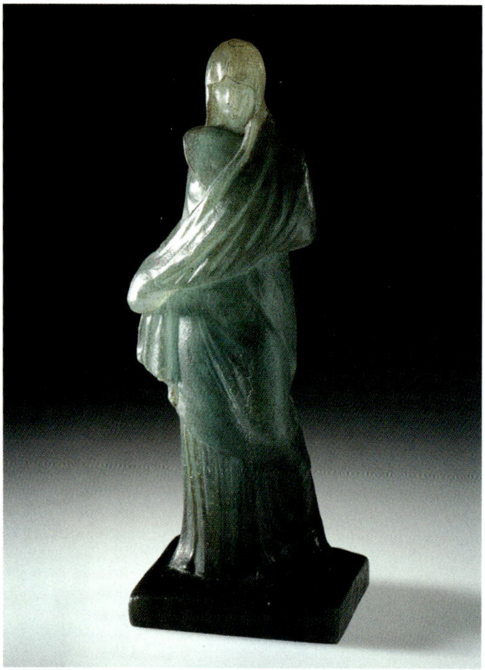

Statuette: Woman with a Fan
Manufactory Daum Frères, Nancy. *c. 1910*
Glass (pâte-de-verre)
H 19.6 cm

CAT. NO. 62

Gallé first showed his works, both as an independent artist and as head of a firm, at the Paris Exposition Universelle of 1878. Despite their high quality of execution, however, noted by the jury at the time, these early objects do not stand out in any artistic sense amongst the mass of products from other contemporary manufacturers.

Over the course of the 1880s, Gallé devoted himself to finding his own style. Taking up the experience of those of his predecessors who had already earned general approval, Gallé combined elements of traditional Venetian glass production, Rousseau's experiments with glass mass, some features of British glassmakers' work with two-layer glass and his own knowledge of the art of China and Japan. One result was that in the late 1870s and 1880s Gallé created a series of vessels with floral forms adorned with polychrome enamel painting, but it was his works using multi-layered glass with very fine colour transitions, achieved by etching away the upper layers of glass to different depths, that were to achieve greatest success.

These vases are adorned with images of flowers, their precise depictions of the structure of each bloom revealing Gallé's serious botanical studies. Those vegetable motifs also often had a symbolic meaning: the thistle signified the town of Nancy, the fern indicated silence and rest, the rose – the beauty of life. In the 1880s and 1890s Gallé created vases that he entitled 'Verreries parlantes' or 'Speaking glass', with lines of verse by his favourite poets – Baudelaire, Maeterlinck and Hugo – woven into the ornament by incising them with a fine needle. Visible only when closely viewed, they further stress the meaning with which Gallé imbued each of his works. 'En ses creusets / Le langage des fleurs et des choses muettes' (In his crucibles / Is the language of flowers and all dumb things) is engraved on one vase in the Hermitage collection.

The Exposition Universelle in Paris in 1889, which included the first extensive display of vases from multi-layered glass, brought Gallé widespread recognition and fame as France's leading glassmaker. The success of his works was facilitated by maximum use of the material's potential, its transparency and wealth of colours, the free arrangement of the design on the vessel's body and the realism of the images, combined with a relevant contemporary message were the key features that were to be copied by numerous followers.

In 1894 Emile Gallé acquired a large glass manufactory on rue la Garenne in Nancy. This marked the start of the firm's industrial production and from the mid-1890s Gallé produced not only exclusive models, made as unique pieces or in very limited editions, but objects intended for a wider circle.

Gallé's style began to gradually change at the end of the 19th century, thanks not only to the start of industrial production but also – indeed largely – to general tendencies affecting the development of Art Nouveau. Gallé was increasingly interested in combining contrasting colours, experimenting with the introduction of metal oxides into the glass mass. His early death in 1904 cut short his further development. Deprived of its leader, the manufactory began to decline, losing its leading position in European glassmaking. It finally closed in 1936.

The Ecole de Nancy

During Gallé's lifetime, in 1901, the School of Nancy was set up under his leadership, bringing together leading artists of the applied arts in Lorraine. Masters of this school were renowned for their work not only with glass, but also with metal, ceramics and furniture. Gallé's closest followers, who also helped set up the School, were the brothers Auguste (1853-1909) and Antonin (1864-1930) Daum. Their father, Jean Daum (1825-85), was amongst those who had settled in Nancy because of discontent under the German occupation of Lorraine. A lawyer by training, in 1878 he acquired a glass manufactory, the Verrerie Sainte-Catherine, which he renamed Verrerie de Nancy. During its early stages the manufactory produced vases and table glassware in the Historicist manner, frequently painted with heraldic symbols of Nancy and Lorraine (the manufactory's trademark was to include the six-pointed cross of Lorraine). Influenced by Gallé's success at the Exposition Universelle in Paris in 1889, the Daum Brothers started to blow items from multi-layer glass, adorning them with flowers and landcapes using the layered etching technique. They sought to compete with Gallé's manufactory in the 1890s but in 1899, partly because of growing competition from foreign manufacturers, the rivals started to collaborate, although this did not prevent the independent development of the two establishments. Despite the stylistic similarities in their products, those produced by the Daum Brothers are more decorative, lacking the philosophical subtext that Gallé gave his works. The manufactory of the Daum Brothers continued to flourish in the 20th century, successfully reacting to changes in trends and tastes.

The work of Emile Gallé and the Daum Brothers exerted a huge influence on glass products in the early 20th century: many manufactories produced works in the 'Gallé style' and centres in France, Britain, Germany and Scandinavia began to put out items in multi-layered glass adorned with flowers and landscapes.

Gallé's influence on European glass production was not, however, limited solely to imitation of his technological processes. His new decorative approach to the arrangement of vegetable ornament over the surface was to become widespread and in Gallé's wake Art Nouveau masters rejected the adornment of their products with traditional bouquets and garlands of stylised flowers, allowing more naturalistic flowers to spread freely across the

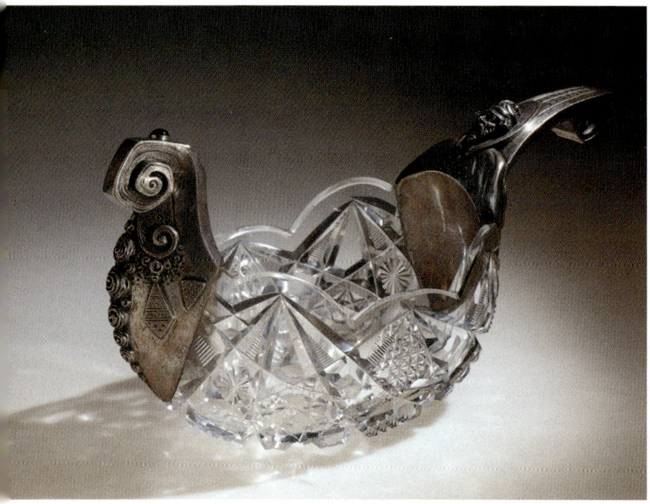

(above) CAT. NO. 86
KOVSH (LADLE) IN THE FORM OF A BOAT
Gus-khrustalny Manufactory,
Vladimir Province. *1910s*
Mount by 14 Artel, Moscow
Kovsh: crystal. Mount: silver, almandine
H 16.7 cm

(right page) CAT. NO. 84
SMALL *VASE POPPY AND BUTTERFLIES*
Imperial Porcelain and
Glass Manufactory, St Petersburg.
Design by K. Krasovsky (?). *1897*
Layered crystal
H 17.8 cm

vessel, giving additional dynamism to its form. The actual technique used to produce the glass was of minor importance, depending as it did solely on the traditions of each individual institution.

New Glass in Russia

In Russia, such vases were produced at the Imperial Glass Manufactory. In Manufactory documents they appear as 'imitation Gallé glass'. The first such pieces were made in St Petersburg in 1893 and indeed, mastery of the multi-layer glass technique was perceived as one of the most important achievements at the factory in the first half of the 1890s. Artists and craftsmen seemed to adopt quite naturally Gallé's principles for applying decoration, but many of the new techniques he had used were not taken up. During the earlier years designs were carved, a technique characteristic of the St Petersburg manufactory, and etching came to be used only in the early 1900s, the chemical being applied with brush in several sittings, which allowed for the creation of smooth tonal transitions.

Most of the Imperial Glass Manufactory's products were unique pieces, intended for the imperial family and their narrow circle. In many ways, the Manufactory's activities were determined by the tastes of these high-ranking clients[6] and it was the imperial family's interest in the work of Emile Gallé that facilitated the development of the new artistic trend in Russia.

In the private apartments of Nicholas II and Alexandra Fyododorovna in the Winter Palace, vases 'in the Gallé genre'[7] stood beside works by the French master himself.

6. T. A. Malinina, *Imperatorskiy Steklyannyy zavod. 1777-1917* [The Imperial Glass Manufactory. 1777-1917], St Petersburg, 2004, pp. 100, 115.
7. Works from the Imperial Glass Manufactory are marked thus in the inventory compiled by N. N. Dementyev, Guardian of the rooms, in 1909, see E. A. Anisimova, 'Vazy raboty Emilya Galle iz lichnykh pokoev Nikolaya II i Aleksandry Fyodorovny v Zimnem dvortse' [Vases by Emile Gallé from the Private Apartments of Nicholas II and Alexandra Fyodorovna in the Winter Palace], in: *Sud'by muzeynykh kollektsiy. Materialy VII Tsarskosel'skoy nauchnoy konferentsii* [The Fate of Museum Collections. Materials from the VII Tsarskoe Selo Scholarly Conference], St Petersburg, 2001, p. 204.

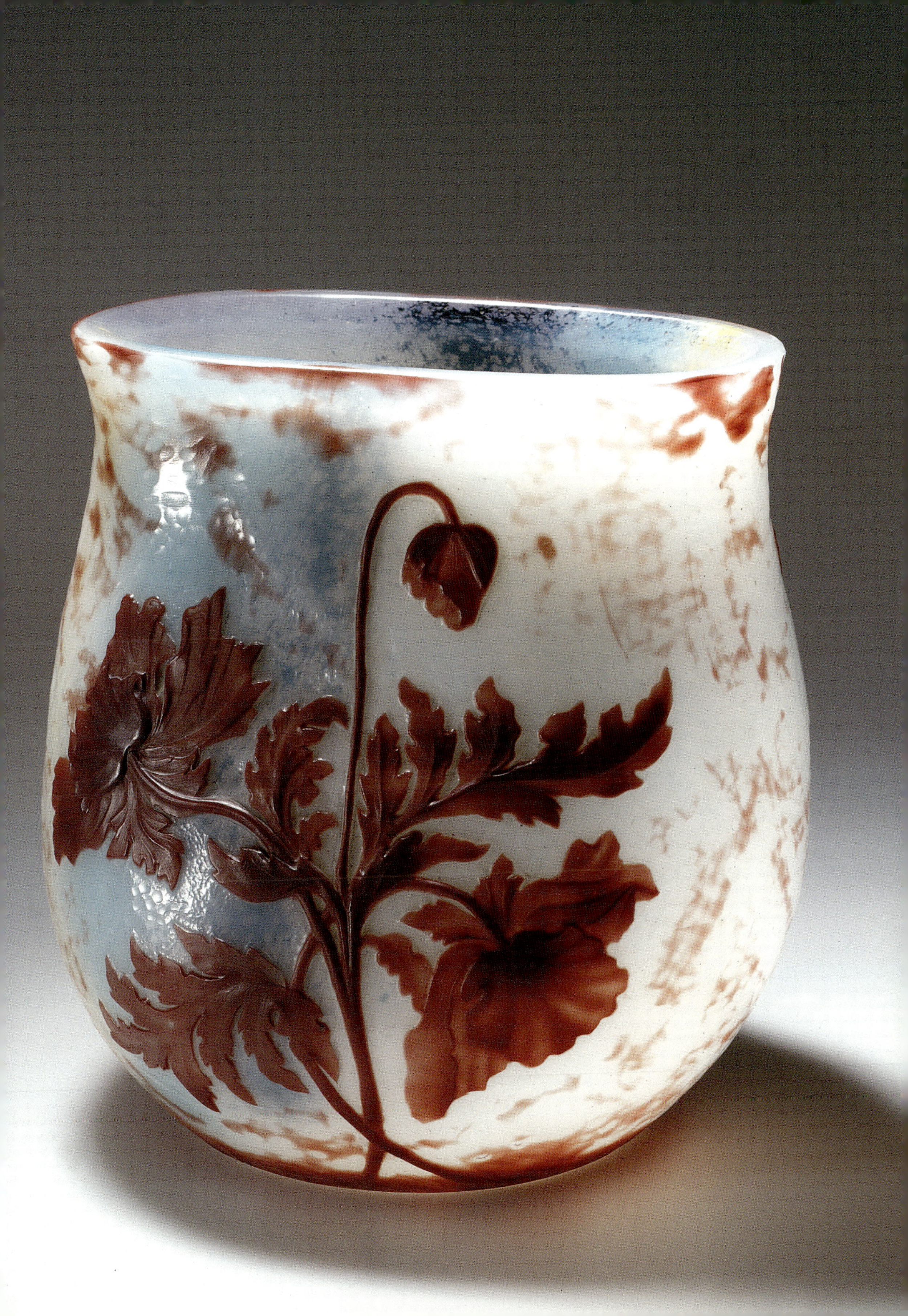

Numerous glass vessels were set out on tables, display cabinets and commodes, a superb example of Art Nouveau style in the royal couple's apartments, which were decorated in accordance with 'historical' taste.

Gallé's works came into the Winter Palace between 1896 and 1900. Two pairs of vases (cats. 26-27), presented to Nicholas and Alexandra during their official visit to Paris in 1896 at the head of a government delegation, stood 'on a bureau which stands by the wall abutting onto the Empire Drawing Room, near the door from this Drawing Room into the Louis XVI Drawing Room to left.'[8] The same document provides a detailed description of the vases, whose mounts were sadly lost in 1917: 'The necks of the vases adorned with oxidised silver fillets made in the form of twigs. Silver stands, oxidised, made in the form of baskets of twigs with on one basket the image of a single gilded lizard and three gilded butterflies, on the other an oxidised snake and a gilded frog.'

Vases by Gallé stood on tables in the Empress's study and were probably much prized. It has been suggested that some of them were acquired during visits to her relatives in Darmstadt.[9] One of the vases (cat. 29) is mistakenly recorded in the inventory as 'in the genre of Gallé', a misunderstanding that arose because the firm's trademark was covered by the object's solid silver mount. An invoice presented by Fabergé to the Imperial Cabinet on 21 February (5 March) 1898 informs us that the mount was made in 1897 – early 1898 and that it cost 70 roubles.[10] It was during restoration in 2000 that the master's signature was discovered beneath the mount: 'Emile Gallé 1892 Nancy fecit.' Until that time, scholars had for many years been incorrect in their dating of the vase and its authorship had been questioned. French scholar François le Tacon sought to identify it with a vase that Gallé had exhibited at the Exposition Universelle in Paris in 1889, described thus: 'Une coupe genre agate rubanée noire passant au verdâtre, à reliefs de fleurs carnées du coloris le plus suave' (A cup of the kind of variegated agate, passing from black to greenish, with relief flowers of the softest skin-coloured tint).[11]

Emile Gallé's works were kept not only in the Empress's rooms: several vases bearing his mark also stood in the Emperor's Study, but all we know of them is the information provided in surviving documents. An inventory of Alexandra's private apartments compiled at the end of the 1890s reveals that they were adorned with the products of another famous firm, that of Louis Comfort Tifffany, although not one of them is in the Museum today.

Louis Comfort Tiffany

American artist Louis Comfort Tiffany (1848-1933) started to compete with Emile Gallé and his followers in the late 1890s. His success in Europe was due above all to original vases in iridescent glass that he showed at exhibitions in Munich in 1897 and in Budapest in 1898, by which time his works were already known on the continent. At the Exposition Universelle in Paris in 1889 Tiffany had shown furniture, carpets and stained glass, and he received five Gold Medals.

Tiffany received an American patent for its famous iridescent glass in 1894. The first vases made in the new technique bear the name given them by the artist, 'Fabrile', an old English word meaning handmade. Soon, Tiffany changed this to 'Favrile', which was to be the name for all of his works covered with

Vase with Snake amidst Clover
Craftsman Sergey Romanov, Imperial Porcelain and Glass Manufactory, St Petersburg
Design by Konstantin Krasovsky (?). *1898*
Two-layer crystal
H 15.5 cm

CAT. NO. 81

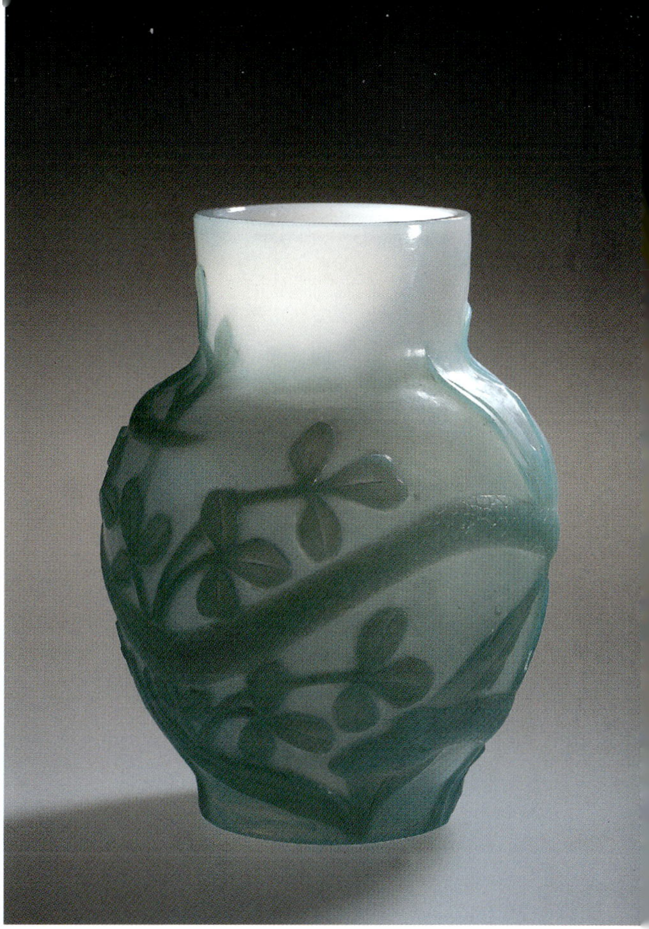

a dusting of metal oxides.[12] In each of his vases, the master experimented with form. His vessels are asymmetrical, their smoothly convex surfaces creating a decorative effect that is reinforced through the arbitrary application of lines of brown, golden, green, white and pale blue. Of all the many different models, greatest fame was enjoyed by Tiffany vases in the form of fantastical flowers.

If it was the Paris Exposition Universelle of 1889 that was decisive in bringing fame to Emile Gallé, it was at the Exposition Universelle of 1900 that Tiffany triumphed. At the start of the 20th century his style was taken up by many European manufactories. The most famous of these was Johann Loetz Witwe[13] in Austria. Founded in 1836 by Johann Baptist Eisner, its products enjoyed repeated success when shown at international exhibitions. In 1900 it began producing vases in iridescent glass, differing from Tiffany's products – which are characterised by warm ochre tones – in the predominance of cool pale bluish-green.

8. See note 7, pp. 204-5.
9. F. Le Tacon, *L'Oeuvre de Verre d'Emile Gallé*, Paris, 1998, p. 62, fig. 39.
10. *Fabergé: Imperial Craftsman and his World*, by Dr Geza von Habsburg with contributions by Alexander von Solodkoff, Dr Robert Bianchi, London-New York, 2000, p. 116, No. 177.
11. F. Le Tacon, *Op. cit.*, p. 62.
12. V. Arwas, *Glas vom Jugendstil zur Art Deco*, Stuttgart, 1987, p. 312.
13. The Manufactory Johann Loetz Witwe (the Widow of Johann Loetz) was founded in Klostermuhle, Southern Bohemia, in 1836 by Johann Baptist Eisner. In 1851 it was taken over by Susanna Loetz, widow of the former manager Johann Loetz. From 1858 the factory used the name Johann Loetz Witwe. It continued to exist until 1947.

René Lalique

As a rule, glassware of the late 19th and early 20th century, regardless of where it was produced, has a bright, intense colour. New forms appeared, the most widespread being a vase for a single flower with a high narrow neck, and fashionable tendencies were reflected in the choice of subjects closely tied to Symbolist art.

A master who was to exert considerable influence on the development of glass in the succeeding period also produced works within the context of Art Nouveau. This was René Lalique (1860-1945), a brilliant representative of the French school who based his work on the experience of his predecessors, François-Eugène Rousseau, Emile Gallé and Henri Cros (1840-1907).

By the end of the 19th century Lalique was one of Paris's leading jewellers. His experiments with glass enamels for jewellery in the 1890s led to an interest in the rich plastic and colouristic potential of glass. Lalique's first vessel in this material was a perfume bottle dating from 1893, created using the cire perdue or lost wax method usually employed for the making of metal objects. He continued to work with this complex technique in the late 19th and early 20th centuries, turning to another complex method of working glass for his jewellery, pâte-de-verre,[14] at the turn of the century.

In 1902 at the Claire Fontaine estate near Paris, René Lalique opened an experimental factory for the production of glass which made vases and small sculptures. The models he produced for the new enterprise reveal his experience as a jeweller. Although large editions were made of each individual piece, they were of high artistic quality. In 1906 Lalique began a collaboration with the perfume company Coty that continued successfully until the 1930s: during that period Lalique produced sixteen models for perfume bottles.

Lalique's glassware of the 1910s combines features of two styles, with elements of decoration characteristic of Art Nouveau and a plasticity of form that was to mark the next stage of artistic development. Indeed, Lalique's greatest period of glass production came in the 1920s and 1930s, the age of Art Deco.

Features of Art Nouveau style continued to appear in the products of most European glass manufactories until the First World War. Many factories were forced to close in 1914 and when the war ended a few years later only a few were to reopen.

Bacchante Vase
René-Jules Lalique, Paris.
Model *c. 1924*
Opalescent glass
H 24.5 cm

cat. no. 80

14. In the pâte-de-verre technique crushed glass is mixed with a binding medium and pressed onto a mould under great pressure. The item is then fired at a relatively low temperature.

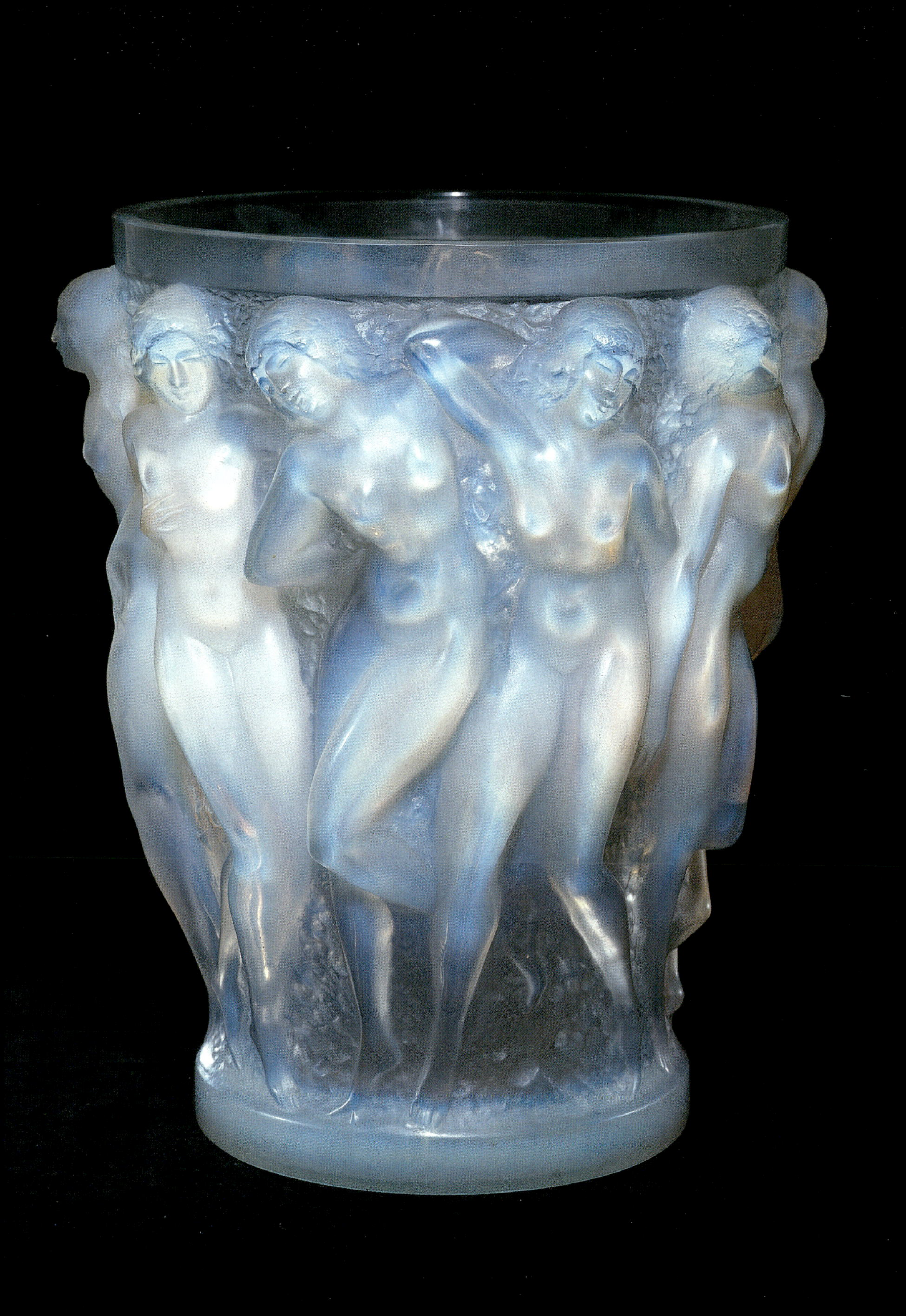

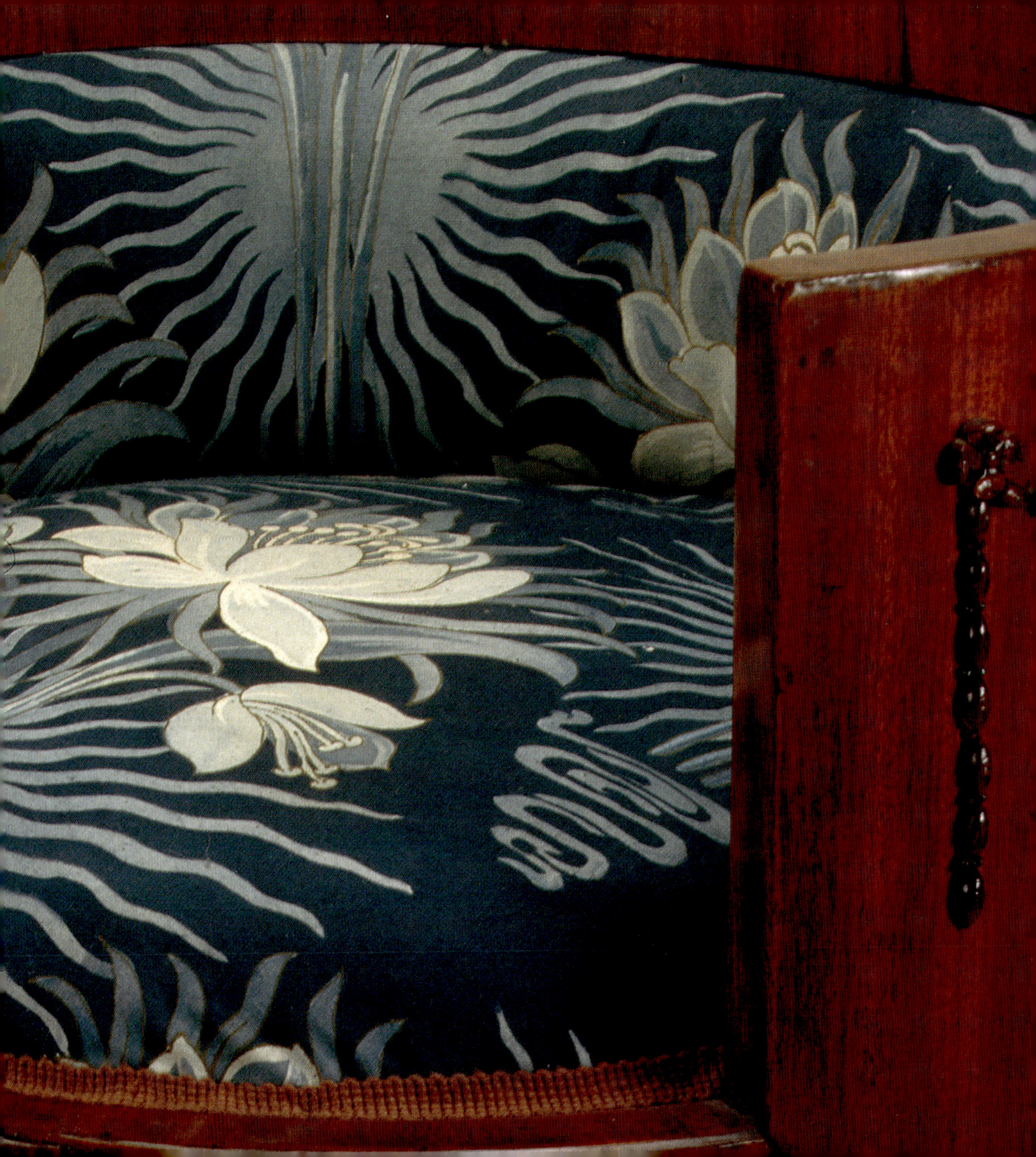

Natalya Guseva

The 'New Style' in Russian Interiors

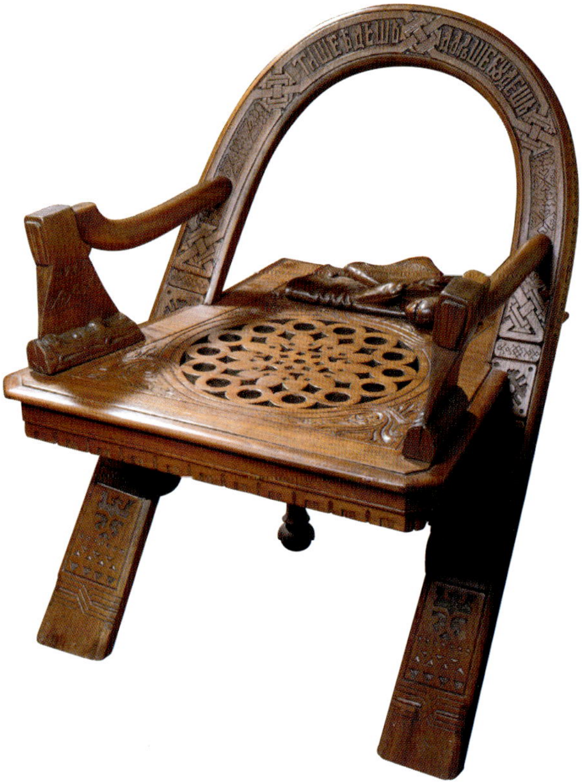

From the second half of the 19th century growth in the international economy – including in Russia – was accompanied by active growth in the urban infrastructure. Apartment blocks, hotels, banks, commercial complexes and new railway stations were being built, bringing in their wake the introduction of new construction materials – reinforced concrete, metal and glass – and all kinds of technical innovations – radio, telephone, electricity, drainage. Demand for a new level of comfort in both private interiors and public buildings stimulated a search for more universal means of aesthetic expression. International artistic and industrial exhibitions, held regularly across Europe after London's celebrated Great Exhibition of 1851, helped spread new ideas.

In Russia the 'new style' was proclaimed by the periodicals *Art and Artistic Industry [Iskusstvo i khudozhestvennaya promyshlennost']* and *The World of Art [Mir Iskusstva]*, both of which first made their appearance at around the same time, in 1898.

In contrast to other European lands, in Russia the formation of Art Nouveau was a somewhat drawn out process. It was closely tied to a rise in national consciousness visible in the wake of the abolition of serfdom in 1861. There was no coincidence in that one of Russia's earliest Art Nouveau monuments, a church in the village of Abramtsevo, built to a design by Victor Vasnetsov of 1882, was inspired by Old Russian architecture.

Another powerful source of inspiration for Russian masters in the 1880s and 1890s came from the European Middle Ages. Adopting elements of the Gothic style, two men in particular gained fame as authors of early Russian Art Nouveau monuments: artist Vasily Polenov built himself a 'cottage' house on the Borki estate near Tula, while architect Fyodor Shekhtel' erected mansions for Zinaida Morozova and Savva Morozov in Moscow. These buildings are brilliant embodiments of the cult of the sinuous line that was to become an international phenomenon.

Such excellent designs, each bearing the stamp of creative personality, demonstrate the Russian atmosphere of advanced artistic experimentation and the introduction of new decorative elements. They did not, however, resolve the key task facing producers: how to create mass-produced items that, whilst remaining affordable, would be practical and convenient and yet not without aesthetic merit. Demand for objects suitable for the adornment of the homes of ordinary citizens of only average means was becoming more and more intense.

Two leading firms in St Petersburg achieved a measure of success in creating quality and fashionable furniture in the 1890s, those of Friedrich (Fyodor) Meltzer and Nikolay Svirskiy. They relatively quickly introduced into their repertoire practical and comfortable items of good artistic design to satisfy the demands of different layers of society.

In 1896, for instance, the Empress's Bathroom in the Winter Palace – still preserved today – was fitted out by the Meltzer firm in the English 'new style'. The greater part of the walls are faced with polished mahogany

(previous page) CAT. NO. 149
DETAIL OF AN ARMCHAIR
F. Meltzer, St Petersburg. *1907-1910s*
Design by Ivan Fomin
Mahogany, chintz

(left page) CAT. NO. 151
ARMCHAIR *YOKE, AXE AND MITTENS*
Russia. *Late 19th century*
Design by Vasily Shutov
Oak
97 x 52 x 58 cm

(below) CAT. NO. 152
TABLE WITH CARVED DRAGONFLY LEGS
Workshop of Emile Gallé, Nancy. *c. 1900*
Pearwood, marquetry of different kinds of wood
76 x 74 x 49 cm

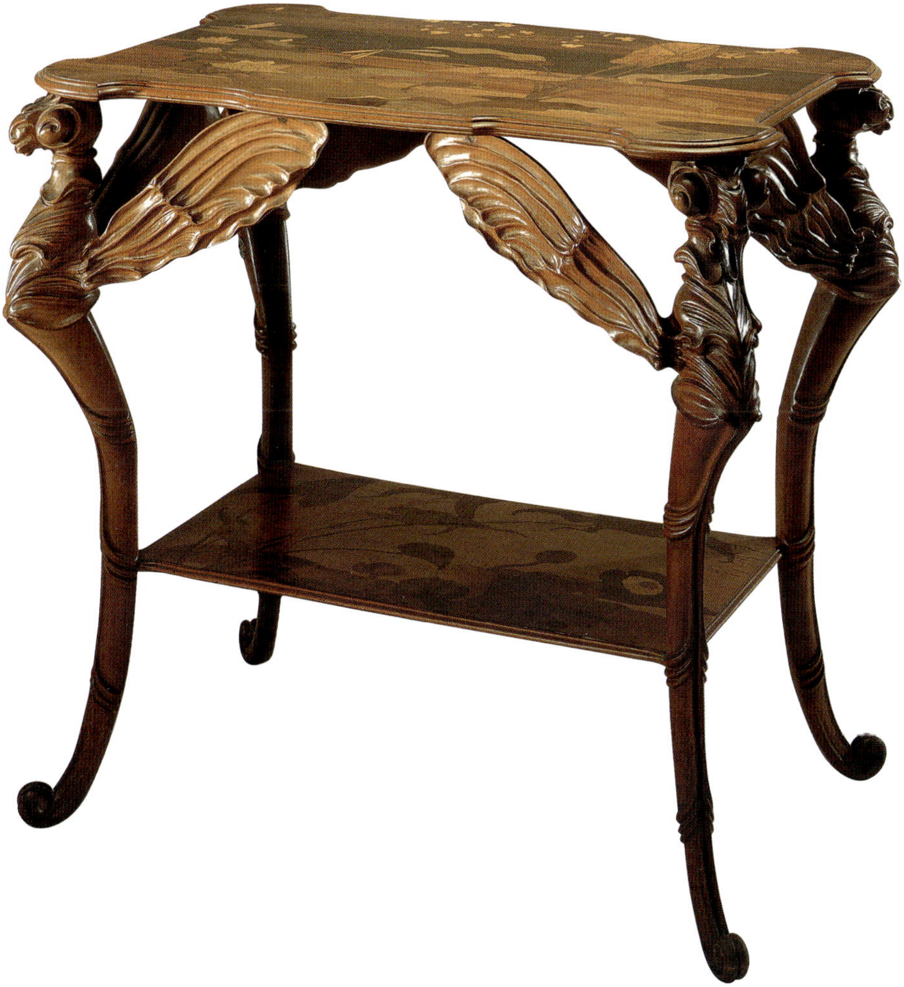

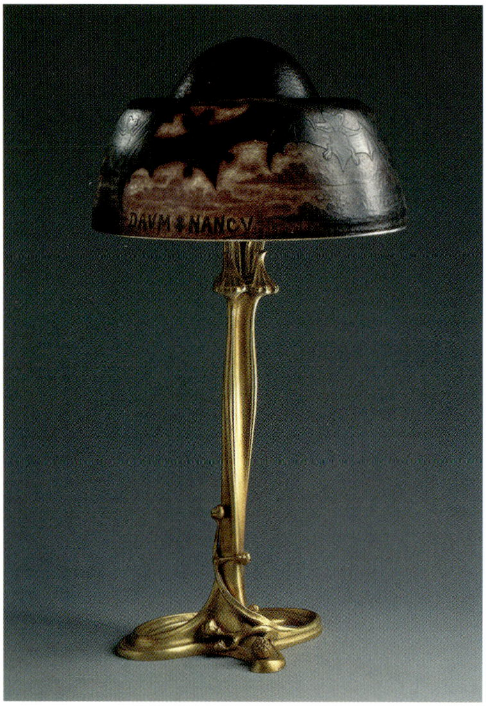

(above) CAT. NO. 59
Table Lamp with Bats
Lampshade: Manufactory Daum Frères, Nancy. *1905-10*. Stand: Louis Majorelle, Nancy
Three-layer glass. Stand: bronze
H 69.5 cm

(right page) CAT. NO. 148
Cabinet Cupboard with bronze decorations
Cabinet: Cleuler, L'Escalier de Cristal, Paris. *1894*
Bronze: Peste. Watercolour: G. Clairin
Design by E. Lièvre, *1894*
Palisander, bronze, watercolour on paper
205 x 115 x 66 cm

panels with built-in corner cupboards; in colour and texture this wood contrasts with the upper walls, covered with white chintz with pale-pink irises. For his own study, adorned with a large Gothic fireplace, Nicholas II chose a severe, unornamented desk, the most attractive detail of which is an electrical lamp with its shade set upon an elegantly curving metal stand.

Another large firm producing works – alongside 'stylised' pieces in various historical modes – was that of Nikolay Svirskiy. In 1896 this produced furniture of rounded forms in pale wood with cotton print upholstery for the Tsar's children and their governess to be used in the imperial train. Thanks to the chintz upholstery of the sofas, walls and ceiling, with a bright flowered pattern against a white ground rather like the products of William Morris, the space had a joyous, optimistic atmosphere.

Svirskiy himself, however, who specialised in marquetry items, had a passion for the work of French designers. He was particularly drawn, for instance, by the floral compositions of masters from the School of Nancy. Showing his works at the Exposition Universelle in Paris in 1889, Svirskiy seemed almost to be trying his strength against Emile Gallé: both received Gold Medals, but while for the French artist this marked the start of his international fame, for the Russian master it was but one in a series of marks of recognition for his considerable professional skill. Surviving works by Svirskiy produced in the 1880s reveal that his marquetry compositions were already reflecting the development of the 'new style'. Gradually moving away from Historicist ornament, he turned to compositions in the Japanese spirit, depicting cranes, tortoises, snakes, butterflies, sunsets and sunrises, motifs that were linked to contemplative observation of nature.

Japanese culture, regularly demonstrated at various international exhibitions from the 1860s onwards, gave a new creative stimulus

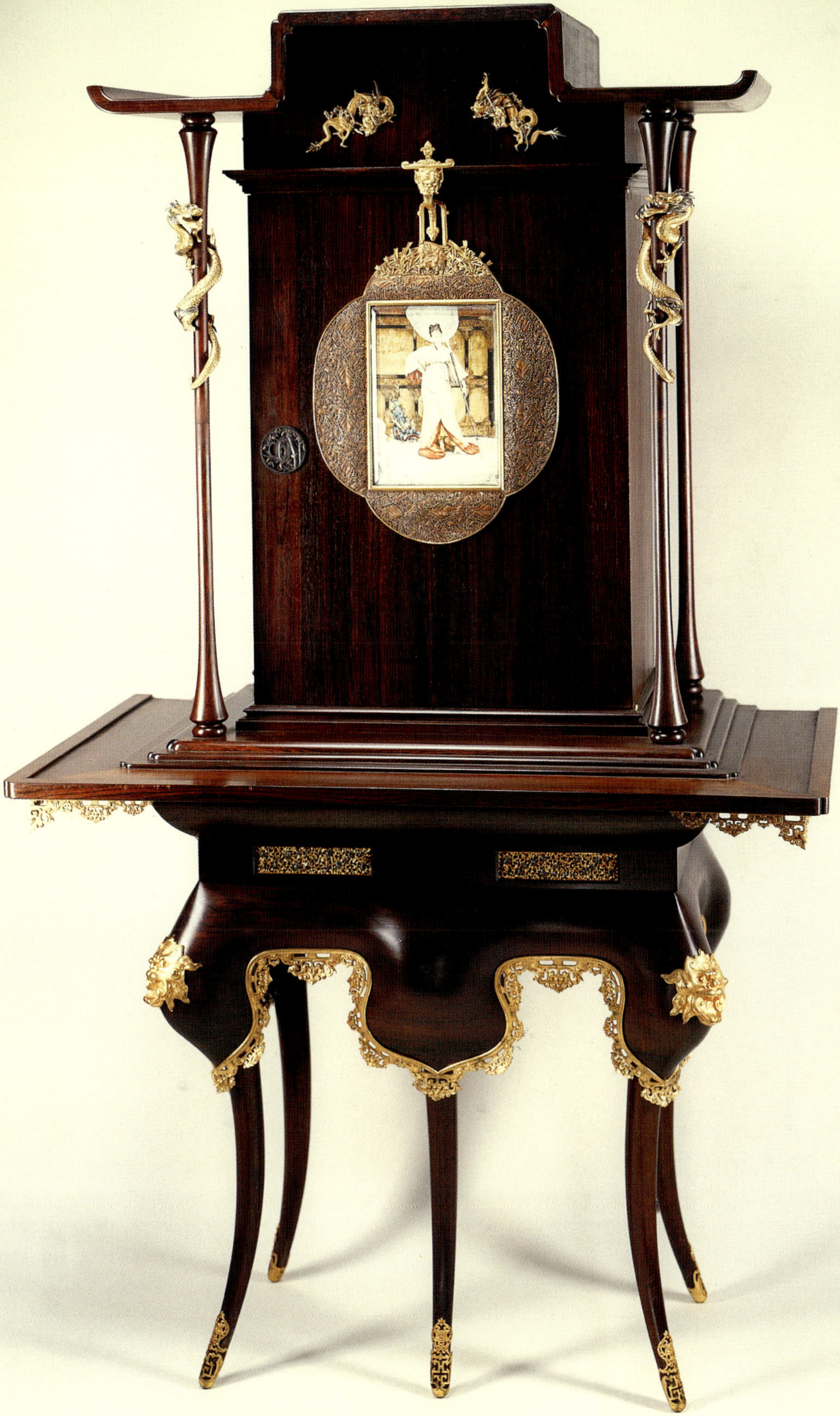

to European art as a whole.[1] It is no surprise, therefore, to discover that identical motifs appear almost simultaneously in the works of both Svirskiy and Gallé: both, for instance, include characteristic Oriental features such as a spider spreadeagled in its web, a motif that was to become more or less symbolic of the Art Nouveau age, an allegory of rationality, solidity and aesthetic perfection.

Seeking beauty in everything that surrounds man, in the most elementary and uncomplicated of natural forms, artists discovered ways of considerably extending their range of decorative motifs. Wild flowers of a kind by no means characteristic of Historicism – thistle, dandelion, poppy, snowdrop, daisy and cornflower – thus entered the Russian cultural repertoire. The theme of water, rich in its potential for half-tonal transitions, also became popular. The flexible stems of lilies, waterlilies and seaweed adorned compositions on chairs, armchairs and sofas, the succulent flowers and buds stretching upwards to appear on the backs.

Sideboards with carved floral ornament and stained glass in the doors came into fashion. Solidly built, they became the key feature of dining rooms, which – because of limited space available in urban apartments – frequently served also as drawing rooms. Here the whole family gathered each evening, an atmosphere of domestic comfort emphasised by dim lighting softly flowing from beneath the large shade of an electric light suspended above the dining table. Tiffany lamps of coloured glass were also fashionable. A handsome sideboard or buffet adorned with carved details, its shelves ranged with expensive crockery, the board set with tasty hors d'oeuvres, became in essence a symbol of the family's prosperity. This single piece of furniture took on a multiple function that was typical of the 'new style', playing the role of both display cabinet and sideboard.

In seeking to reduce the cost of pieces through mass production, manufacturers were forced to increase the amount of work done by machines. This in turn led designers to simplify the technological processes, devising furniture constructions that were easily assembled – and dismantled – and that employed interchangeable details. Each prototype was thus transformed into an abstract composition combining convex details and simple geometrical forms.

No single style achieved such a level of unity across its many products. Mathematically precise templates with flexible lines attractive to the eye allowed for mass production of identical details. As was so rightly noted by Serge Diaghilev, such objects allowed one to 'adjust oneself directly to life and create for modern man an environment in which his cares would be relieved, relaxation made more possible, and the whole of life more comfortable and joyous.'

The universality of the 'new style' made it possible to give aesthetic form even to such utilitarian spaces as the insides of post offices, banks and stations. Meltzer's furniture company, for instance, developed a range of office desks.

In St Petersburg and other Russian towns, great popularity was enjoyed by a particular kind of office furniture patented in the United States. It arrived in Russia mainly via Sweden and the Baltic countries, where local production was established on licence from American firms. The advantage of this 'Swedish-American' furniture lay in that, as we read in the catalogues, 'nothing can disappear from your desk. You can go away at any moment, leaving everything on the surface. You have only to put down the lid and your desk, together with all the drawers, is locked.'

While some retrospective features were incorporated into objects made in the 'new style', there were also many examples of furniture with a national romantic resonance. St Petersburg, for instance, produced some interesting examples of 'northern Art Nouveau', introducing into an apparently international framework details such as an empty shore with pines, a square with a town hall, a snowy landscape or a bear hunt... Seeking to escape the monotony and lack of character which inevitably threatened mass produced objects, craftsmen deliberately turned to Scandinavian monuments in which, in the words of architect Andrey Ol', they were drawn by 'the clear energetic spirit' and 'the strong link with folk traditions'.

It was these features that had been inherent in Russian decorative and applied art for centuries, features that were most vividly manifested in the work of painter Sergey Malyutin: developing entirely within the Art Nouveau stream, his art was synthetic in nature, interweaving motifs from Russian folk heritage with archaic elements, with Oriental and medieval European features.

Overall, the furniture market in Russia's capital, St Petersburg, at the turn of the 19th and 20th centuries offered a great variety of interpretations of Art Nouveau. Genuine creative innovations, as is the case in any sphere, were hard to find amongst the mass of products put out by the different factories and workshops and much in demand among the urban populace. Moreover, a large quantity of furniture was still produced in the styles of past eras. Seeking to give some guidance to ordinary craftsmen in this huge stream of products, the periodicals *The Joiner [Stolyar]* and *Crafts Newspaper [Remeslennaya gazeta]* continually published examples of the very latest fashions taken from foreign sources.

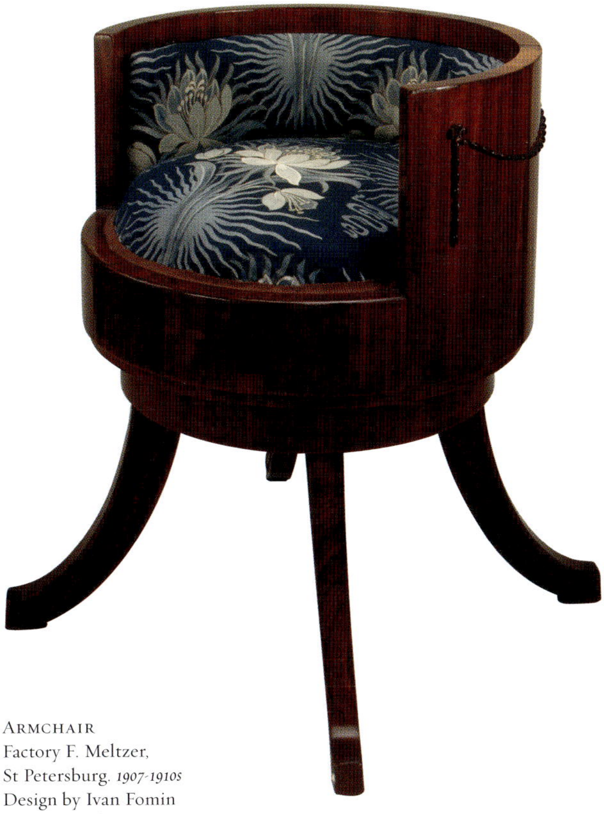

ARMCHAIR
Factory F. Meltzer,
St Petersburg. *1907-1910s*
Design by Ivan Fomin
Mahogany, chintz
68 x 60 x 60 cm

CAT. NO. 149

With the aim of further propagandising the most recent achievements of craftsmen and designers, a large exhibition was held in Moscow between November 1902 and January 1903, *Architecture and Artistic Industry in the New Style*. The organisers invited not only well

1. In 1861 Japan liberated its restrictions on external trade and Japanese goods flooded onto the European market.

known Russian masters Ivan Fomin, William Walcott, Fyodor Shekhtel and Konstantin Korovin but also European celebrities, among them designers such as the Austrian Joseph Maria Olbrich and the Scot Charles Rennie Mackintosh. Overall the exhibition was dominated by rationality: a monumental constructional approach clearly prevailing over floral, more decorative and handmade items.

Almost at the same time, in January 1903, an exhibition entitled *Contemporary Art* opened in St Petersburg. Its main participants were the artists who were the main ideologues of the influential periodical *The World of Art [Mir Iskusstva]*, whose aim was to demonstrate 'their taste for the elegant and a sense of style – everything that has been totally lost in everyday life in St Petersburg'. It was hoped that the interior designs presented to the public would be a striking and amazing surprise to local citizens. The members of the World of Art group sought to create an ideal environment, seemingly drawn from some elegantly stylised picture. Their exhibition enjoyed a certain resonance, mainly amongst the creative classes, forcing them to think seriously about strengthening the role of professional designers in industrial production.

Of greatest potential were the designs by architects who took part in the Moscow exhibition, notably Ivan Fomin. Skilfully perephrasing Empire Style models, Fomin created original pieces of furniture adorned with relief decoration in the form of twisted hoops, spirals and acorns. He created models for the Meltzer brothers, with whom he worked for many years, that seem to represent an accumulation of the best features of the 'new style' in St Petersburg: functional comfort, clear logical construction and a light sprinkling of Empire retrospective.

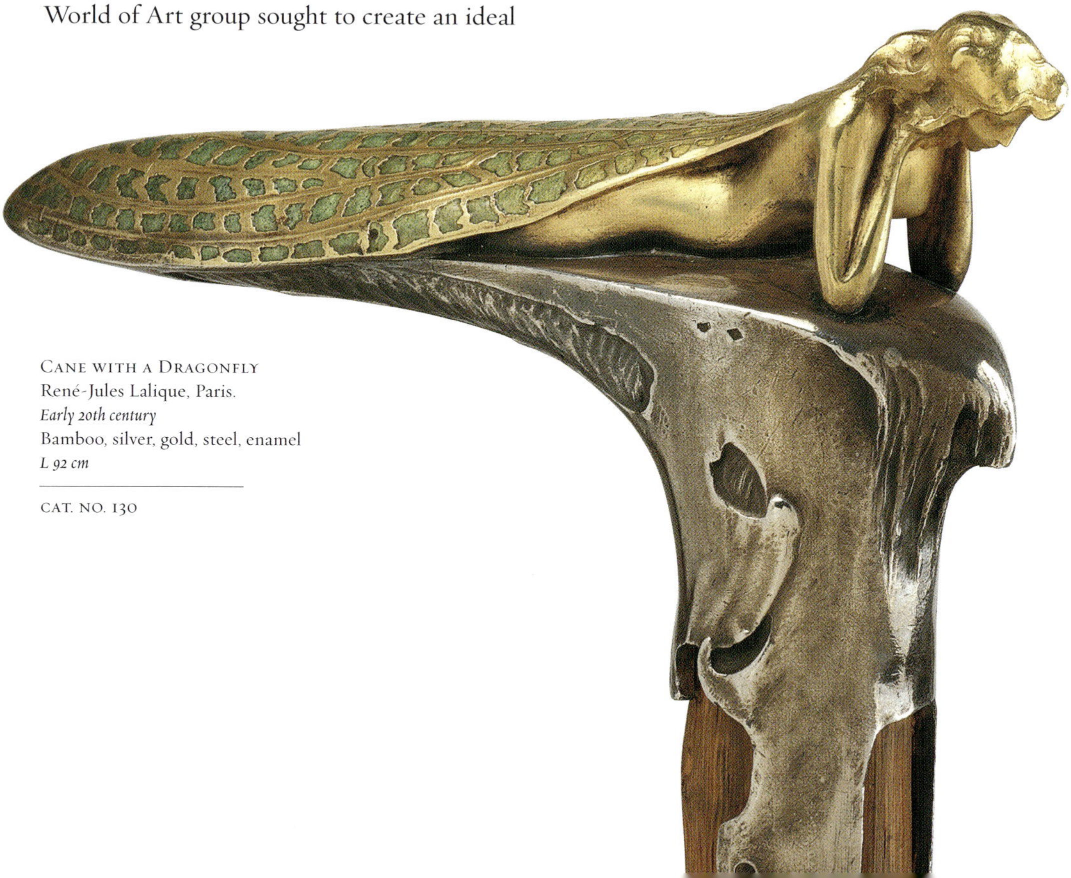

Cane with a Dragonfly
René-Jules Lalique, Paris.
Early 20th century
Bamboo, silver, gold, steel, enamel
L 92 cm

CAT. NO. 130

Such works in the 'new style' were to be produced not only by leading firms in the capital. They also appeared amongst the range of products on offer from many workshops around Russia, as was superbly demonstrated by an international artistic and construction exhibition held in St Petersburg in May 1908. Amongst the producers of furnishings particular mention was given to the Stroganov Art School in Moscow, displaying rooms in very different historical styles, and the Ivan Platonov factory for artistic furniture and joinery works. The 'interior for a drawing room in the English style of white pearwood' made at the Platonov factory was one of a number of widespread variations on openwork geometrical constructions in the spirit of Charles Rennie Mackintosh. A special section at the exhibition was made up of 'crafts from Finland'. Remarkable for their notably Art Nouveau tendencies – seeking increasing simplification of form whilst maintaining a very high level of execution – were the Finnish Factory for Bent and Turned Furniture, the Joint-stock Company of Finnish Joiners, and the Buman Factory in the town of Abo. At the start of the 1910s, all of Russia's most talented masters turned to this unfussy approach, using form and mass to give maximum expression.

Even the elite production of the Imperial Porcelain Manufactory was affected by Art Nouveau's penetration into the urban environment. Between 1882 and 1894 it produced large quantities of pieces decorated using the underglaze painting technique, employing two artists who had formerly worked at the Royal Copenhagen Manufactory and who had been specially invited to St Petersburg, Carl Mortensen and Carl Liisberg. Modest landscapes of Russia's northern and central areas, animals and birds, simple vegetation, all conveyed with soft lyricism, were the main subjects of the painting, combining naturally with forms that tended towards concentration on the rounded simple masses of the pure white porcelain mass.

Russian glassmakers also achieved great success in mastering the techniques developed by the celebrated Frenchman Emile Gallé. Images were produced on the glass using etching or engraving through several layers of coloured glass to different depths. Particular skill was displayed by masters at the Imperial and Maltsov Glass Manufactories. If the forms and motifs used to decorate both glass and porcelain vases were often very similar, this can be explained in that for many years the Imperial Porcelain and Glass Manufactories were run by a single administration, under a single artistic manager.

By the turn of the 19th and 20th centuries there were dozens of private ceramics workshops in Russia, as well as centres teaching ceramics production. Of the latter, the leading schools were the Stieglitz School of Technical Drawing and the Society for the Encouragement of the Arts, both in St Petersburg, and the Stroganov Art School in Moscow. The teaching programme included 'design in styles', which was very much in keeping with contemporary demands. Meanwhile there were two key centres spearheading the renaissance in Russian folk art within the context of current creative trends and experimentation, organised on the estates of two artistic patrons, that of the Savva Mamontov at Abramtsevo, near Moscow, and that of Princess Maria Tenisheva at Talashkino, near Smolensk. Overall Art Nouveau was a notable phenomenon in Russia in all kinds of art.

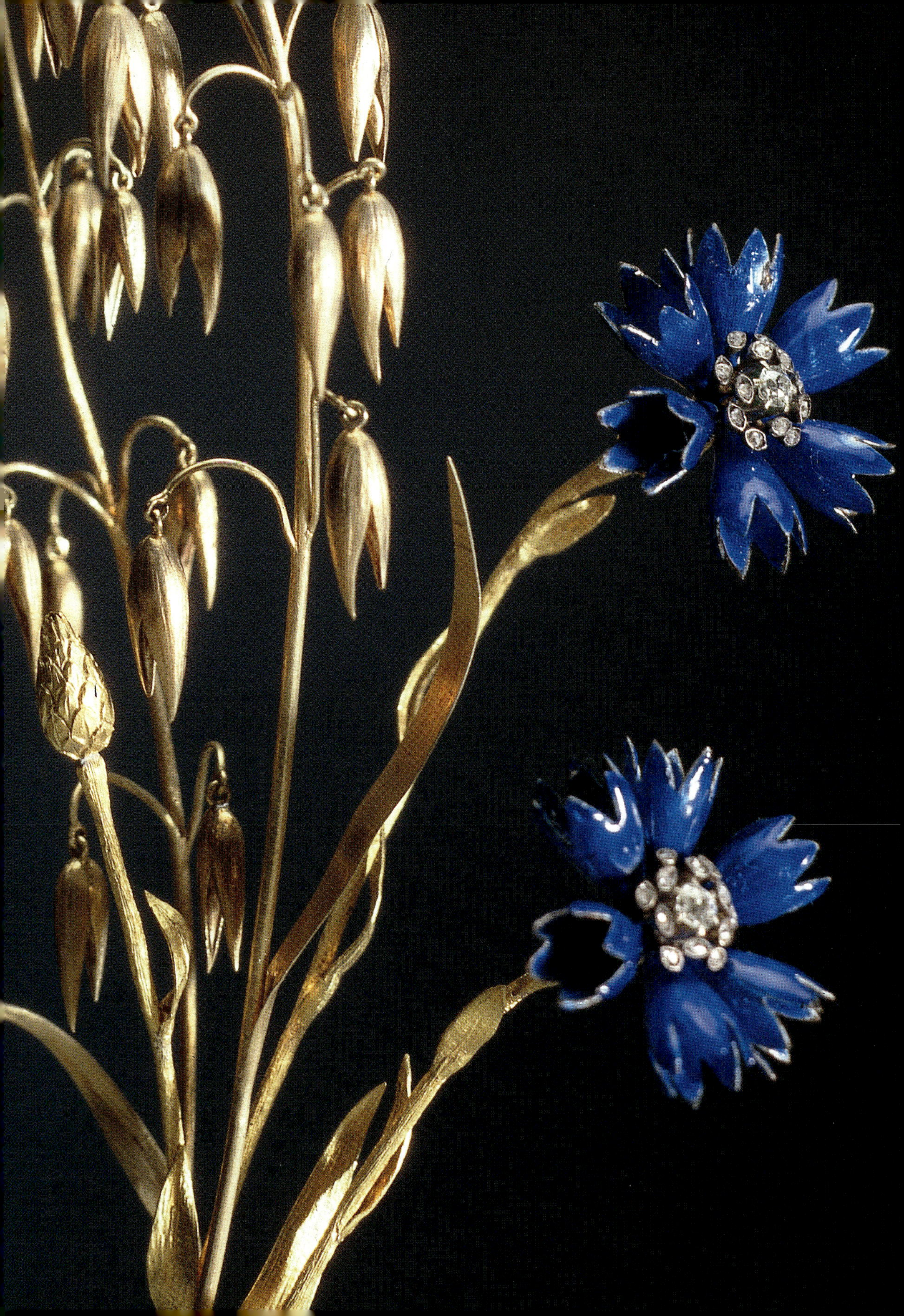

Marina Lopato

Fabergé and Art Nouveau

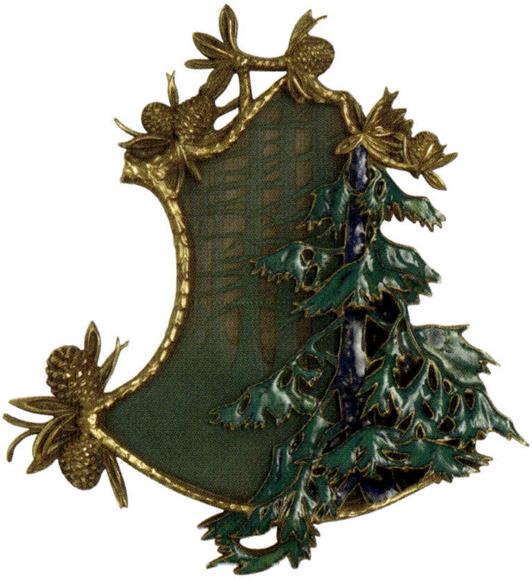

(pevious page) CAT. NO. 112
DETAIL OF AN OBJET DE VERTU
Firm of Carl Fabergé, St Petersburg.
Late 19th century
Gold, diamond, enamel, rock crystal

(left) CAT. NO. 126
FIR-TREE PENDANT
René-Jules Lalique, Paris. *1900-1*
Gold, enamel, glass
H 7.2 cm

(right page) CAT. NO. 132
MIRROR IN THE FORM OF A FAN
Firm of Alphonse Giroux – Veuve
Ferdinand Duvinage, Paris. *1877-82*
Different varieties of wood, ivory, brass
H 31 cm

Fabergé was the first St Petersburg jeweller to create Art Nouveau works. His earliest precisely dated piece in this 'new style' was the Lily-of-the-Valley Easter Egg of 1898, a gift from Nicholas II to his mother, Dowager Empress Maria Fyodorovna. The last piece of known date was the Clover Easter Egg of Empress Alexandra, made in 1902. Just four years lie between them, but during that time the artist traversed a stylistic path from proto-Art Nouveau to the fully developed style. His celebrated vase of smoky quartz in a silver setting (cat. 128), its rocaille tendrils clearly transformed into Art Nouveau elements, is also dated to 1898.[1] Both Rococo and Mannerist ideas lie behind the composition carved into the vase's body.

These early works clearly reveal the origins of the new style that the firm's artists were only cautiously mastering. Art Nouveau features are visible above all in the naturalistic motifs, the flowers that were so characteristic. Not for nothing were such works much criticised at the Paris Exposition Universelle of 1900 for being 'without artistic or decorative feeling'. 'We have before us,' complained critic René Chanteclair, 'a photograph of nature without the artist having impressed his own style upon it.'[2] Perhaps the critic was right and these works do rather capture all aspects of nature in a manner characteristic of the second half of the 19th century. Perhaps, though, the style itself lies in that 'photographic manner', a suggestion that seems particularly clear when we compare these objects with imitative works by 20th-century masters.

Resolved in a very different spirit were Fabergé's flower compositions influenced by Japanese art – so popular in the second half of the 19th century. These so-called Ikebani also stand on the border between naturalism and Art Nouveau.

Artists creating Art Nouveau pieces for Fabergé also took various Classical styles and, above all, Rococo as their inspiration. Rocaille motifs were much favoured by the firm's leading master, Mikhail Perkhin, dominating his art until his death in 1903. This love of Rococo was a feature of the French arts during the 1890s. Relations were quite close after an exhibition of luxury items from France, held in St Petersburg in 1890, and particularly in the wake of the conclusion of the Franco-Russian alliance in 1894. Naturally artists and craftsmen producing luxury items were affected by this atmosphere of friendly exchange.

Despite his loyalty to varying historical styles, Carl Fabergé turned to Art Nouveau as a result of his own creative flexibility, his feel for the market and his sensitivity to what was going on around him. Fabergé and his sons, three of whom became artists, were well aware of current artistic trends. It is notable that the brief period of Fabergé's interest in Art Nouveau almost coincides with the lifetime of the celebrated St Petersburg periodical *The World of Art [Mir Iskusstva]*. Alexandre Benois, artist and publisher of *The World of Art*, and perhaps Konstantin Somov, leading artist of the World of Art movement, were to be met at exhibitions, in drawing rooms and indeed inside the Imperial Hermitage. Somov's Harlequins are to be seen on several items produced for Fabergé.

But there were far more important individuals, whose opinions and requirements were law unto Fabergé. His main client, for instance, Empress Alexandra Fyodorovna, whose love for the Art Nouveau style is well known. Her brother, Ernst Ludwig, Grand Duke of Hesse, founded a colony of artists in Darmstadt where they sought to create 'collective works of art'. Inspired by the artistic atmosphere of this society, the Empress began to collect works by Gallé and Tiffany, Rörstrand ceramics and Royal Doulton. In the private apartments of the Alexander

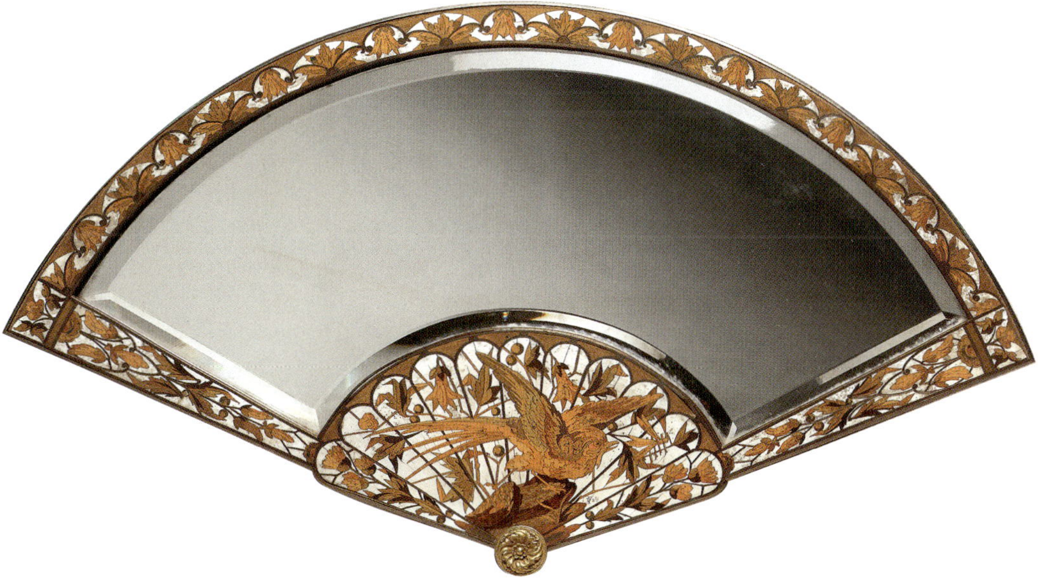

1. Marina Lopato, 'Notes on the Lapidary work of the Fabergé Firm', *Fabergé: Imperial Craftsman and his World*, by Dr Géza von Habsburg with contributions by Alexander von Solodkoff, Dr Robert Bianchi, London-New York, 2000, pp. 298-301.
2. Géza von Habsburg, 'Fabergé and the Paris 1900 Exposition Universelle', in: Géza von Habsburg, Marina Lopato, Fabergé Imperial Jeweller, exh. cat., London, 1993, p. 122.

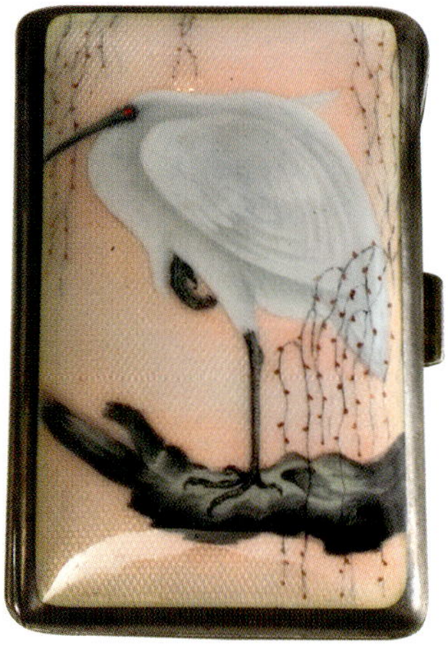

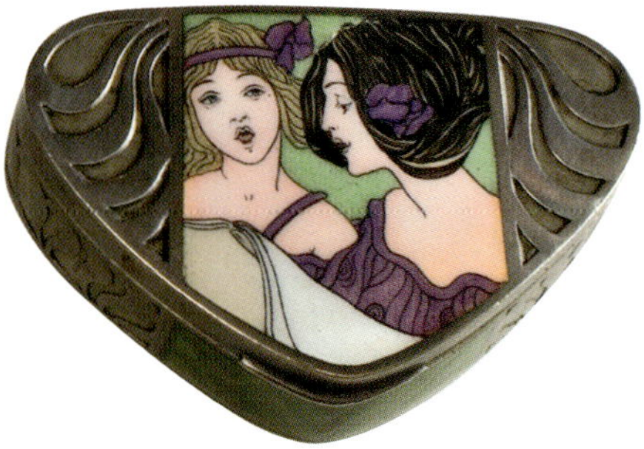

(left) CAT. NO. 119
PORTE-CIGAR WITH A HERON
Western Europe. *Before 1919*
Silver, enamel
H 8 cm

(right) CAT. NO. 127
TOILET BOX WITH
TWO LADIES SINGING
Austria (?). *Late 19th – early 20th century*
Silver, enamel
H 2.1 cm

Palace at Tsarskoe Selo, redesigned by Roman Meltzer in the 'new style', these objects stood alongside sentimental knick-knacks of the Victorian age. One of the first invoices from Fabergé, kept amongst archive documents relating to The Cabinet of His Imperial Highness, is for 'silver mounts to three Gallé vases', dated 17 (29) May 1897, for a sum of 185 roubles. Six months later Fabergé presented an invoice for works that are today to be found in the Hermitage and in Pavlovsk Palace Museum. An invoice of 21 February (5 March) 1898 lists: '3829 Small maiolica vase for flowers with a frog and lizard – 17 r. 50. Glass Gallé vase with swamp plants and ephemerals: silver mount with ephemerals – 70 r. Gallé 'bamboo' vase: silver mount with leaves – 200 r. Gallé vase with lilies – electric lamp: silver mount, swamp plants – 240 r. Vase with sphinxes – 100 r.'[3] As a rule Fabergé's mounts did not draw attention to themselves, serving only to emphasise the form or main decorative motif. In creating mounts and settings for items produced by other craftsmen, Fabergé's masters revealed a keen sense of the style of each piece, subordinating their own work to it with considerable tact. Works of crystal glass, for instance, adorned with precise geometrical carving, were given mounts of similarly precise design, mainly in Neoclassical style. Items of smooth glass and softly rounded forms were placed in rocaille mounts.

While the St Petersburg branch of Fabergé created pieces oriented mainly towards Western versions of the style, the Moscow branch developed its own Russian version of Art Nouveau. Henry Charles Bainbridge, employee of Fabergé in London, wrote that the 'Moscow House made use of this style almost

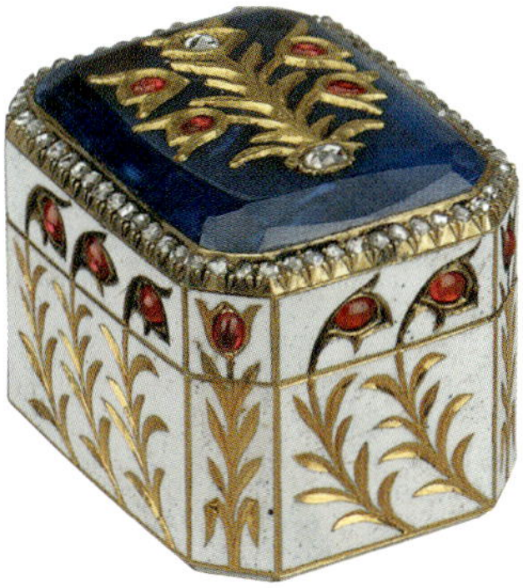

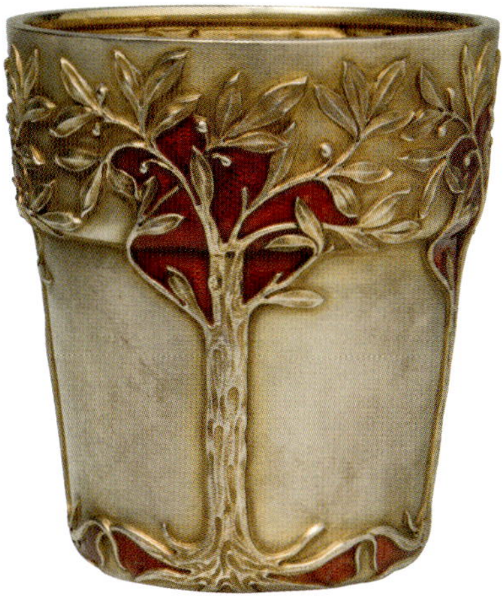

ad infinitum in silver work of every kind such as tankards, bratini, icons, bowls, cigarette cases, etc., and in silver work associated with Siberian stones. These objects were made much use of as presentation gifts to Emirs and Khans, visiting foreign potentates, statesmen, etc.'[4]

Artists working for the Moscow branch created works that reveal at least two main trends within the broader range of Neo-Russian Art Nouveau. One of these derives from Historicism and is most brilliantly embodied in works by the celebrated owner of a small manufactory for silver objects, Ignaty Sazikov. Historical and legendary figures appeared on these early 20th-century items in less concrete form than before, reflecting a romanticised perception of the past. Western authors have seen in these works a melding of 'Art Nouveau, Slavic Revival and Symbolism'.[5] Representing this trend are the Boris Godunov Writing Set,

(left) CAT. NO. 114
SMALL BOX
Craftsman Mikhail Perkhin, Firm of Carl Fabergé, St Petersburg. *1890s*
Gold, enamel, diamond, ruby, sapphire
H 2.8 cm

(right) CAT. NO. 118
CUP
Craftsman Konstantin Linke, Firm of Karl (Carl) Edvard Bolin, Moscow. *1899-1906*
Silver, enamel
H 7.4 cm

possibly designed by the Russian painter and mysticist Nicholas Roerich, and the Ivan Kalita Cup. The prototype for the latter may have been found amongst the painter and ceramicist Mikhail Vrubel's ceramic sculptures, produced at the Abramtsevo workshops near Moscow. Certainly it was the creative experiments of the Abramtsevo circle that formed the basis for another trend, in which Moscow craftsmen working for Fabergé made wide use of characteristic stylised Old

3. RUSSIAN STATE HISTORICAL ARCHIVE, FUND 468, *OPIS'* 13, *DELO* 2190.
4. H. C. BAINBRIDGE, *PETER CARL FABERGÉ*, LONDON, 1966, P. 132.
5. H. WATERFIELD, *FABERGÉ FROM THE FORBES MAGAZINE COLLECTION*, NEW YORK, 1973, P. 115.

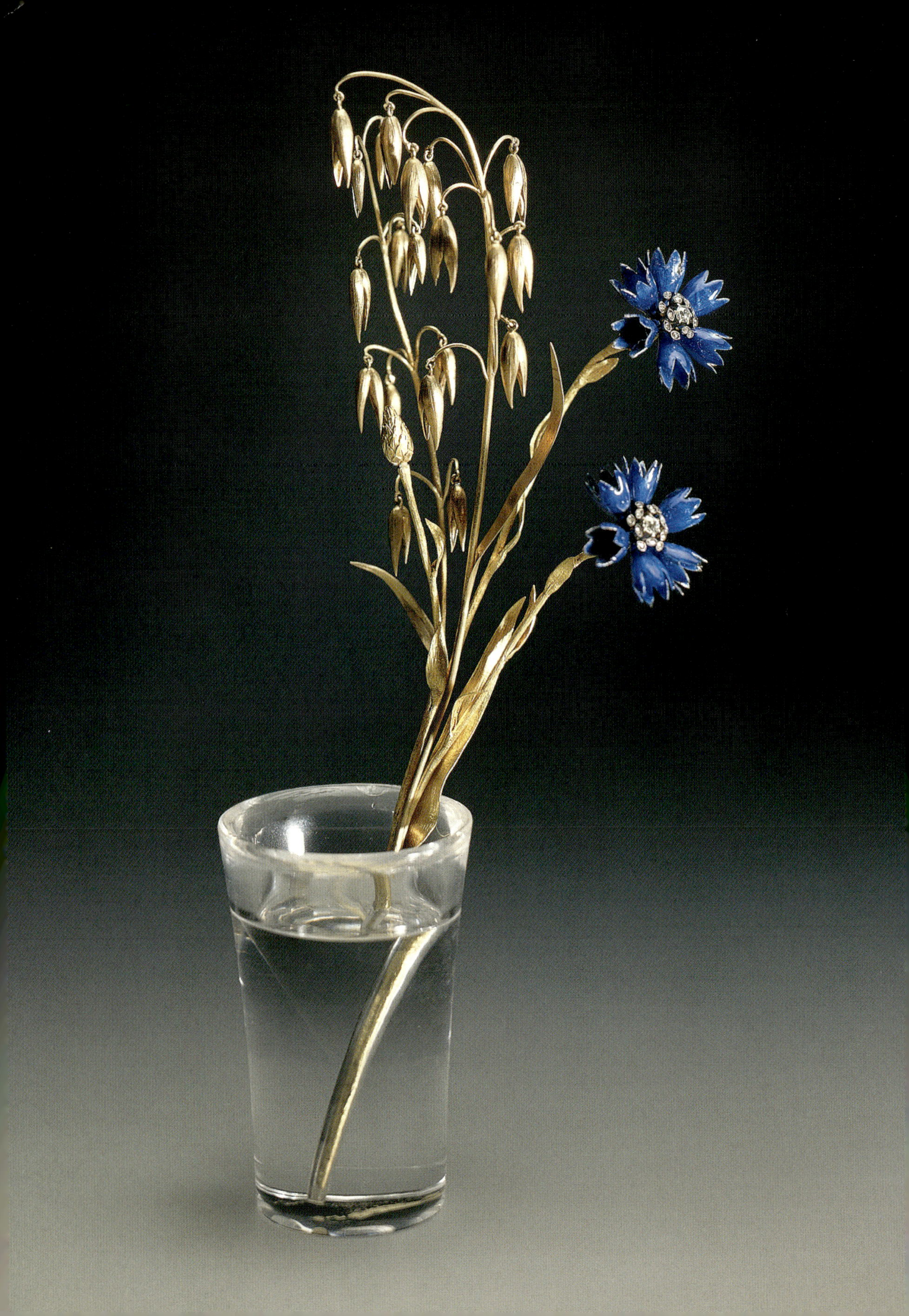

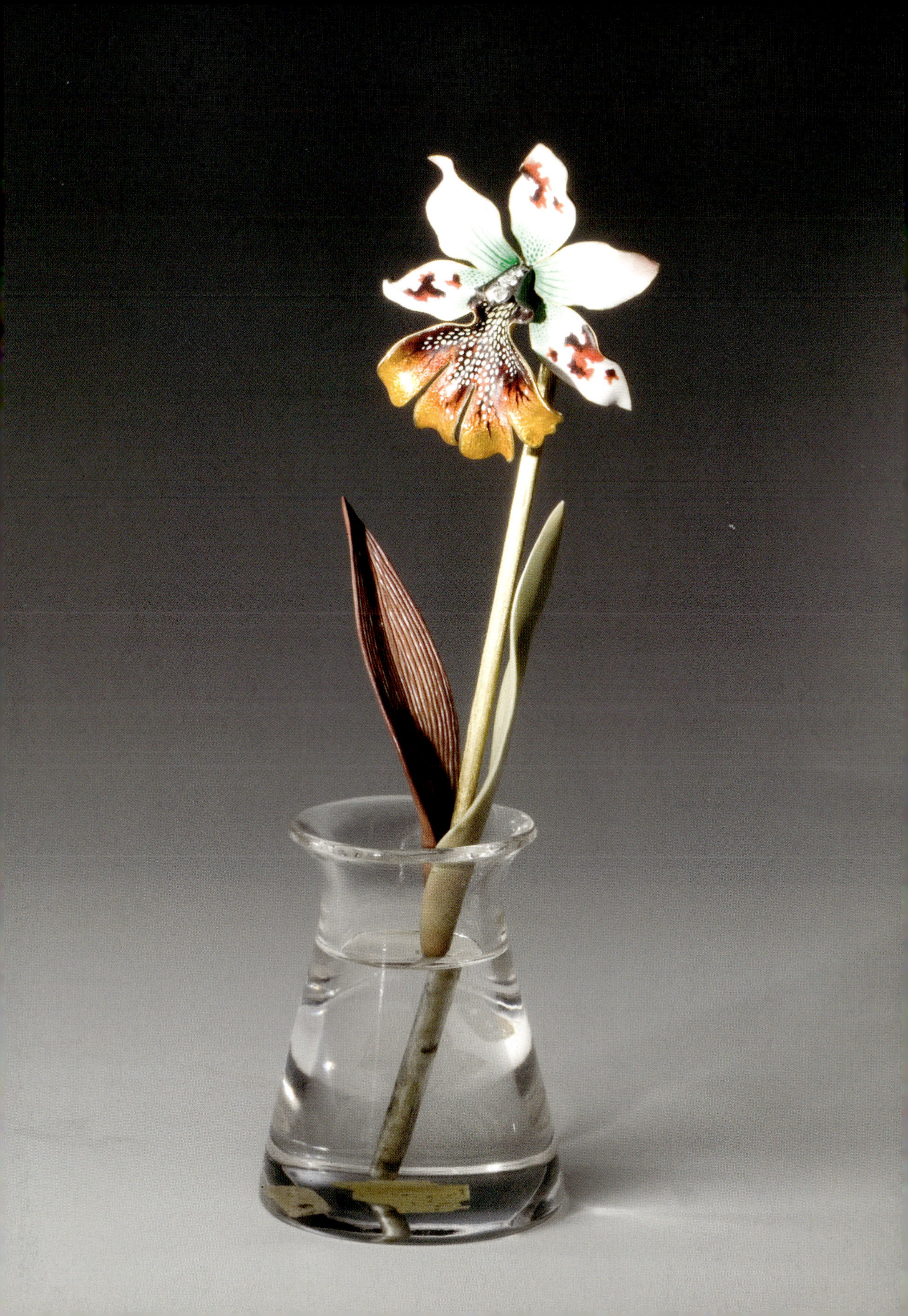

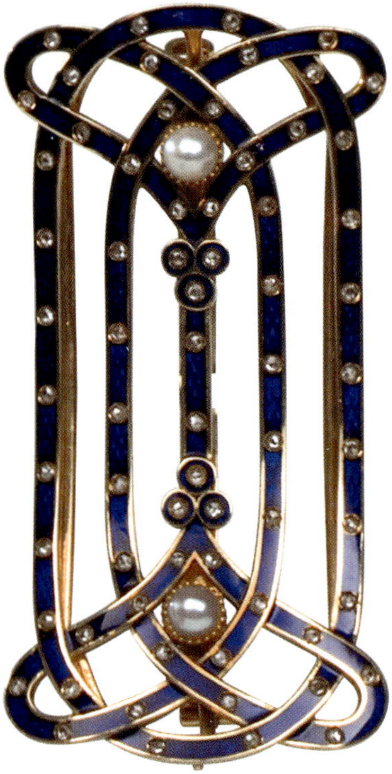

Russian forms and decorative motifs, emphatically exaggerated, their colour intensified. All kinds of little boxes, tea and coffee services were adorned with a kind of cloisonné enamel in deep local colours. Filigree metal formed the walls of the pools of enamel, arranged in a geometrical pattern founded on characteristic Russian wood carving motifs (cat. 118). Fabergé's Moscow output frequently includes stylised images of birds, plants and berries borrowed from works produced in the artists' colonies at Abramtsevo or Talashkino or from the illustrations of Ivan Bilibin. In some cases the filigree patterns seem to recall paintings by Gustav Klimt.[6]

Some explanation for the extremely high quality of designs used by the Fabergé craftsmen is to be found in Carl Fabergé's links with professional artists such as Baron Klodt von Jurgensburg, Jan Lieberg-Nieberg, Mikhail Ivanov, Sergey Adrianov, Robert Bach, Ivan Gal'nbek, Fyodor Grunberg-Salnkans, Vasily Kritskiy, and of course Leonty and Alexandre Benois, amongst others. No less close were the links between Fabergé and teachers and pupils at the Stieglitz School for Technical Drawing in St Petersburg and the Stroganov Art School in Moscow. From there he selected not only craftsmen, metal-workers, carvers, engravers and jewellers but also talented draughtsmen to work in his own studio. Moreover, Fabergé frequently provided support for pupils at the school, having their exhibition works mounted in silver in his workshops.

A small number of Art Nouveau designs are to be found amongst the works on paper surviving from the Fabergé firm. Several groups of jewellery designs appear in an album in the Hermitage,[7] mainly pendants, brooches and hairpins intended for the middle-range buyer. Similar pieces also feature in a collection of drawings sold at auction through Christie's in 1989.[8] There a complete mix of styles is visible in drawings for cups, chalices, kovshes (a kind of traditional low Russian vessel), basins, beakers and other

6. Anne Odom, 'Fabergé's Moscow Workshops', in: Géza von Habsburg, Marina Lopato, *Fabergé: Imperial Jeweller*, Hermitage, St Petersburg, Fabergé Arts Foundation, Paris; London, 1993, p. 113.
7. M. N. Lopato, 'Al'bom risunkov yuvelirnykh izdeliy firmy "K. Faberzhe"', *Soobshcheniya Gosudarstvennogo Ermitazha* [Proceedings of the State Hermitage], issue LXII, 2004, p. 27-33.
8. *Designs from the House of Carl Fabergé*, Christie's, London, Thursday 27 April 1989.

utensils. Most original of all are twelve designs for goblets by a single hand the motifs on which seem to this author to derive not only from Old Russian examples but also from Scandinavian models. Such a level of stylisation places these designs on a different level, revealing something of the tendencies that were to be seen in the next stage of stylistic development, the evolution of Art Deco. Several pieces obviously produced under the influence of similar ideas to those behind these drawings seem to me to confirm that Art Deco too had its place in the creative experiments of the firm of Fabergé.

(previous spread, left) CAT. NO. 112
OBJET DE VERTU
Firm of Carl Fabergé, St Petersburg.
Late 19th century
Gold, diamond, enamel, rock crystal

(previous spread, right) CAT. NO. 120
OBJET DE VERTU
Paris. *Late 19th century*
Gold, diamond, enamel, jasper, rock crystal
H 17.5 cm

(left page) CAT. NO. 108
BUCKLE/BROOCH
Craftsman Mikhail Perkhin,
Firm of Carl Fabergé,
St Petersburg. *Early 20th century*
Gold, diamond, pearl, enamel
H 7.2 cm

(below) CAT. NO. 121
BROOCH
St Petersburg (?). *Late 19th century*
Gold, silver, diamond, sapphire, enamel
H 3.8 cm

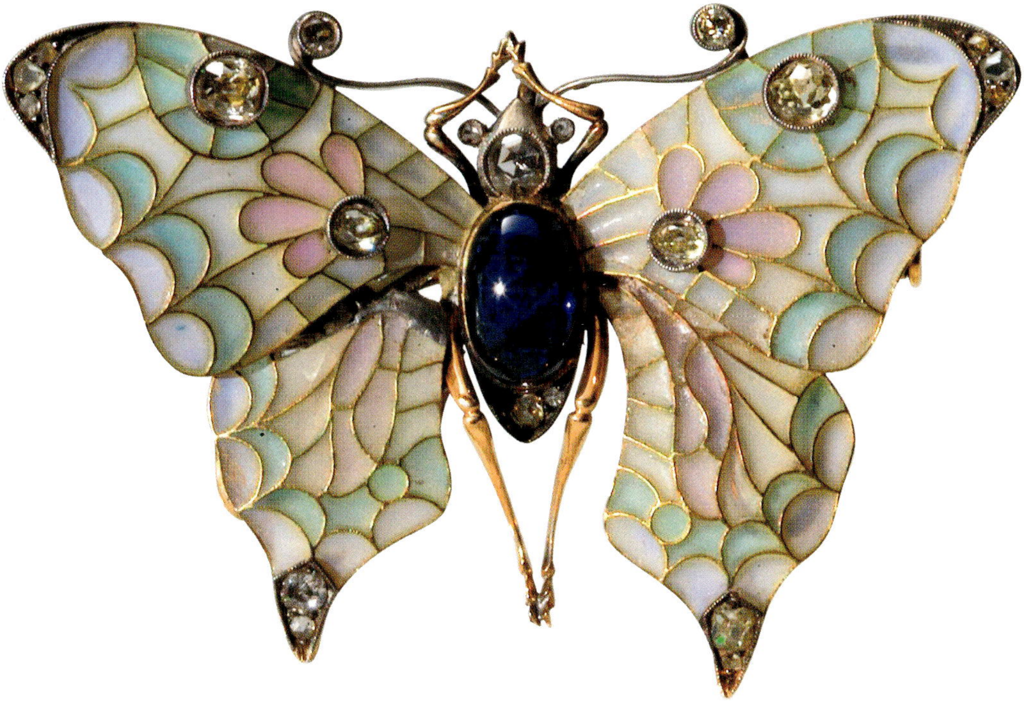

Catalogue

1

Jug with a Snake-shaped Handle
Salviati Dottore Antonio, Venice. *c. 1878*
Decolourised, transparent green, aventurine and opaline glass; opaque pink, yellow, red, white and black glass; free-blown and modelled
Height 26.5
Inv. No. Kr 1438
Provenance: 1878 acquired by Alexander Polovtsov at the Exposition Universelle in Paris, kept in his collection in St Petersburg; 1886 to the Stieglitz Museum; 1933 transferred to the Hermitage from the 1st Branch of the Hermitage (formerly the Stieglitz Museum), Leningrad.
Literature: Leningrad 1985, No. 341; Japan 2006-7, No. 1.

The renaissance of Venice's famed glass production is linked with Doctor Antonio Salviati (1816-90). A lawyer by training, he abandoned legal practice in 1859 to found a mosaic workshop on the island of Murano. In the second half of the 1860s the Salviati company started to produce vessels of all kinds, in 1877 taking the name Salviati Dottore Antonio.
Alexander Alexandrovich Polovtsov (1832-1909), a friend of Tsar Alexander III, was for many years Secretary to the State Council. A Russian manufacturer and politician, he was also a renowned patron. It was thanks to him that the Central School for Technical Drawing of Baron Stieglitz assembled, over the course of the 1880s and 1890s, one of Russia's best collections of applied art.
E.A.

2

Glass with a Large Moulded Flower
Giuseppe Barovier, Salviati Dottore Antonio, Venice. *c. 1878*
Colourless and dark-blue transparent glass; yellow, milk and aventurine threads; green, yellow and opaque pink glass; free-blown and modelled
Height 27.5; diameter of the body 10.4
Inv. No. Kr 1435
Provenance: 1878 acquired by Alexander Polovtsov at the Exposition Universelle in Paris, kept in his collection in St Petersburg; 1886 to the Stieglitz Museum; 1933 transferred to the Hermitage from the 1st Branch of the Hermitage (formerly the Stieglitz Museum), Leningrad.
Literature: Leningrad 1967 (ex-catalogue); Leningrad 1985, No. 337; St Petersburg 1996, No. 358; Japan 2006-7, No. 2.

Here the glass – with a long stem and small bowl – is presented as a flower emerging from a vase. Technical devices of different periods were used to make it, with filigree glass threads and modelled details. Because it is so overloaded with decorative elements the glass can only really be used to adorn an interior.
E.A.

3

Two-handled Flat Vase
Salviati Dottore Antonio, Venice. *c. 1878*
Decolourised glass, aventurine threads; free-blown
Height 27.5; width 10.8
Inv. No. Kr 1386
Provenance: 1878 acquired by Alexander Polovtsov at the Exposition Universelle in Paris, kept in his collection in St Petersburg; 1886 to the Stieglitz Museum; 1933 transferred to the Hermitage from the 1st Branch of the Hermitage (formerly the Stieglitz Museum), Leningrad.
Literature: Leningrad 1967 (ex-catalogue); Japan 2006-7, No. 3.

This vase uses elements characteristic of applied arts of the Venetian Renaissance: handles attached to the body with rosette shapes with stamped round projections and a slightly flattened knop between the body and foot.
E.A.

4

Tall Conical Glass on a Snake-shaped Stem
Probably by Giuseppe Barovier. Salviati Dottore Antonio, Venice. *c. 1878*
Decolourised, ruby, green and aventurine glass; free-blown and modelled
Height 24.6
Inv. No. Kr 1442
Provenance: 1878 acquired by Alexander Polovtsov at the Exposition Universelle in Paris, kept in his collection in St Petersburg; 1886 to the Stieglitz Museum; 1933 transferred to the Hermitage from the 1st Branch of the Hermitage (formerly the Stieglitz Museum), Leningrad.
Literature: Leningrad 1967 (ex-catalogue); Leningrad 1985, No. 346; Japan 2006-7, No. 4.
E.A.

5

Vase
Venice, probably Salviati Dottore Antonio. *Last quarter of the 19th century*
Aquamarine and colourless glass; mould-blown, iridescence, appliqués à chaud
Height with handles 16.1; diameter of body 6.1
Inv. No. Kr 2728
Provenance: 1923 transferred to the Hermitage from the Stieglitz Museum, Petrograd.
Literature: Leningrad 1967 (ex-catalogue).

There are several known versions of this model made using different coloured glasses.
The vase is made in the form of a vessel for warming rose water, an almorratxa. The almorratxa form emerged in Catalonia as an imitation of similar vessels exported from Damascus in the 14th century. By the 16th century Catalonian almorratxas were widely exported, including to Venice (Alice Wilson Frothingham, *Spanish Glass,* New York, 1963, p. 41). It was the unusual form that attracted the craftsman at Salviati as they sought to revive some of the traditions of past ages.
E.A.

6

Vase
J. & L. Lobmeyer, Vienna. *c. 1878*
Made by Meyer Glassworks; painted by the Vimperk painting studio. Model by Machytka and Schmoranz. *1877.* On the bottom in white enamel the firm's mark *JLLW* and the gold number *6*
Colourless glass; mould-blown, painted with coloured enamels – dark and pale blue, turquoise, green, white and gold
Height 20.5
Inv. No. Kr 1337

Provenance: 1878 acquired at the Exposition Universelle in Paris for the Stieglitz Museum, St Petersburg; 1933 transferred to the Hermitage from the 1st Branch of the Hermitage (formerly the Stieglitz Museum), Leningrad.
Literature: St Petersburg 2005, No. 1.2.31; Japan 2006-7, No. 8.

We know that the model for this piece was executed 5 November (Olga Drachotova, 'From Neo-Classical Taste to Historicism', *Bohemian Glass. 1400-1989*, edited by Sylva Petrova and Jean-Luc Olivie, New York, 1990, pp. 72, 239) and several repetitions were produced. The vase is painted in 'Persian style' with vegetable ornament composed of stylised cornflowers, a design deriving from decorative motifs widely used in Ottoman ceramics of the 16th and 17th centuries. A similar motif was used by William de Morgan (1839-1917), an artist working with William Morris; from 1875 de Morgan studied Ottoman ornament with the aim of using it to decorate English ceramics (Annette Hagendorn, *Auf der Suche nach dem neuen Stil. Der Einfluss der osmanischen Kunst auf die europäische Keramik im 19. Jahrhundert,* Staatliche Museen zu Berlin, 1998, p. 77). In the 1880s 'Persian cornflowers' featured on many decorative tiles (*Kunsthandwerk und Kunstgewerbe. Staatliche Kunstsammlungen Kassel. Katalog, Bd. 2, Historismus. Angewandte Kunst im 19. Jahrhundert,* Kassel, 1989, No. 417).
E.A.

7

Vase in the Form of a Mosque Lamp
Philippe-Joseph Brocard, Paris. *1878*
In the lower part of the body a mark, a double *B*, in gold; mark in gold on the base: *Brocard 1878*
Decolourised glass; mould-blown, painted with coloured enamels – dark and pale blue, red, green, pink yellow and gold
Height 25.9; diameter of the body 18.5
Inv. No. Kr 1410
Provenance: 1878 acquired by Alexander Polovtsov at the Exposition Universelle in Paris, kept in his collection in St Petersburg; 1886 to the Stieglitz Museum; 1933 transferred to the Hermitage from the 1st Branch of the Hermitage (formerly the Stieglitz Museum), Leningrad.
Literature: Japan 2006-7, No. 6.

Philippe-Joseph Brocard (died 1896) started his career as a restorer of glass.
Lamps hung in archways formed an obligatory part of the decoration of any mosque, the light they shed having both a theological and mystical meaning that derived from the celebrated ayat in the Koran, 'Light' (Koran, sura 24, ayat 35).
During the second half of the 19th century vases in the form of mosque lamps became extremely popular, being produced at many European and Russian manufactories.
Brocard reproduced – with some distortions – a standard inscription of the kind frequently found on applied and decorative arts objects made for Mameluk rulers: 'Glory to our Sovereign Sultan, experienced and energetic, Maliq al Naser' (inscription read by Anton Pritula of the Hermitage).
In the lower part of the body are depictions of three cups or 'wine goblets' set in circles, the arms of court cup-bearers (one of the most important posts at court, where nomadic banqueting traditions were preserved).
E.A.

8

Vase in the Form of a Mosque Lamp
Philippe-Joseph Brocard, Paris. *1878*
Mark in gold on the base: *Brocard 1878*
Transparent yellow glass; mould-blown, painted with coloured enamels – dark blue, red, pink, white, green, yellow, brown and gold
Height 14.6; diameter of the body 10.8
Inv. No. Kr 1409
Provenance: 1878 acquired by Alexander Polovtsov at the Exposition Universelle in Paris, kept in his collection in St Petersburg; 1886 to the Stieglitz Museum; 1933 transferred to the Hermitage from the 1st Branch of the Hermitage (formerly the Stieglitz Museum), Leningrad.
Literature: Japan 2006-7, No. 7.

Like cat. 7, this vase takes the form of a mosque lamp. In this case the decoration includes vegetable ornament and traditional colours characteristic of Islamic glass-painting of the first half of the 14th century.
E.A.

9

Jug
L'Escalier de Cristal, France. *1852-57*
On the base a paper label with the inscription: *LAHOCHE PARIS ESCALIER DE CRISTAL PALAIS ROYAL 162 & 164*
Decolourised and aquamarine glass; vetro a reticello
Height with handle 32.5; diameter of the body 13.5
Inv. No. Kr 2707
Provenance: after 1904 acquired by the Society for the Encouragement of the Arts, St Petersburg; 1933 transferred to the Hermitage.
Previously unpublished.

L'Escalier de Cristal was a firm known for its furniture, ceramics and glass. From 1852 to 1857 it was run by Lahoche.
Around the middle of the 19th century there was a revival of interest in Venetian 16th-century glass in Europe. Much admired in particular was the filigree technique, using a mesh of glass strands known as *vetro a reticello,* a technique first mentioned in 1549.
E.A.

10

Drop-shaped Vase
Appert Frères, Clichy. *c. 1889*
Model by Ernest-Baptiste Léveillé, Paris
Inscription incised with a needle on the base: *Paris E Léveillé*
Decolourised glass with two opalescent spots of brown, blue and yellow; free-blown
Height 27.6; diameter 8.4
Inv. No. Kr 1350
Provenance: 29 October 1889 acquired by Alexander Alexandrovich Polovtsov in Paris , kept in his collection in St Petersburg; 1894 to the Stieglitz Museum; 1933 transferred to the Hermitage from the 1st Branch of the Hermitage (formerly the Stieglitz Museum), Leningrad.
Literature: Leningrad 1967, ill. 56; Leningrad 1974, No. 254; Japan 2006-7, No. 9.

The model for this vase was probably developed by Léveillé around 1889. The free combination of colours reflected his interest in the art and culture of Japan.
Like his teacher François-Eugène Rousseau, Léveillé worked with the brothers Adrien and Léon Appert at Clichy, near Paris. Their choice of their manufactory was determined by its advanced technological potential.
E.A.

11
Vase
Appert Frères, Clichy. *1886-89*
Model by Ernest-Baptiste Léveillé, Paris
Signature engraved on the bottom: *E Léveillé / Paris*
Two layers of yellowish decolourised glass, with between them inclusions of beige, red and black glass, with tiny pieces of gold foil; artificial craquelure; mould-blown
Height: 26.7; body 17 x 9.6
Inv. No. Kr 1376
Provenance: 29 October 1889 acquired by Alexander Polovtsov in Paris, kept in his collection in St Petersburg; 1894 to the Stieglitz Museum; 1933 transferred to the Hermitage from the 1st Branch of the Hermitage (formerly the Stieglitz Museum), Leningrad.
Literature: Leningrad 1974, No. 256; Japan 2006-7, No. 10.

Archive documents reveal that this vase was one of five objects purchased by Alexander Polovtsov via the Maison Rousseau et Léveillé. Polovtsov's wife, Nadezhda Mikhaylovna, then transferred it on 18 (30) July 1889 as part of a group of 93 objects given to the Museum of the Baron Stieglitz School of Technical Drawing (Hermitage Archives, Fund 1, *opis'* 47, *delo* 9, f. 204).
Such vases were produced in three sizes. The form derives from Chinese rectangular vessels in various materials such as rock crystal and jasper. Ricke places the creation of the models for the 'Vase plat à tête de chimère' in 1880, when the firm of Alfred Appert patented a method of mechanically blowing glass that made possible the creation of thick-walled items. On 16 December 1885 Rousseau sold to Léveillé the forms for objects he had himself developed, among them the form for this vase (Ricke, Schmitt 2004, p. 81, No. 2). Léveillé's mark on the base is evidence that the vase was produced after that sale.
E.A.

12
Vase
Appert Frères, Clichy. *1886-89*
Model by F.E. Rousseau and E.B. Léveillé, Paris
Signature engraved on the bottom: *E Léveillé / Paris*
Two layers of yellowish decolourised glass, with between them inclusions of beige, red and black glass, with tiny pieces of gold foil; artificial craquelure; mould-blown
Height: 27.3; body 12.9 x 9.9
Inv. No. Kr 1377
Provenance: 29 October 1889 acquired by Alexander Polovtsov in Paris, kept in his collection in St Petersburg; 1894 to the Stieglitz Museum; 1933 transferred to the Hermitage from the 1st Branch of the Hermitage (formerly the Stieglitz Museum), Leningrad.
Literature: Leningrad 1974, No. 255; Japan 2006-7, No. 11.
E.A.

13
Vase with a Spray of Flowering Plum
Appert Frères, Clichy. *c. 1889*
Model by F.E. Rousseau and E.B. Léveillé, Paris
Engraved on the bottom: *E. Rousseau / E Léveillé;* pink oval label with black letters, around the oval: *E.Léveillé / Rousseau;* around the centre: *paris;* and running across: *74 bt haussmann*
Semi-transparent greyish-white glass with an overlay of yellow glass; mould-blown, etched and engraved
Height 15.3; body 11.9 x 10.6
Inv. No. Kr 1344
Provenance: 29 October 1889 acquired by Alexander Polovtsov in Paris, kept in his collection in St Petersburg; 1894 to the Stieglitz Museum; 1933 transferred to the Hermitage from the 1st Branch of the Hermitage (formerly the Stieglitz Museum), Leningrad.
Literature: Leningrad 1974, No. 258; Japan 2006-7, No. 12.

Rousseau and Léveillé often used a combination of semi-transparent greyish-white and yellow glass in the making of different models during the 1880s and 1890s. The depiction of branches of flowering plum recalls motifs used in Japanese lacquer carvings.
E.A.

14
Vase with a Spray of Rosehips
Thomas Webb and Sons factory, Stourbridge. *c. 1889*
Stamped into the base the mark: *thomas webb & sons;* label: *T. Goode & CO / South / Audley Street / London/ Grosvenor Square*
Greenish-blue glass with a milky layer; mould-blown, etched, engraved, acid matt finish of the outside surface
Height 22.6; diameter 14.8
Inv. No. Kr 1341
Provenance: 23 October 1889 acquired at the Exposition Universelle in Paris for the Stieglitz Museum, St Petersburg; 1923 transferred to the Hermitage from the Stieglitz Museum.
Literature: Leningrad 1967 (ex-catalogue); Leningrad 1974, No. 170; Japan 2006-7, No. 13.

Thomas Webb & Sons was one of England's leading glass manufacturers in the 1870s. Its first works of multi-layer 'cameo' glass can be dated to 1876.
This vase (as well as cat. nos. 15-18) was one of nine objects acquired at the Exposition Universelle in Paris via the shop Thomas Goode & Co. for the Stieglitz Museum in St Petersburg.
E.A.

15
Vase with a Spray of Datura
(datura arborea)
Thomas Webb and Sons factory, Stourbridge. *c. 1889*
Stamped into the base the mark: *thomas webb & sons;* label: *T. Goode & CO / South / Audley Street / London / Grosvenor Square*
Yellow glass with an overlay of milky glass; mould-blown, etched, engraved, acid matt finish of the outer surface
Height 16.9; diameter 17.1
Inv. No. Kr 1340
Provenance: 23 October 1889 acquired at the Exposition Universelle in Paris for the Stieglitz Museum, St Petersburg; 1923 transferred to the Hermitage from the Stieglitz Museum.
Literature: Leningrad 1967 (ex-catalogue); Leningrad 1974, No. 172; Hermitage English Art 1979, No. 341; Japan 2006-7, No. 14.

Thomas Webb & Sons put out both original pieces and limited edition mass produced items, of which this is an example. The decoration includes traditional elements such as stylised flowers around the neck and the rhythmic arrangement of leafy ornament around the base, contrasting with the free arrangement of the stem of thorn apple around the shoulders of the vase. Such naturalism in the depiction of vegetation became firmly established in the decoration of glassware only in the 1890s, thanks to the work of Emile Gallé.
E.A.

16
VASE WITH A ROSE
Thomas Webb and Sons factory, Stourbridge. *c. 1889*
Stamped into the base the mark: THOMAS WEBB & SONS, CAMEO; traces of a round stamp in black with part of the firm's title
Four-layer glass; milky glass with yellow, dark pink and an overlay of milky glass; mould-blown, multi-layer etching, engraved, acid matt finish of the outside surface
Height 15; body 13 x 7.6
Inv. No. Kr 1343
Provenance: 23 October 1889 acquired at the Exposition Universelle in Paris for the Stieglitz Museum, St Petersburg; 1923 transferred to the Hermitage from the Stieglitz Museum.
Literature: Leningrad 1967 (ex-catalogue); Leningrad 1974, No. 173; Hermitage English Art 1979, No. 342; Japan 2006-7, No. 17.

An example of Webb's industrial output. In form the vase recalls contemporary Chinese flasks for holding snuff, also made of layered glass.
E.A.

17
VASE WITH DECORATION IN CHINESE STYLE
Thomas Webb and Sons factory, Stourbridge. *c. 1889*
Stamped into the base the mark: THOMAS WEBB & SONS; label: *T. Goode & CO / South / Audley Street / London / Grosvenor Square*
Three-layer glass: yellowish-milky with a ruby layer; mould-blown, multi-layer etching
Height 18.5
Inv. No. Kr 1347
Provenance: 23 October 1889 acquired at the Exposition Universelle in Paris for the Stieglitz Museum, St Petersburg; 1923 transferred to the Hermitage from the 1st Branch of the Hermitage (formerly the Stieglitz Museum).
Literature: Leningrad 1967 (ex-catalogue); Leningrad 1974, No. 171; Hermitage English Art 1979, No. 339; St Petersburg 1996, No. 331; Japan 2006-7, No. 15.

Chinese and Japanese glass was very popular in 19th-century England. The firm of Thomas Webb was inspired to make objects in carved 'cameo' glass by Chinese snuff flasks, made using this technique. Working in the oriental style in the firm's workshops were Daniel (1817-1907) and Lionel (1852-1926) Pearce, both of whom started work there in 1884. Daniel Pearce was also in charge of the design workshop.
E.A.

18
VASE WITH MOORISH ORNAMENTAL MOTIFS AND FLOWERS
Thomas Webb and Sons factory, Stourbridge. *c. 1889*
Stamped into the base the mark: THOMAS WEBB & SONS; label: *T. Goode & CO / South / Audley Street / London / Grosvenor Square*
Three-layer glass: semi-transparent green with opaque grey and milky overlay; mould-blown, multi-layer etching, partially engraved
Height 24.6; diameter 15.6
Inv. No. Kr 1358
Provenance: 23 October 1889 acquired at the Exposition Universelle in Paris for the Stieglitz Museum, St Petersburg; 1923 transferred to the Hermitage from the Stieglitz Museum.
Literature: Leningrad 1967 (ex-catalogue); Leningrad 1974, No. 175; Japan 2006-7, No. 16.

An example of the firm's industrial output.
E.A.

19
VASE, THE LID DECORATED WITH A GARLAND OF FORGET-ME-NOTS AND RIBBONS
Meisenthal (?)
Model Emile Gallé, Nancy. *c. 1867*
Signature on the bottom: *Gallé / à / Nancy*
Colourless transparent glass; painted with opaque enamel in dark and pale blue, white, green and yellow; mould-blown
Height with lid 16.2; diameter 15.1
Inv. No. Kr 2676
Provenance: before 1904 acquired by the Society for the Encouragement of the Arts, St Petersburg; 1933 transferred to the Hermitage.
Literature: Catalogue 1904, No. 295; Leningrad 1974, No. 222; Ivanova 1983, p. 129; St Petersburg 1996, No. 423; St Petersburg 1999, No. 1; Japan 2006-7, No. 18.

Forms for a series of glass tableware objects decorated in the style of Louis XVI were developed by Gallé around 1867. Ph.-T. Charpentier, on the basis of the painting technique, links their production with the manufactory in Meisenthal (Paris 1985-86, No. 62). The model was repeated on many occasions up to the end of the 1870s. Charpentier considers that the signature 'Gallé à Nancy' which appears on a number of items in the group (including the Hermitage vase) is characteristic of the period before 1877, when the firm was run by Charles Gallé, father of Emile. In 1877 Emile Gallé became head of the firm and objects were henceforth marked not only with the surname but also with the craftsman's first name. Charpentier also suggested that the decoration was conceived to mark Charles Gallé's receipt in 1866 of a licence as supplier to the Court of Napoleon III, identifying the insects set amidst the garland as the bees that form part of Napoleon's arms (Paris 1985-86, No. 62).
E.A.

20
TRAY WITH HERALDIC SYMBOLS OF NANCY
Emile Gallé, Nancy. *1889*
On the back in two places, the engraved mark: E G and a Cross of Lorraine, with the signature *Emile Gallé / Nancy / Exposition 1889*
Transparent yellowish-brown glass; engraved, painted with opaque enamels and gold
38.8 x 29.6 x 3.9
Inv. No. ZF 27877
Provenance: 2001 acquired via the Hermitage Purchasing Commission.
Literature: Japan 2006-7, No. 20.

In the 1880s Gallé frequently used the heraldic symbols of Lorraine on his products. Alongside stylised thistles – symbol of the city of Nancy – are freely arranged arms of different lands that once belonged to the Dukes of Lorraine and those to which they laid claim. Two fish swim in the same direction – arms of the Province of Bar; the heraldic lilies set into the ornament are the arms of Sicily; lions walking in opposite directions form the arms of the neighbouring duchies of Geldern and Jülich, which played an important political role in the 13th century; the cross signifies Jerusalem, while the bands of differing width forming the background are the stylised arms of Hungary and Aragon. Lorraine's claim to most of these lands came via the Anjou dynasty which ruled the state for many years, above all René of Anjou (le bon roi René, 1409-80) who held the titles duc de Guise, duc de Bar, duc de Lorraine (1431-53), duc d'Anjou, Touraine and Calabria, comte de Provence, and who laid claim to the thrones of Aragon and Valencia (1434), was crowned King of Jerusalem in 1435 and was King of Naples 1438-42.
E.A.

21

Decanter with a Stopper in the Form of an Orchid (Cypripendium calceolus)
Emile Gallé, Nancy. *c. 1889*
Signed on the bottom: *E.Gallé / Nancy / depose*
Transparent, yellowish-brown glass; mould-blown, ground, painted in coloured enamels – yellow, pale violet, dark violet, green and white
Height with stopper 25.5; 12.2 x 9
Inv. No. ZF 27703 a,b
Provenance: 1994 acquired via the Hermitage Purchasing Commission.
Literature: St Petersburg 1997, No. 143; St Petersburg 1999, No. 2; Japan 2006-7, No. 19.

This item formed part of a service with 'flower forms' consisting of two decanters, twelve glasses and a leaf-shaped tray. Several such services were produced. One was shown at the Exposition Universelle in Paris in 1889, representing the floral trend or 'vegetable style' in Gallé's work of the period. Its decoration employs an enamelling technique new to Gallé, by which each paint was fired at a different temperature.
E.A.

22

Vase with a Toad and a Dragonfly
Emile Gallé, Nancy. *1888*
Signed on the body: *E*, a Cross of Lorraine and the letter G
Relief inscription on the body's pale ground with brown spots: *Souci de plaire* [the desire to please]; engraved on the bottom: *Exposition 1889 Galerie d'honneur; Emile Gallé / fecit. Nancy / 1888; C'est / mon Souci* ['Tis my desire] with a snail and a leaf
Two-layered glass, colourless with an overlay of brown; a turquoise spot applied to the colourless glass, a blue spot on the brown; mould-blown, deep etching and multi-layer engraving; acid matt finish of the inside surface
Height 16.1; body 16.3 x 9.7
Inv. No. Kr 1345
Provenance: 1889 acquired by Alexander Polovtsov at the Exposition Universelle in Paris, entered the Stieglitz Museum, St Petersburg, on 9 (21) November 1889; 1923 transferred to the Hermitage from the Stieglitz Museum.
Literature: Leningrad 1974, No. 223; Ivanova 1983, p. 128; Stieglitz Museum 1994, No. 12; St Petersburg 1999, No. 3; Japan 2006-7, No. 21.

The sketch for the model, produced in 1888, survives (Duncan 1984, p. 113, No. 162). In the drawing, the left side of the décor consists of a toad eyeing a dragonfly as it flies past, identical to that on the Hermitage vessel, but the right side is different, the design lacking the flowers in the foreground and having different inscriptions. The drawing includes lines from a poem by Charles-Marie-René Leconte de Lisle 'Echappez vous des ombres immobiles' (Avoid immobile shadows). Closest to the design is a vase in the Kunstindustrimuseet, Copenhagen (Paris 1985-86, No. 102).
Gallé repeated the model several times with certain changes in the decoration (Kunstindustrimuseet, Copenhagen; Museum of Fine Arts, Boston). The main subject, present in all versions, is explained by Philippe Thiébaut as the battle between the forces of good – embodied by the dragonfly – and evil – embodied by the toad eyeing it greedily (Paris 1985-86, No. 102).
E.A.

23

Vase with Ribbons, Vegetable Motifs and Dragonflies
Emile Gallé, Nancy. *c. 1889*
Engraved on the bottom: *Em.Gallé / Nanceiis fecit N 308* and a depiction of leaves
Two-layer glass, colourless with the addition of oxides (turquoise, green and black) and opaque pink overlay; mould-blown, multi-layer engraving, carving
Height 21.5; diameter 17.8
Inv. No. Kr 1346
Provenance: 1889 acquired by Alexander Polovtsov at the Exposition Universelle in Paris; 1923 transferred to the Hermitage from the Stieglitz Museum.
Literature: Leningrad 1967 (ex-catalogue); Leningrad 1974, 1974, No. 225; Ivanova 1983, p. 128; St Petersburg 1999, No. 4; Japan 2006-7, No. 22.

The vase was influenced by vessels in Islamic style. Gallé almost entirely repeats the form of the body and the arrangement of the ornamental bands, the main difference lying in the lack of the broad foot and the loops for suspension. The ribbons, vegetable motifs and dragonflies recall the carving on 18th-century Chinese vessels from two-layer glass.
E.A.

24

Vase with Butterflies and Dragonflies
Emile Gallé, Nancy. *1889*
Engraved on the bottom: *Emile Gallé / Nancy / Exposition 1889; E* with a Cross of Lorraine and the letter G, depiction of a butterfly
Three-layer glass – transparent with coloured spots of oxides and gold foil with cherry and lilac overlays; mould-blown, deep etching, partially engraved, hand-polished in places
Height 23; diameter 30
Inv. No. Kr 1434
Provenance: 1889 acquired by Alexander Polovtsov at the Exposition Universelle in Paris, entered the Stieglitz Museum, St Petersburg, 11 (23) November 1889; 1923 transferred to the Hermitage from the Stieglitz Museum.

Literature: Leningrad 1967 (ex-catalogue); Leningrad 1974, No. 224; Ivanova 1983, p. 130; St Petersburg 1999, No. 5; Japan 2006-7, No. 23.

When this vase was made Gallé was experimenting with different techniques for the decoration of glass. Fine transitions from cold tones to warm were achieved by retaining all three layers of glass in the ornamental areas but etching through one or two layers in the background, a particularly remarkable effect being created by the tiny pieces of metal foil set between the layers.

The decoration combines two stylistic traditions: the heavy, somewhat stocky form and bands of lobes along the upper and lower edges are characteristic of Historicism, but the ornamental frieze composed of large moths, dragonflies and beetles is very much in the Art Nouveau manner.

E.A.

25

Vase with a Passion Flower (passiflora)

Emile Gallé, Nancy. *c. 1889*

Relief inscription etched on the foot: *Gallé*; engraved on the bottom: *'...Pour tirer un soleil de nos coeurs, et pour faire / De nos pensers brûlants une tiède atmosphère / Baudelaire'* [...To draw the sun from our hearts and make / Of our burning thoughts a warm atmosphere / Baudelaire]

Body of five-layer glass – lilac, olive green, pale blue with pink and brown overlays; mould-blown, multi-layer etching, polished, acid matt finish of the inside surface. Foot of two-layered glass, colourless and red; etched, with inclusions of metal foil and glass incrustation

Height 63.5; body 17.7 x 9.5; diameter of foot 16.6

Inv. No. FB 1633

Provenance: 1949 via the State Museums Fund.

Literature: Ivanova 1983, pp. 128-37; Duncan 1984, ill. 110; Babin 1994, No. 480; Nancy 1999, No. 109; St Petersburg 1999, No. 7; Japan 2006-7, No. 40.

One of Gallé's 'Verreries parlantes'. The text derives from Charles Baudelaire's poem 'Paysage', part of the 'Tableaux parisiens' cycle in the book *Les Fleurs du mal.* Gallé slightly rephrased the original, which reads '...De tirer un soleil de mon coeur, et pour faire / De mes pensers brûlants une tiède atmosphère' [... To draw the sun from my heart and make / Of my burning thoughts a warm atmosphere].

The vase was produced at a time when Gallé was experimenting with both form and technique.

There is a photograph of the vase taken before it was despatched to Russia (Duncan 1984).

Closest in form to the Hermitage vase is another in the Hentrich collection in the Kunstmuseum Düsseldorf, dated 1884-89 (Helga Hilschenz, *Das Glas des Jugendstils. Katalog Der Sammlung Hentrich im Kunstmuseum Düsseldorf (Kataloge des Kunstmuseums Düsseldorf,* Bd. 1), Munich, 1973, vol. 1).

E.A.

26

Vase with an Orchid (phalenopsis aphroditae)

Emile Gallé, Nancy. *1889-90*

Setting: Bapst & Falise, Paris

Engraved inscription on the body: *O beauté des choses qui meurent! Les grandes ailes de la mort / qui, sans les blesser, les effleurent / leur donne [sic] un charme plus fort... / Emile Hinzelin* [Oh beauty of all that dies! The broad wings of death which brush across them without wounding / gives them a greater charm / Emile Hinzelin]

Engraved inscription: *habitaculum vetus et fragile quam fragilioris / Enimulat / Nanceils Em.Gallé faciebat Vitratius ann. 1889-90;* on the bottom the letter *E,* a Cross of Lorraine, shells and the letter G

Mark on the silver setting: head of a warrior in profile set into an octagon; *Bapst & Falise, Paris*

Two-layer glass, colourless with the introduction of oxides (blue, green, brownish-black), opaque pink; mould-blown, multi-layer etching, engraved. Setting of silver; cast, chased, carved, parcel-gilt.

Height with lid 27.5; diameter 12.5

Inv. No. ZF 23414 a,b

Provenance: 1896 presented to Tsar Nicholas II and Alexandra Fyodorovna during their visit to Paris; 1931 transferred to the Hermitage.

Literature: Champier 1896, No. 16; Shelkovnikov 1962; Leningrad 1967 (ex-catalogue); Leningrad 1974, No. 226; Ivanova 1983, pp. 128-37; Duncan 1984, No. 186; Rappe 1991, pp. 18-24; St Petersburg 1994, Nos. 330, 331; le Tacon 1998, fig. 32; St Petersburg 1999, No. 8; Anisimova 2001, p. 204; Japan 2006-7, No. 34.

With cat. 27 presented to the royal couple but the pair was made several years before their visit to Paris, with no intention then that they be used as a diplomatic gift.

At the end of the 19th century Bapst & Falise was one of France's leading jewellery firms. Emile Gallé collaborated with them on many occasions, ordering settings for his glassware. The orchid is often seen as symbolising evil and scholars have placed a gloomy interpretation on such vases (Ivanova 1983, p. 128), thanks also to the quotation from Hinzelin. It is possible, however, that we should see the decoration as an illustration of Emile Gallé's scholarly study of the theory of the evolution, based on the example of orchids.

The orchids on this vase come from the Philippines but they were one of the most popular glass-house flowers in Europe in the late 19th and early 20th centuries.

E.A.

27

Lidded Vase with an Orchid (angraecum suescuipedale)

Emile Gallé, Nancy. *1889-90*

Setting: Bapst & Falize, Paris

Engraved inscription on the bottom: *Emile Gallé ft. Nanceiis;* depiction of a shell

Two identical marks on the silver setting: the head of a warrior in profile set into an octagon; *Bapst & Falise, Paris*

Two-layer glass, colourless with the introduction of oxides (blue, green, brownish-black), opaque pink overlay down to the stem; mould-blown, multi-layer etching, engraved. Setting of silver; cast, chased, carved, parcel-gilt

Height with lid 28; diameter 12.3

Inv. No. ZF 23413 a,b

Provenance: 1896 presented to Tsar Nicholas II and Alexandra Fyodorovna during their visit to Paris; 1931 transferred to the Hermitage from the Winter Palace.

Literature: Champier 1896, No. 16; Shelkovnikov 1962; Leningrad 1967 (ex-catalogue); Leningrad 1974, No. 227; Ivanova 1983, pp. 128-37; Duncan 1984, No. 186; Rappe 1991, pp. 18-24; St Petersburg 1994, Nos. 330, 331; le Tacon 1998, fig. 32; St Petersburg 1999, No. 9; Anisimova 2001, p. 204; Japan 2006-7, No. 35.

A major role was played in decoration of these vases by the parcel-gilt settings of the base produced by one of Paris' leading jewellers, Lucien Falise. In 1917, however, the settings were partly lost. We can judge the overall composition only from a reproduction in the *Revue des arts décoratifs* for 1896 (No. 16). There, however, the vases are mistakenly dated to 1896 and the setting is described as being of gold, errors repeated in Duncan's monograph on the work of Gallé (Duncan 1984, No. 186).
The orchid depicted on this vase comes from Madagascar, Eastern Africa and Reunion.
E.A.

28
Vase with an Orchid (cypripedium calceolus)
Emile Gallé, Nancy. *1895-96*
Relief inscription etched on the base, on the flower: *Cristallerie/ d'Emile Gallé à Nancy*
Three-layer glass, colourless, milky and yellow; mould-blown, engraved over etching
Height 14.5; diameter 12.5
Inv. No. ZF 24911
Provenance: 1937 via the State Museums Fund.
Literature: Leningrad 1967 (ex-catalogue); Leningrad 1974, No. 242; St Petersburg 1999, No. 10; Japan 2006-7, No. 46.
E.A.

29
Vase with Water Anemones and Dragonflies in Flight
Emile Gallé, Nancy. *1892*
Setting: Yury Rapoport, firm of Carl Fabergé, St Petersburg
Engraved inscription by the edge of the vase: *Vegetations de Symboles;* on the upper ring: *Palmes lentes de mes désirs. Nepuphars mornes des plaisirs. Mousses froides, lianes molles... Maurice Maeterlinck* [Slow palms of my desires. Sad lilies of pleasure. Cold mosses, soft lianes... Maurice Maeterlinck]
On the base beneath the setting the signature and date: *Emile Gallé 1892 Nancy fecit*
Marks on the silver setting: on the bottom a two-headed eagle in a circle; *fabergé* [in Russian]; *i.r.* [mark of Yury / Iury Rapoport]; fineness mark *88* and crossed anchors and a sceptre
Four-layer glass – milky, with pink, colourless and black overlays; mould-blown, multi-layer engraving, acid matt finish of the inside surface. Silver mount; wrought, chased and carved
Height with setting 20.5
Inv. No. ZF 23410
Provenance: by 1909 in the private apartments of Empress Alexandra Fyodorovna, Winter Palace, St Petersburg; 1931 transferred to the Hermitage from the Winter Palace.
Literature: Leningrad 1974, No. 245; St Petersburg-Paris-London 1993, p. 111; Speyer 1994, pp. 126-27; le Tacon 1998, fig. 39; St Petersburg 1999, No. 6; Fabergé 2000, No. 177; Anisimova 2001, p. 206; Japan 2006-7, No. 24.

An 'Inventory of items belonging to their Imperial Highnesses and kept in the Winter Palace' compiled in 1909 records that these vases stood on the Empress' desk in her study.
For many years the setting hid the maker's signature. Therefore in the 1909 inventory Gallé's authorship was questioned and the item was described as 'in the Gallé genre'. In the exhibition catalogue Leningrad 1974 an attribution to Gallé was made solely on the basis of artistic analysis. In 2000, however, conservation undertaken in the Hermitage's laboratories revealed not only the signature that confirmed Gallé's authorship but also the date, 1892.
Philippe le Tacon, citing a letter from Gallé to Robert Montesquieu of 14 October 1896, considers that this vase was that presented by the craftsman to Empress Alexandra Fyodorovna during her stay with relatives in Darmstadt in 1896 (le Tacon 1998, p. 62).
Maeterlinck was one of Gallé's favourite authors. The craftsman started to included quotations from poems by various writers on his vases, thus giving the image a symbolic resonance, in 1884. Such pieces came to be called 'Verreries parlantes'.
E.A.

30
Lidded Vase with Lotus (nymphaea lotus or Tiger Lotus)
Emile Gallé, Nancy. *1897*
Engraved inscription on the body: *Gallé / Paris Nancy*
Two-layer glass – colourless and brownish-orange; mould-blown, deep etching, acid matt finish of the inside surface
Height with lid 11.5; diameter 9.1
Inv. No. ZF 23409 a,b
Provenance: by 1909 in the private apartments of Empress Alexandra Fyodorovna, Winter Palace, St Petersburg; 1931 transferred to the Hermitage from the Winter Palace.
Literature: Leningrad 1974, No. 231; Ivanova 1983, p. 128; Speyer 1994, p. 126; St Petersburg 1999, No. 12; Anisimova 2001, p. 205; Japan 2006-7, No. 25.

This vase can be identified with one described in archive documents as having stood on the Empress's desk in the Winter Palace: a small vase 'in the form of a white mushroom with a lid, of cloudy yellow colour (the ground) with relief flowers in brown. With the mark of Gallé.' The description was later corrected in pencil, with the addition after the word 'vase' of 'glass, two-layer', the words 'brown colour' crossed out and replaced with 'orange' (Anisimova 2001, p. 205).
Gallé developed a decoration of lotus flowers and leaves in 1897 for a vase exhibited at Le Grand Dépôt, Emile Bourgeois's shop in Paris (Hilschenz-Mlynek 1985, Nos. 232-34). It was later used to produce series of vases.
E.A.

31
Vase with Dahlias
Emile Gallé, Nancy. *1898*
Setting: Yury Rapoport, firm of Carl Fabergé, St Petersburg
Engraved on the body, against the background of a cross of Lorraine: *Emile Gallé*
Marks on the bottom of the mount: a two-headed eagle in a circle; *fabergé* [in Russian]; *i.r.* [mark of Yury / Iury Rapoport]; fineness mark *88* and crossed anchors and a sceptre
Three-layer glass – yellowish-green, colourless and violet-brown; mould-blown, etched, engraved, glass intarsia. Silver mount: cast, chased, carved
Height with setting 25.8
Inv. No. ZF 23411
Provenance: kept in the Louis XVI Drawing Room in the Winter Palace, St Petersburg; 1931 transferred to the Hermitage from the Winter Palace.
Literature: Leningrad 1974, No. 234; Ivanova 1983, p. 128;

St Petersburg-Paris-London 1993, No. 56; St Petersburg 1999, No. 13; Fabergé 2000, No. 179; Anisimova 2001, p. 205; Japan 2006-7, No. 26.

Formerly kept in the Louis XVI Drawing Room in the Winter Palace (Anisimova 2001, p. 205).
The vase's body is made in the form of a stick of bamboo, against the background of which there are dahlia stems, leaves and flowers. According to Emile Gallé's original concept the model was to have a bronze setting at the base and a drawing for that setting appears in an album of the craftsman's completed works, dated to 5 March 1898 (Ricke, Schmitt 2004, pl. 15). Its modest forms clearly did not suit the vase's owners, however, and they commissioned a new one. Hermitage curator Marina Lopato discovered an invoice from the firm of Fabergé to the Imperial Cabinet dated 21 February (5 March) 1898 for the making of a silver setting for a vase in the form of a stick of bamboo (Fabergé 2000, No. 179).
Several variations of the model are known.
E.A.

32
Vase with Irises
Emile Gallé, Nancy. *1898*
Gilded engraved inscription on the body: *Gallé;* engraved on the stem: *Nous monterons vers la lumière* [We rise up towards the light]
Two-layer glass, transparent and lilac; mould-blown, deep multi-layer etching and engraving, hand-polished
Height 35.5; body 22.3 x 17.2
Inv. No. ZF 24912
Provenance: 1937 via the State Museums Fund.
Literature: Leningrad 1974, No. 233; St Petersburg 1999, No. 14; Schizuoka 2005, p. 203; Japan 2006-7, No. 48.

Two copies of this vase are known today, the other being in the Hentrich collection, Kunstmuseum Düsseldorf (Hilschenz-Mlynek 1985, No. 257). It is not possible to determine which of them was exhibited in the Salon du Champ de Mars in 1898 (E. Gallé, 'Mes envois au Salon', *Revue des arts décoratifs*, Paris, 1898, No. 18).
Part of the group known as 'Verreries parlantes', the phrase engraved on the stem deriving from a poem by the French writer Théodore de Banville (1823-91), although the original reads slightly differently: 'Nous monterons enfin vers la lumière [At last we rise up towards the light] (Hilschenz-Mlynek 1985, No. 257). Philippe Garner sees the quotation as a reflection of Gallé's pacifist views. While he admits the controversial nature of such an assertion, he nonetheless thus groups it with other objects bearing quotations from Baudelaire and Hugo that are markedly anti-war in tone (Garner 1990, p. 55). Such an understanding of the decoration is not contradicted by the traditional symbolism of the iris, known in Europe as the sword-lily because of its sharp leaves.
E.A.

33
Vase with Chrysanthemum
Emile Gallé, Nancy. *1900*
Engraved inscription on the body: *Emile Gallé 1900;* engraved and gilded inscription on the base: *Cristallerie de E.Gallé Nancy* on a relief image of a chrysanthemum
Four-layer glass – colourless, yellow, orange and brown; mould-blown, multi-layer etching, partial engraving, acid matt finish of the background and inside surface
Height 26.1; diameter 26.4
Inv. No. Kr 1356
Provenance: acquired in Emile Gallé's shop in Nancy in 1900 for the Stieglitz Museum, St Petersburg; 1923 transferred to the Hermitage from the Stieglitz Museum.
Literature: Leningrad 1967 (ex-catalogue); Leningrad 1974, No. 230; St Petersburg 1999, No. 15; Japan 2006-7, No. 27.

In the decoration of this vase we see an example of the craftsman's reinterpretation of Far Eastern art. In Japan, for instance, the chrysanthemum is a traditional seasonal motif symbolising autumn.
E.A.

34
Vase with Begonias (Begonia de Lemoine)
Emile Gallé, Nancy. *1900*
Engraved and gilded inscription on the body: *Gallé 1900;* paper label on the bottom: *Cristallerie / d'art / 37508 / Emile Gallé / Nancy. Paris*
Four-layer glass – colourless, ruby, violet and olive; mould-blown, engraved over multi-layer etching
Height 16.1; diameter 9
Inv. No. Kr 1348
Provenance: 1900 acquired in the shop of Emile Gallé in Nancy for the Stieglitz Museum, St Petersburg; 1923 transferred to the Hermitage.
Literature: Leningrad 1967 (ex-catalogue); Leningrad 1974, No. 229; Ivanova 1983, p. 134; St Petersburg 1999, No. 16; Japan 2006-7, No. 28.

The vase was photographed before it was sent to Russia (Duncan 1984, pp. 21, 59, ill. 61). This may be the vase shown at the Exposition Universelle in Paris in 1900.
E.A.

35
Vase with Symbols of Night
Emile Gallé, Nancy. *1900*
Engraved inscription on the body: *Emile / Gallé / 1900*
Two-layer glass – colourless and violet, lower part with an overlay of brown glass, colourless bubbled glass with violet, lilac and yellow lights, with inclusions of metal foil and coloured oxides, in two places glass incrustation; mould-blown, engraved, the colourless glass with internal craquelure, partly gilded, engraved
Height 30.5; diameter 8.6
Inv. No. Kr 1371
Provenance: 1900 acquired in the shop of Emile Gallé in Nancy for the Stieglitz Museum, St Petersburg; 1923 transferred to the Hermitage.
Literature: Leningrad 1967 (ex-catalogue); Leningrad 1974, No. 240; St Petersburg 1999, No. 17; Japan 2006-7, No. 29.

Attributes of night make up the decoration: poppy heads on long stems against a ground studded with night stars and moths, while below, partly hidden between the stems and insects, a fallen star sheds its last rays.
A similar vase (Duncan 1984, pp. 21, 61) bears the inscription 'Dans le ciel des ailes, des ailes / Pierre Guillard' [Wings, wings in the sky / Pierre Guillard].
E.A.

36
Vase with the Sea Bed
Emile Gallé, Nancy. *c. 1900*
Engraved inscription on the body: *Gallé*
Two-layer glass – colourless with green, brown and black oxides, milky-lilac; mould-blown, engraved, partly etched with acid matt finish of the background
Height 13.6; diameter 23.2
Inv. No. ZF 24913
Provenance: 1937 via the State Museums Fund.
Literature: Leningrad 1967 (ex-catalogue); Leningrad 1974, No. 244; Ivanova 1983, p. 133; St Petersburg 1999, No. 18; Japan 2006-7, No. 47.

Possibly part of a small series of vases similar in form and technique decorated with different aspects of the force of Nature and created around 1900. Philippe Thiébaut considers that the basis for the concept lay in four works by French historian Jules Michelet dating from 1856-68, *L'Oiseau, L'Insecte, La Mer, La Montagne* (Paris 1985-86, No. 129). The Hermitage vase was clearly intended to illustrate the subject of the sea.
E.A.

37
Vase with Irises
Emile Gallé, Nancy. *c. 1903*
Three-layer glass – colourless, violet and brown; mould-blown, multi-layer etching, engraved, acid matt finish of the inside surface
Relief inscription etched on the body: *Gallé*
Height 38; diameter 17.4
Inv. No. ZF 27116
Provenance: 1978 acquired via the Hermitage Purchasing Commission.
Literature: Leningrad 1979, No. 37; St Petersburg 1999, No. 19; Japan 2006-7, No. 51.

Here the images of irises are subordinated to rules that would seem to have been influenced by the Japanese art of ikebana. Firstly, the iris leaf is turned flat towards the viewer, never sideways on as that would recall the blade of a sword turned with its sharp edge to the enemy.
E.A.

38
Vase with Magnolias
Emile Gallé, Nancy. *c. 1900*
Engraved mark on the body: *Gallé*; inscription engraved on the bottom: *Cristallerie de Gallé à Nancy*
Three-layer glass – colourless, milky and an overlay of ruby glass; mould-blown, relief multi-layer matt engraving with partial hand polishing, intarsia
Height 27.3; diameter 8.7
Inv. No. FB 1200
Provenance: 1927 via the State Museums Fund.
Literature: Leningrad 1967 (ex-catalogue); Leningrad 1974, No. 239; St Petersburg 1999, No. 22; Japan 2006-7, No. 45.

Images of magnolias similar in terms of the colour of the glass, the composition and technique, appear on a group of vessels of different forms produced in Gallé's workshop between 1896 and 1900.
E.A.

39
Vase with a Landscape with a Lake
Manufactory of Emile Gallé, Nancy. *c. 1904*
Relief mark etched on the body: *Gallé*
Four-layer glass – colourless, yellow, blue and brown; mould-blown, multi-layer etching, partly engraved, acid matt finish of the background and inside surface
Height 61.8; diameter 19
Inv. No. ZF 26725
Provenance: 1963 acquired via the Hermitage Purchasing Commission.
Literature: Leningrad 1967 (ex-catalogue); Leningrad 1974, No. 235; St Petersburg 1999, No. 24; Japan 2006-7, No. 53.
E.A.

40
Vase with Ferns (polypodium vulgare)
Manufactory of Emile Gallé, Nancy. *c. 1904*
Engraved mark on the body: *Gallé*
Four-layer glass – colourless, pink, green and brown; mould-blown, etched, acid matt finish of the background and inside surface
Height 39; body 11.3 x 9.6
Inv. No. ZF 26780
Provenance: 1963 acquired via the Hermitage Purchasing Commission.
Literature: St Petersburg 1999, No. 25; Japan 2006-7, No. 54.

Decoration using fern fronds was developed before 1904, being used to adorn table lamps in the 'demi-riche' series, which consisted of limited edition items.
E.A.

41
Vase with a Landscape with a Lake
Manufactory of Emile Gallé, Nancy. *1904-6*
Etched mark on the body: *Gallé* with a small star
Three-layer glass – colourless, yellow and brown; mould-blown, etched, acid matt finish of the background and inside surface
Height 23.3; body 18.5 x 9.3
Inv. No. ZF 27212
Provenance: 1981 transferred to the Hermitage from the October Regional Finance Department [Rayfinotdel] by decision of the Main Cultural Administration of the city of Leningrad.
Literature: St Petersburg 1999, No. 26; Japan 2006-7, No. 55.

Landscapes of similar composition appeared in the decoration of Gallé's products between 1904 and 1914, the industrial period of the Gallé manufactory.
E.A.

42
Vase with Flowering Eryngium
Manufactory of Emile Gallé, Nancy. *1904-6*
Etched mark on the body: *Gallé* with a small star
Three-layer glass – colourless, pink and green; mould-blown, etched, acid matt finish of the background and inside surface
Height 11.2; body 7.3 x 6.1
Inv. No. ZF 27705
Provenance: 1993 acquired via the Hermitage Purchasing Commission.
Literature: St Petersburg 1997, No. 145; St Petersburg 1999, No. 27; Japan 2006-7, No. 60.
E.A.

43
VASE WITH CLEMATIS
Manufactory of Emile Gallé, Nancy. *1904-6*
Relief mark on the body: *Gallé* with a small star
Three-layer glass – pink, colourless and violet; mould-blown, etched, polished, acid matt finish of the background and inside surface
Height 11.9; body 8.2 x 6.5
Inv. No. ZF 27228
Provenance: 1982 acquired via the Hermitage Purchasing Commission.
Literature: Leningrad 1983, No. 40; St Petersburg 1999, No. 29; Japan 2006-7, No. 58.

The form was developed in the early years of the 20th century and was produced in different sizes with varied decoration.
E.A.

44
VASE WITH FLOWERING TOBACCO (NICOTIANA)
Manufactory of Emile Gallé, Nancy. *1907-14*
Relief mark on the body: *Gallé*
Three-layer glass – colourless, yellow and brown; mould-blown, etched, polished, acid matt finish of the background and inside surface
Height 49.9; diameter 18.1
Inv. No. ZF 26743
Provenance: 1964 acquired via the Hermitage Purchasing Commission.
Literature: St Petersburg 1999, No. 31; Japan 2006-7, No. 61.

Vases of this form, but in different sizes and of different coloured glass, were put out in quantities at the manufactory during its period of industrial mass production.
E.A.

45
VASE WITH AN ORCHID (OPHRYS)
Manufactory of Emile Gallé, Nancy. *1907-14*
Etched mark on the body: *Gallé*
Two-layer glass – milky and brown; mould-blown, etched, polished, acid matt finish of the background and inside surface
Height 16.8; body 8.4 x 4.9
Inv. No. ZF 27286
Provenance: 1983 transferred to the Hermitage from the Moscow Regional Finance Department [Rayfinotdel] via Pulkovo Customs, Leningrad Airport.
Literature: Leningrad 1984, No. 30; St Petersburg 1999, No. 36; Japan 2006-7, No. 64.

This form was developed around 1904 for mass produced items. The decoration is composed of orchids. These flowers are frequently found in Gallé's work, reflecting his serious interest in botany, influenced by the works of Charles Darwin. Emile Gallé was the author of several scientific studies on the evolution of the species, using the orchids of Lorraine as the basis for his analysis.
E.A.

46
VASE WITH AN ALPINE LANDSCAPE
Manufactory of Emile Gallé, Nancy. *1907-14*
Relief mark on the body: *Gallé*
Four-layer glass – colourless, violet, yellow and brown; mould-blown, etched, acid matt finish, polished
Height 46.2; diameter 18.1
Inv. No. ZF 24972
Provenance: 1937 acquired via the Hermitage Purchasing Commission.
Literature: St Petersburg 1999, No. 38; Japan 2006-7, No. 63.

A similar form was used on numerous occasions during the manufactory's period of mass production.
E.A.

47
VASE WITH A SPRAY OF HAWTHORN AND CLUSTERS OF HAWS (CRATAEGUS)
Manufactory of Emile Gallé, Nancy. *c. 1914*
Relief mark etched on the body: *Gallé*
Three-layer glass – colourless, yellow and red; mould-blown, etched, engraved, polished, acid matt finish of the background and inside surface
Height 23.9; diameter 11.6
Inv. No. ZF 27293
Provenance: 1984 acquired via the Hermitage Purchasing Commission.
Literature: St Petersburg 1999, No. 40; Japan 2006-7, No. 68.

Decoration composed of hawthorn was used at the Gallé manufactory between 1904 and 1914 on varied mass produced items.
E.A.

48
VASE WITH VIOLETS
Manufactory of Emile Gallé, Nancy. *1930s*
Mark etched on the body: *Gallé*
Three-layer glass – colourless, orange-yellow and lilac; mould-blown, multi-layer etching, acid matt finish of the background and inside surface, polished
Height 11; body 9.4 x 9.3
Inv. No. ZF 26480
Provenance: 1953 transferred to the Hermitage from the USSR State Museum of the Revolution, Leningrad.
Literature: St Petersburg 1999, No. 44; Japan 2006-7, No. 72.

To judge by both the nature of the letters that make up the firm's mark and the use of opalescent glass, the vase was produced in the 1930s. The vase was among gifts presented to Joseph Stalin (1878-1953).
E.A.

49
PLANT POT IN THE FORM OF A PARROT
Emile Gallé, Nancy. *c. 1890*
On the bottom an inscription in red enamel: *E. Gallé Nancy*
Faience, polychrome overglaze painting, gilding, glass
Length 43.5
Inv. No. ZF 27909
Provenance: 2003 acquired via the Hermitage Purchasing Commission.
Literature: Japan 2006-7, No. 75.

Many ceramic pieces produced to designs by Gallé demonstrate the characteristic features of Historicism. He most frequently turned to 18th-century porcelain forms, among them that of a parrot. Such works were painted with a bright range of colours specially developed by Gallé.
This plant pot relates in style to an earlier group of objects of the late 1870s, united by their colourful decoration over a white glaze, inspired by Japanese art of the early Meiji Period (1868-1912). Flowering sakura is combined with Gallic cockerels and chickens in a naïve attempt to combine two different artistic and cultural traditions.
E.I.

50
Vase with Tulips
Manufactory Daum Frères, Nancy. *1895*
Mark on the base framed by tulips: *Daum* and a Cross of Lorraine, beneath it *Nancy 1895*; round label: *Au vase etrusque / 20 Bd Malesherbes / Paris*
Five-layer glass – opaque pale blue, yellow, colourless, ruby and brown; mould-blown, multi-layer deep engraving over the whole of the outer surface, acid matt finish of the outside surface
Height 16.1; diameter 17.7
Inv. No. ZF 23435
Provenance: 1931 transferred to the Hermitage from the Museum of the Academy of Arts, Leningrad.
Literature: Leningrad 1967, ill. 54; Leningrad 1974, No. 246; Ivanova 1983, pp. 131, 135; St Petersburg 1999, No. 45; Japan 2006-7, No. 76.

In the mid-1890s the manufactory of the Daum brothers periodically put out simple, unfussy forms recalling the ceramics of Antiquity. This vase – as we can tell from the label it bears – is in Etruscan style of the 4th to 2nd centuries BC.
Artists at the Daum manufactory repeatedly used the tulip motif in the late 19th and early 20th centuries.
E.A.

51
Vase with a Spray of Bleeding Heart (dicentra)
Manufactory Daum Frères, Nancy. *c. 1899*
Mark engraved on the bottom: *Daum, Nancy* and a Cross of Lorraine
Two-layer glass – pink and green; mould-blown, etched, copper-wheel engraving
Height 14.5
Inv. No. ZF 27295
Provenance: 1984 acquired via the Hermitage Purchasing Commission.
Literature: St Petersburg 1999, No. 46; Japan 2006-7, No. 77.

The form of this vase, with its tall neck slightly narrowed at the centre, is characteristic of the period around 1899. Artists at the Daum manufactory were inspired by the dicentra motif not only at this time but also later, in the 1900s and 1910s, using it in decorative compositions on a variety of vases.
E.A.

52
Vase with a Spray of Lunaria
Manufactory Daum Frères, Nancy. *c. 1899*
Mark etched on the bottom: Daum, Nancy and a Cross of Lorraine
Two-layer glass – pink and green; mould-blown, etched, copper-wheel engraving
Height 14.2
Inv. No. ZF 27498
Provenance: 1987 acquired via the Hermitage Purchasing Commission.
Literature: St Petersburg 1999, No. 47; Japan 2006-7, No. 78.

Inspired by nature, Art Nouveau revealed the beauty of flowers and plants that had previously escaped the attention of artists. One such plant was lunaria, its unusual form and fragile sprays captured by craftsmen of the School of Nancy on items in glass, metal and wood.
E.A.

53-55
Three Tumblers with Fuchsia
Manufactory Daum Frères, Nancy. *c. 1900*
Mark in gold paint on the bottom: *Daum* with a Cross of Lorraine, *Nancy*
Two-layer colourless glass with a milky and violet tint between them; mould-blown, etched, painted in gold and coloured enamels (blue, purple, green), polished
Height 11.7; diameter 6.2. Inv. No. ZF 24918
Height 11.8; diameter 6.4. Inv. No. ZF 24919
Height 11.6; diameter 6.2. Inv. No. ZF 24920
Provenance: 1937 via the State Museums Fund.
Literature: Leningrad 1967 (ex-catalogue); Leningrad 1974, No. 248; St Petersburg 1999, No. 19, 48; Japan 2006-7, Nos. 79-81.

This combination of layered glass and painted enamels is characteristic of works produced by Daum Frères in the 1890s to 1910s.
The bases of the glasses have gold painting over polished glass to create the effect of a mount or setting, a device found on items produced between 1895 and 1905.
E.A.

56
Table Lamp with Trees in the Rain
Manufactory Daum Frères, Nancy. *c. 1900*
Mark in black paint on the base: *Daum, Nancy,* a Cross of Lorraine, *1578*
Four-layer glass – colourless, green, pink and colourless; mould-blown, etched, acid matt finish of the background, black enamel paint, engraved, polished. Setting: bronze; cast, chased
Height 41.7; lampshade 17.5 x 17.7
Inv. No. ZF 27100 a,b
Provenance: 1976 acquired for the Hermitage by the USSR Ministry of Culture.
Literature: Leningrad 1977, No. 267; St Petersburg 1999, No. 49; Japan 2006-7, No. 88.

Around 1900 the Daum manufactory developed several decorative variations on a landscape theme specially for table lamps. In all the different versions the stem of the lamp bears an image of tree trunks, the lampshade thus playing the role of the trees' crowns.
E.A.

57
Table Lamp with Birch Trees
Manufactory Daum Frères, Nancy. *c. 1900*
Mark in purple on the base: *Daum, Nancy* and a Cross of Lorraine, *1802*
Two-layer glass – colourless and pink opalescent, on the foot an overlay of purple and yellow glass; mould-blown, etched, painted with coloured enamels (green, black, brown), acid matt finish, polished
Height 41.3; lampshade 18.2 x 18.4
Inv. No. ZF 27347 a,b
Provenance: 1984 acquired via the Hermitage Purchasing Commission.
Literature: St Petersburg 1999, No. 50; Japan 2006-7, No. 89.
E.A.

58
Chandelier with Blackcurrant (ribes nigrum)
Manufactory Daum Frères, Nancy. *1900-3*
Mark etched on the body: *Daum, Nancy* and a Cross of Lorraine
Three-layer glass – colourless, green and blue; mould-blown, multi-layer etching, polished, acid matt finish. Framework: iron (?); wrought, chased
Height 9.1; diameter 30.6; height when suspended 80.9
Inv. No. ZF 27812 a,b
Provenance: 1995 acquired via the Hermitage Purchasing Commission.
Literature: St Petersburg 1997, No. 147; St Petersburg 1999, No. 51; Japan 2006-7, No. 90.

Whereas table lamps were often produced by the Daum manufactory, chandeliers were much less common. In design and execution this example recalls a series of vases produced to designs by Henri Bergé (Petry s.a., Nos. 37-43).
E.A.

59
Table Lamp with Bats
Manufactory Daum Frères, Nancy. *1905-10*
Bronze stand by Louis Majorelle
Relief mark etched on the lampshade: *Daum,* a Cross of Lorraine, *Nancy*
Three-layer glass – milky, violet and an orange overlay in the upper part; mould-blown, etched, multi-layer deep engraving over the whole surface, acid matt finish of the inside surface. Stand: bronze; cast, chased, gilded
Height 69.5; diameter of lampshade 34.7
Inv. No. ZF 27243 a,b
Provenance: 1982 acquired via the Hermitage Purchasing Commission.
Literature: Leningrad 1983, No. 37; St Petersburg 1999, No. 52; Japan 2006-7, No. 87.

One of the best Art Nouveau lamps produced at the Daum manufactory. The model for the bronze stand was produced in 1905 by Louis Majorelle (1859-1926), one of the leading artists of the School of Nancy, and it was originally intended for use on a table lamp with three branches (Macklowe Gallery, New York; Arwas 1987, ill. p. 78). Here, however, only the base and support remain from that more extensive stand. Emile Gallé was the first artist of the School of Nancy – around 1890 – to use depictions of bats in his work. This attribute of night (according to the European tradition), was seen in China as a symbol of good fortune.
E.A.

60
Small Vase with a Winter Landscape
Manufactory Daum Frères, Nancy. *1900-7*
Mark in black paint on the bottom: *Daum, Nancy* and a Cross of Lorraine
Three-layer glass – two layers of colourless glass with between them intercalary vitrification of yellow and orange glass, then brown glass; mould-blown, etched, painted in white enamel, acid matt finish of the background
Height 8; diameter 6.2
Inv. No. ZF 27229
Provenance: 1982 acquired via the Hermitage Purchasing Commission.
Literature: Leningrad 1983, No. 38; St Petersburg 1999, No. 54; Japan 2006-7, No. 82.

Between 1900 and 1907 the Daum manufactory produced a series of vases in orange-yellow tones showing winter landscapes. These items are all made of cased glass with enamel painting.
E.A.

61
Small Vase with a Seascape
Manufactory Daum Frères, Nancy. *c. 1910*
Mark in black paint on the bottom: *Daum, Nancy* and a Cross of Lorraine
Four-layer glass – colourless, pink, yellow and black; mould-blown, etched, acid matt finish of the background, polished, painted in black enamel
Height 5.4; diameter 3.7
Inv. No. ZF 27804
Provenance: 1994 acquired via the Hermitage Purchasing Commission.
Literature: St Petersburg 1997, No. 146; St Petersburg 1999, No. 56; Japan 2006-7, No. 84.

Artists at the Daum manufactory were drawn by images of seascapes with sailboats and barely visible horizons in the background in the years around 1910.
E.A.

62
Statuette: Woman with a Fan
Manufactory Daum Frères, Nancy. *c. 1910*
Inscription engraved on the base: *Daum, Nancy* and a Cross of Lorraine
Pale bluish-green glass; cast in a mould, pâte-de-verre
Height 19.6
Inv. No. ZF 27213
Provenance: 1981 acquired via the Hermitage Purchasing Commission.
Literature: St Petersburg 1999, No. 57; Japan 2006-7, No. 99.

The firm produced its first cast glass sculptures in 1906, the result of collaboration between Antonin Daum, Henri Bergé – one of the manufactory's leading craftsmen – and Amalric Walter.
This figure repeats the famous painted terracotta figurines of the late 4th and early 3rd centuries BC from the town of Tanagra in Boetia. The figurines were discovered in the 1870s and immediately became popular with collectors.
E.A.

63
Vase with Hydrangeas, Butterflies and Dragonflies
Manufactory Daum Frères, Nancy. *c. 1910*
Mark engraved on the bottom: *Daum, Nancy* and a Cross of Lorraine
Three-layered glass, two layers of colourless glass tinted within with coloured pink and yellow powdered glass, opaque milky glass with coloured powdered glass in blue and green; mould-blown, etched
Height 14.4; diameter 15.8
Inv. No. ZF 24915
Provenance: 1937 via the State Museums Fund.
Literature: Leningrad 1967 (ex-catalogue); Leningrad 1974, No. 247; Ivanova 1983, p. 135; St Petersburg 1999, No. 58; Japan 2006-7, No. 98.

This technique, involving the use of powdered glass in pastel tones and the introduction of metal oxides, was characteristic of works produced at the Daum manufactory during the period 1910-14.
E.A.

64
Vase with Gilly-flowers (matthiola)
Manufactory Daum Frères, Nancy. *c. 1910*
Mark etched on the body: *Daum, Nancy* and a Cross of Lorraine
Five-layer glass – yellow, green and pink glass between two layers of colourless glass; mould-blown, etched, painted
Height 33.2; diameter 15.2
Inv. No. ZF 27398
Provenance: 1984 acquired via the Hermitage Purchasing Commission.
Literature: Minsk 1989, No. 97; St Petersburg 1999, No. 59; Japan 2006-7, No. 91.

It is possible to relate this vase to Daum products of 1909-10 on the basis of its use of multi-layer glass with powdered glass and painting. It was probably produced under the influence of Henri Bergé, who during this period created designs for the decoration of vases showing flowers and shrubs.
E.A.

65
Small Vase
Manufactory Daum Frères, Nancy. *c. 1910*
Mark engraved on the bottom: *Daum, Nancy* and a Cross of Lorraine
Four-layer glass – colourless, yellow, red and green; mould-blown, etched, polished, acid matt finish of the background
2.9 x 4.9 x 3.3
Inv. No. E 9341
Provenance: 1925 via the State Museums Fund.
Literature: St Petersburg 1999, No. 60; Japan 2006-7, No. 86.

Close in technique to a group of vases produced to designs by Henri Bergé.
E.A.

66
Vase
Manufactory Daum Frères, Nancy. *1907-10*
Engraved mark on the body by the base: *Daum, Nancy* and a Cross of Lorraine
Three-layer glass – colourless, pink and yellow, with by the base a scattering of dark cherry-red and green powdered glass; mould-blown, etched, acid matt finish
Height 71.5
Inv. No. ZF 27221
Provenance: 1981 acquired via the Hermitage Purchasing Commission.
Literature: St Petersburg 1999, No. 61; Japan 2006-7, No. 97.

Vases of similar form, with a high narrow neck, appeared at the manufactories of both Daum and Gallé around 1900. Around 1910 the Daum manufactory started to produce such vases adorned solely with a play of different areas of colour.
E.A.

67
Vase with a Landscape with a Lake
Manufactory Daum Frères, Nancy. *c. 1910*
Mount: France
Marked etched on the body: *Daum, Nancy* and a Cross of Lorraine
On the mount three marks: a head in a circle, the fineness mark *84*, *R 5* in a rectangle
Four-layer glass – colourless, yellow, red and brown; mould-blown, etched, polished, acid matt finish. Mount: silver; chased
Height 21; diameter 20.7
Inv. No. ZF 27500
Provenance: 1987 acquired via the Hermitage Purchasing Commission.
Literature: St Petersburg 1999, No. 62; Japan 2006-7, No. 94.

One of a series of vases with landscape depictions, like cat. nos. 68-70. When compared with other vases, however, this example proves to be considerably finer in terms of finish, etching and nuances of colour transition. It is also set apart from the overall body of mass products by its silver mount.
E.A.

68
Vase with a Landscape with a Lake
Manufactory Daum Frères, Nancy. *After 1910*
Mark etched on the body: *Daum, Nancy* and a Cross of Lorraine
Four-layer glass – colourless, yellow, red and brown; mould-blown, etched, polished, acid matt finish of the inside surface
Height 48.8; diameter of neck 17.7; diameter of base 14.2
Inv. No. ZF 27701
Provenance: 1993 acquired via the Hermitage Purchasing Commission.
Literature: St Petersburg 1997, No. 149; St Petersburg 1999, No. 63; Japan 2006-7, No. 93.

A number of different firms producing objects in cased glass used images of trees in the foreground and a landscape unfolding beyond in the 1910s. Similar compositions were used to decorate objects from the Gallé, Legras and later the de Vez manufactories.
E.A.

69
Vase with a Landscape with a Lake
Manufactory Daum Frères, Nancy. *After 1910*
Mark etched on the body: *Daum, Nancy* and a Cross of Lorraine
Four-layer glass – colourless, yellow, red and brown; mould-blown, etched, polished, acid matt finish of the inside surface

24.7 x 21.4 x 17.3
Inv. No. ZF 27702
Provenance: 1993 acquired via the Hermitage Purchasing Commission.
Literature: St Petersburg 1997, No. 150; St Petersburg 1999, No. 64; Japan 2006-7, No. 95.
E.A.

70
BASE WITH A LANDSCAPE WITH A LAKE
Manufactory Daum Frères, Nancy. *c. 1910*
Mark etched on the body: *Daum, Nancy* and a Cross of Lorraine
Four-layer glass – colourless, yellow, red and brown; mould-blown, etched, polished, acid matt finish of the inside surface
Height 48.8; diameter of neck 12.2; diameter of base 13.7
Inv. No. ZF 27700
Provenance: 1993 acquired via the Hermitage Purchasing Commission.
Literature: St Petersburg 1997, No. 148; St Petersburg 1999, No. 65; Japan 2006-7, No. 92.
E.A.

71
VASE WITH FLOWERING TOBACCO
Manufactory Daum Frères, Nancy. *c. 1913*
Mark on the base: *Daum, Nancy* and a Cross of Lorraine
Four-layer glass – colourless, yellow, red and brown; mould-blown, etched, worked with a wheel, acid matt finish
Height 31.2
Inv. No. ZF 27875
Provenance: 2001 acquired via the Hermitage Purchasing Commission.
Literature: Japan 2006-7, No. 96.

The Daum manufactory started to produce vases of this form around 1905. The decoration of tobacco leaves and flowers emerged considerably later, around 1910 (Hilschenz-Mlynek 1985, No. 116).
E.A.

72
SMALL VASE WITH A LANDSCAPE
Manufactory Daum Frères, Nancy. *1905-14*
Mark on the base: *Daum, Nancy* and a Cross of Lorraine
Three-layer glass – colourless with overlays of blue and green; mould-blown, etched, painted with black enamel
Height 4.1
Inv. No. ZF 27386
Provenance: 1985 acquired via the Hermitage Purchasing Commission.
Literature: Japan 2006-7, No. 85.

Vases of such form were produced by the Daum manufactory in different sizes from 1905.
E.A.

73
FEMALE MASK
Henri Cros, France. *c. 1896*
Signature on the back: *H. Cros*
Opaque glass; pâte-de-verre
23 x 22
Inv. No. ZF 23401
Provenance: 1896 presented to Nicholas II and Alexandra Fyodorovna by the French government; 1931 transferred to the Hermitage from the Winter Palace, Leningrad.
Literature: Leningrad 1967 (ex-catalogue); Leningrad 1974, No. 250; Rappe 1991, p. 24; St Petersburg 1994, No. 332; Japan 2006-7, No. 36.

One of the gifts presented to the Russian Emperor and Empress during their visit to Paris in 1896, it was kept in a special case in the royal couple's bedroom in the Winter Palace. Henri Cros was a Parisian sculptor and medal-maker whose first experiments with glass were conducted in 1894. His reliefs were produced in the pâte-de-verre technique, in which a ceramic form is filled with powdered glass tinted with metal oxides and then fired. Many French craftsmen working with glass were to take up this technique, among them artists of the School of Nancy.
E.A.

74
VASE-BOWL
Louis Comfort Tiffany, New York. *c. 1897*
Round label on the bottom: in the centre the monogram *TGDCO* [Tiffany Glass and Decorating Company] and running round the outside: *TIFFANY.FAVRILE.GLASS.REGISTERED.TRADE. MARK*; rectangular label with the number *4790*
Transparent yellow glass inside with cyclamen-red and greenish shades outside and silvery-blue-pearly iridescent hues outside (Tiffany-Favrile Glass)
Height 14.1; diameter 20.7
Inv. No. Kr 1372
Provenance: 14 August 1897 acquired for the Stieglitz Museum, St Petersburg; 1933 transferred to the Hermitage from the 1st Branch of the Hermitage (formerly the Stieglitz Museum).
Literature: Leningrad 1967 (ex-catalogue); Leningrad 1974, No. 216; Japan 2006-7, No. 102.

Archive documents reveal that 'a glass bowl (Tiffany Favorile [sic] glass)' was acquired from the gallery L'Art Nouveau. This Paris shop sold paintings, sculptures and applied art. It was established in 1895 by Siegfried Bing (1838-1905), taking its name from the style that was so popular in the last years of the 19th century and early years of the 20th. Amongst the works available through the shop were products from Gallé and other masters of the School of Nancy. Bing was also the main agent in Paris for the sale of glass from Tiffany.
E.A.

75
VASE
Johann Loetz Witwe, Klostermühle, Austria. *c. 1900*
Mark engraved on the bottom: *Loetz / Austria*
Colourless glass with iridescent yellowish-brown powdered glass, the décor in powdered greenish-blue glass; mould-blown
Height 21.7; diameter 10.2
Inv. No. ZF 27241
Provenance: 1982 acquired via the Hermitage Purchasing Commission.
Literature: Japan 2006-7, No. 105.

From 1851 the glass manufactory in Klostermühle (now Klášterský Mlýn, Czech Republic) was run by Susanna Loetz, widow of its former manager, and her second husband Franz Gerstner, a doctor of jurisprudence. In 1858 the firm was reg-

istered under the name Johann Loetz [Lötz] Witwe. Along with all kinds of tableware the manufactory produced high quality and expensive glass, for which it received a Grand Prix at the 1900 Exposition Universelle in Paris, where other prizewinners included Gallé and Tiffany. From 1904 the firm worked closely with artists from the Wiener Werkstätte.
E.A.

76
Vase with a Silver Mount
Johann Loetz Witwe, Klostermühle, Austria. *c. 1900*
Mark engraved on the bottom: *Loetz / Austria*
Colourless glass with iridescent blue and pale-green powdered glass; mould-blown. Mount: silver-gilt
Height 15.3; diameter 7.2
Inv. No. ZF 27346
Provenance: 1984 acquired via the Hermitage Purchasing Commission.
Literature: Japan 2006-7, No. 106.

The firm Johann Loetz Witwe was the first European manufactory to imitate Tiffany, and the most successful. The technique of making iridescent glass in the Tiffany style, by applying a scattering of metal salts to the hot glass, was patented by the Loetz manufactory in 1898.
Silver and bronze mounts using characteristic Art Nouveau style mounts are often found on vases produced by the Austrian manufactory.
E.A.

77
Decanter with a Stopper
René-Jules Lalique, Paris. *c. 1914*
Mark etched on the base: *Lalique*
Colourless glass; mould-blown, painted with blue enamel
Height with stopper 31; body 15.8 x 8.1
Inv. No. ZF 23436 a,b
Provenance: 1931 transferred to the Hermitage from the Museum of the Academy of Arts, Leningrad.
Literature: Leningrad 1974, No. 251; Japan 2006-7, No. 114.

The form of this decanter with its round body flattened on two sides and its high narrow neck was characteristic of different tableware items produced by the Lalique manufactory around 1912 (Hodge 1999, p. 82). This piece is adorned with vegetable ornament – composed of stylised flowering plum – that accentuates that form. Ornament in this new Art Deco style, which emerged around 1910, reflects the influence of Japanese art on Lalique's work.
E.A.

78
Vase with Six Female Figures
René-Jules Lalique, Paris. *Model: 1912*
Mark carved on the foot: *R. LALIQUE*
Transparent brownish glass; cast under pressure together with the decoration, acid matt finish, ground and polished
Height 24.5; diameter 19.4
Inv. No. ZF 27158
Provenance: 1980 acquired via the Hermitage Purchasing Commission.
Literature: Japan 2006-7, No. 113.

Reflections of the late Art Nouveau style are seen in the decoration of this piece. Beneath each of the six female figures adorning the vase is a horned mascaron, while each character is framed with ivy (the plant identified with Bacchus). Thus the subject is one of bacchanalia, frequently found in the work of Lalique.
E.A.

79
Lunaria Vase ('Monnaie du Pape')
René-Jules Lalique, Paris. *Model c. 1913*
Mark on the base: *R. LALIQUE*
Pale blue transparent glass; mould-blown, acid matt finish of the outside surface, ground
Height 22.7; diameter 17.1
Inv. No. ZF 27544
Provenance: 1988 acquired via the Hermitage Purchasing Commission.
Literature: Japan 2006-7, No. 115.

The model for the 'Monnaie du Pape' vase was one of the first that Lalique developed to be blown in a mould (Hodge 1999, p. 20). It is notable for its high neck.
E.A.

80
Bacchante Vase
René-Jules Lalique, Paris. *Model c. 1924*
Engraved mark on the base: *R. LALIQUE / FRANCE / No 9.997*
Semi-transparent opalescent glass; cast under pressure in a form, etched, acid matt finish, ground
Height 24.5; diameter 18.6
Inv. No. ZF 27402
Provenance: 1985 acquired via the Hermitage Purchasing Commission.
Literature: Japan 2006-7, No. 116.

The Bacchante vase was one of the most important of all Lalique's figured reliefs. The model was created around 1924 and is still in production today. Woven in a mad dance, the figures recall sculptural groups by Auguste Rodin.
Opalescent glass, such as that from which this vase is made, is produced by introducing phosphate into the glass mass, along with a small amount of cobalt to give it a bluish sheen.
E.A.

81
Vase with Snake Amidst Clover
Sergey Romanov, Imperial Porcelain and Glass Manufactory, St Petersburg. *1898*
Design by Konstantin Krasovsky (?)
On the base a carved mark: *N[ikolay] II* below an imperial crown and the date *1898*
Two-layer matt green crystal; blown, carved, engraved, ground and polished
15.5 x 11.3 x 11.3
Inv. No. ERS 1617
Provenance: Gatchina Palace Museum, near St Petersburg; 1941 transferred to the Hermitage from the State Museum of Ethnography of Peoples of the USSR, Leningrad.
Literature: Corning 1989, No. 59; St Petersburg 2004, No. 492.

Among the artists working at the Imperial Porcelain and Glass Manufactory in the late 1890s was Sergey Romanov, graduate of the Stieglitz School for Technical Drawing,

admirer of the work of Gallé and author of many works in Art Nouveau style. Documents record that in imitation of the famous French craftsman Romanov adorned his vases not only with flowers and plants but also with a variety of animals and insects. There would seem to have been some problems at the Imperial Manufactory in developing new forms for the layered vases that were based on examples in Japanese art; therefore Russian craftsmen made a close study of works by Gallé and his workshop. Even during this early period in the use of layered glass at the Imperial Manufactory, its products reveal a desire – despite similarities of form and dimensions to original pieces by Gallé – to create something independent and original, using a very different range of colours and design.
The round form derives from a celebrated vase with a toad and dragonfly (cat. 22) produced in the workshop of Emile Gallé in Nancy in 1888.
T.M.

82
IRIS VASE
Alexander Zotov, Imperial Porcelain and Glass Manufactory, St Petersburg. *1900*
Design by Konstantin Krasovsky
On the base a carved mark: *N[IKOLAY] II* below an imperial crown and the date *1900*
Layered matt lilac crystal; blown, carved, engraved, ground and polished
30.5 x 20 x 20
Inv. No. ERS 2432
Provenance: private apartments of Empress Alexandra Fyodorovna in the Winter Palace, St Petersburg; transferred to the Hermitage from the Winter Palace.
Literature: Leningrad 1974, No. 202; St Petersburg 1994, No. 156; Nicholas & Alexandra 1998, No. 245; St Petersburg 2004, No. 503.

This vase stood in the Boudoir of Empress Alexandra Fyodorovna in the Winter Palace.
Craftsmen at the Imperial Manufactory were of course aware that pinkish-lilac tones were the Empress' favourite, preferred by her not only in her own attire but also for all kinds of furnishings and interior decoration. Vases produced for the imperial family thus frequently include lilac or dense violet colours in the design. Problems were, however, encountered by Manufactory chemists and technicians when trying to achieve the necessary shades. During this period violet hues were achieved not by the usual method of adding manganese to the glass, but by adding a mixture of gold and cobalt (Russian State Historical Archive, Fund 503, *opis'* 1 [491\2128], *delo* 88, 1901, f. 67).
T.M.

83
EUPHORBIA VASE
Grigory Omorokov, Imperial Porcelain and Glass Manufactory, St Petersburg. *1908*
Design by Rudolph Wilde
Colourless crystal; blown, engraved, ground and polished
17 x 17.8 x 12
Inv. No. ERS 3409
Provenance: 1992 acquired via the Hermitage Purchasing Commission.
Literature: St Petersburg 2004, No. 538.

Attributed to Omorokov by T. V. Petrova on the basis of a photograph in the factory Museum (No. 91/1662).
T.M.

84
SMALL VASE, POPPY AND BUTTERFLIES
Imperial Porcelain and Glass Manufactory, St Petersburg. *1897*
Design by Konstantin Krasovsky (?)
On the base a carved mark: *N[IKOLAY] II* below an imperial crown and the date *1897*
Layered crystal – milky, yellowish-blue and brownish-red; blown, carved, engraved, ground and polished
Height 17.8
Inv. No. ERS 1629
Provenance: 1941 transferred to the Hermitage from the State Museum of Ethnography of Peoples of the USSR, Leningrad.
Literature: Leningrad 1967, ill. 78; Shelkovnikov 1967, fig. 6; Leningrad 1974, No. 203; St Petersburg 2004, No. 484

One of the earliest examples of layered glass to be produced in St Petersburg. The vase's form recalls items from the workshop of Emile Gallé. It is possible that the decoration was designed by one of the senior 'flower-artists' at the Imperial Manufactory, Konstantin Krasovsky, nephew of the greatest master of the genre, Fyodor Krasovsky. In the 1890s I. Murinov and Sergey Romanov worked on developing vases in layered glass, both of them owing much to Emile Gallé even while creating new and original forms.
Archive documents reveal that on 14 (26) December 1896 a number of glass items were presented to the Dowager Empress Maria Fyodorovna, among them what may perhaps have been the two very first vases 'in layers' (as there were described).
T.M.

85
VASE WITH A CRIMEAN LANDSCAPE
Gus-khrustalny Manufactory, Vladimir Province, Russia. *Late 19th – early 20th century*
Marks: *Yu. S. N M n Gus Khrust* [Yu. S. Nechaev-Maltsov heir, Gus-khrustalny]
Layered glass; blown, etched
41.3 x 10.2 x 19
Inv. No. ERS 3292
Provenance: 1985 acquired via the Hermitage Purchasing Commission.
Previously unpublished.

The Gus-khrustalny Glass Manufactory, east of Moscow, was founded by Yury Stepanovich Nechaev-Maltsov, a leading Russian industrialist who also enjoyed a reputation as a patron, using his money to found museums, libraries and art schools. Around the turn of the century his factory actively acquired examples of work by the leading Russian and foreign glass manufactories, and of course craftsmen at Gus-khrustalny were not indifferent to the products of Gallé's workshop. In turn they found their own approach in creating items in the Art Nouveau style.
The Crimea, in what is now Ukraine, was one of Nechaev-Maltsov's favourite places. He had there an extremely handsome estate. Southern landscapes thus often feature on vases produced at his factory.
T.M.

86

Kovsh (Ladle) in the Form of a Boat
Gus-khrustalny Manufactory, Vladimir Province, Russia. *1910s*
Mount by 14 Artel, Moscow
Colourless crystal; blown, carved. Mount: silver; cast, almandine
33.5 x 16.7 x 16.7
Inv. No. ERS 3357
Provenance: 1998 acquired via the Hermitage Purchasing Commission.
Previously unpublished.

A *kovsh* is a traditional Russian ladle. This example is made in imitation of the forms of an Old Russian boat, with half-length male figures wearing 17th-century costume in relief on the handle.
The owners of private Moscow silver workshops sometimes commissioned crystal insets for expensive special orders from the large glass manufactory at Gus-khrustalny. Moreover, already finished vases, bowls and other crystal objects might be selected by the silver workshops to be given rich mounts.
T.M.

87-89

Three Cups
Lavr Orlovsky, Imperial Porcelain and Glass Manufactory, St Petersburg. *Late 19th century*
Engraved monogram: *N II A* [Nicholas II Alexandrovich] and the two-headed eagle, symbol of the Russian Empire
Colourless glass; blown, engraved, ground painted, gilded
16,7 x 7,3 x 7,3 cm; Inv. no. ERS 1131
20 x 9,1 x 9,1 cm; Inv. no. ERS 3029
20 x 9,1 x 9,1 cm; Inv. no. ERS 3030
Provenance: 1941 transferred to the Hermitage from the State Museum of Ethnography of Peoples of the USSR, Leningrad.
Literature: London 1998, No. 241.

Orlovsky was one of the most celebrated masters working at the Imperial Glass Manufactory in the late 19th and early 20th century.
These cups are made to imitate 17th-century Baroque examples. They were used in the imperial residences at banquets and at celebrations surrounding the presentation of various awards.
T.M.

90

Bratina (Loving Cup)
Elizaveta Bem, Dyatkovo Crystal Factory, Bryansk Province, Russia. *1880s*
Inscription around the edge: *Postoronis' dusha – obol'yu* ('Stand aside – or I shall splash you')
Golden glass; blown, painted enamel, iridescences, gilded
Height 17.6
Inv. No. ERS 1678
Provenance: 1941 transferred to the Hermitage from the State Museum for the Ethnography of Peoples of the USSR, Leningrad.
Previously unpublished.

In the 1870s and 1880s artists working at Russian manufactories created many items 'in the Russian manner', reworking Byzantine and Old Russian designs and turning to Russian folklore for inspiration. Bem was an artist of varied talents who worked in many different techniques and genres. She created for the Dyatkovo Crystal Factory a series of works inspired by Russian folk art that were extremely popular at the imperial court.
T.M.

91

Jug with the Sea Bed and Fishermen
Imperial Porcelain and Glass Manufactory, St Petersburg. *1908-1910s*
Firm of Carl Fabergé
Marks: of the Fabergé firm on the lid, of Moscow assay office
Colourless crystal; blown, engraved. Mount: silver
Height 26
Inv. No. ERS 3187
Provenance: 1983 acquired via the Hermitage Purchasing Commission.
Literature: Corning 1989, No. 72; Aarhus 1990, No. 137.
T.M.

92-93

Pair of Vases with the Russian State Eagle
Horace Bieuville, Sèvres Porcelain Manufactory. *1896*
Mould by Albert-Ernest Carrier-Belleuse. *1880*
Marks: in black, *S 96*, for the decoration *1896*
Hard paste porcelain; overglaze painting, gilding
Height 82.5
Inv. Nos. ZF 21129, ZF-21130
Provenance: 1922 transferred to the Hermitage from the Winter Palace, Petrograd.
Literature: USA 1998-2001, No. 236; Kazakevitch 2002; Tokyo-Kobe-Gunma 2003, Nos. 68, 69; Japan 2006-7, Nos. 38, 39.

To judge by the date this vase was made it may have been produced specially to mark the visit of the last Russian Emperor, Nicholas II, and Empress Alexandra Fyodorovna, to France, 5-10 (17-22) October 1896. This was the first official visit by a Russian ruler in the history of the French Republic.
The model for this form was created in 1880 to a design by the Sèvres Manufactory's artistic director, Albert-Ernest Carrier-Belleuse and the painting was by Horace Bieuville (Kazakevitch 2002, p. 86). The black two-headed eagle against a yellow ground was that found on the Emperor's personal banner.
J.V.

94

Bust Portrait of Emperor Nicholas II
Léopold Bernhard Bernstamm (Léopold-Bernhard Leibber), Sèvres Porcelain Manufactory, *1897*
Marks: on the shoulder in the top left corner: *Sèvres 1897*; in the lower right corner on the overcoat: *L. Bernstamm*
Biscuit porcelain
46 x 38 x 21
Inv. No. ERSk 236
Provenance: Winter Palace, St Petersburg; 1920s transferred to the Hermitage via the State Museums Fund.
Literature: Tezi, Rotenstern 1909, pp. 8-10; Bernstamm 1913, p. 22; Librovich 1913; Severyukhin 1993; St Petersburg 1994, No. 88; USA 1998-2001, No. 132.

Léopold Bernstamm studied in St Petersburg in the workshop of David Ivanovich Jensen and then at the Drawing School of the Society for the Encouragement of the Arts. From 1879 to

1881 he attended classes at St Petersburg's Academy of Arts, continuing his education under A. Rivalti in Florence and then in Rome (1884). In 1885 he moved to Paris, exhibiting at the Salon regularly from 1887; in 1890 he was appointed chief artist at A. Grévin's Museum of Wax Figures there. Bernstamm produced numerous portraits of public figures in Russia and France. In 1891 he was made a Knight of the Légion d'honneur, in 1908 Commander.
In late 1895 – early 1896 the sculptor received a commission for busts of members of the Russian imperial family. 'The marble busts of the imperial couple served as a superb prototype for mass-produced sculptural images and earned the author the sovereign's good will for many years' (Severyukhin 1993, p. 252). The sculptor's work sketches from life found reflection in Nicholas II's diary: '20 September. Wednesday. 1895 ... After breakfast I sat for more than an hour while I was modelled by Bernstamm, on whose behalf Bogolyubov had asked my favour'; '21 September. Thursday. Again sat to the sculptor' (*Dnevniki Nikolaya II* [The Diaries of Nicholas II], Moscow, 1991, pp. 103-4).
Sèvres Porcelain Manufactory commissioned busts of the imperial couple, Nicholas II and Alexander Fyodorovna, after their visit to Paris in 1896. The cloth has been modelled in the Art Nouveau manner.
E.T.

95
MEDALLION WITH PROFILE PORTRAIT OF NICHOLAS II AND ALEXANDRA FYODOROVNA
Jules-Clément Chaplain, Sèvres Porcelain Manufactory. *1896*
Inscriptions: *NICOLAS II ALEXANDRA;* on the reverse: *LL. MM. l'Empereur et l'Imperatrice de Russie visitant la Manufacture National de Sèvres – 8 octobre 1896*
Hard paste porcelain, biscuit porcelain
Diameter 9
Inv. No. ZF 22293
Provenance: 1920 transferred to the Hermitage from the former collection of Illarion Ivanovich Vorontsov-Dashkov, Petrograd.
Literature: Brunet, Préaud 1978, p. 272; Kazakiewitsch 1997; Kazakevich 2003, pp. 221-33.

From the time of its foundation, it was rare that important guests of the city of Paris omitted to make a visit to the Sèvres Porcelain Manufactory, a fact of which its administration was very proud. On 8 (20) October 1896 Nicholas II and his wife visited Sèvres. In commemoration of that event two medallions were made, *France et Russie* and *Empéreur et Impératrice de Russie,* from models by Chaplain (Brunet, Préaud 1978). Two portrait medallions were presented to the Emperor and Empress.
J.V.

96-99
PIECES FROM THE DANCE WITH SCARVES (LE JEU DE L'ECHARPE)
Agathon Léonard van Weydeveldt, Sèvres Porcelain Manufactory. *1900*
Hard paste porcelain, biscuit porcelain

FEMALE FIGURE WITH TORCHES
Marks: *AL, LG* (form maker Louis Gueneau)
Height 57
Inv. No. GCh 12406

STAND
Decoration mark *for 1900*
15.8 x 20
Inv. No. GCh 12414

FEMALE DANCER WITH A TAMBOURINE
Height 51.5
Inv. No. GCh 12412

FEMALE DANCER WITH A BRACELET ON HER RIGHT ARM
Marks: *AL*
Height 45.8
Inv. No. GCh 12403

Provenance: April 1901 presented by the French government to Nicholas II and Empress Alexandra Fyodorovna and transferred to the Hermitage from the Hofmarshal's Department of the Winter Palace, St Petersburg.
Literature: St Petersburg 1994, No. 328; Leonard 2000; Kazakevich 2003, pp. 221-33; Vilensky 2006, pp. 129-33.

Agathon Léonard van Weydeveldt (1841-1923) produced this table decoration, known as *Le jeu de l'Echarpe* or *Dance with Scarves,* consisting of fifteen female figures. It was shown at the Exposition Universelle in Paris in 1900, in which the Sèvres Manufactory played an active role. In producing these sculptures, Léonard was influenced by the dancing of the American Loïe Fuller. Each of the fifteen pieces was conceived as an independent sculptural work united by a common idea, the result being a unique example of Sèvres sculpture that was to become a symbol of the Art Nouveau age. These porcelain dancers not only form a carefully conceived composition but they seem to present some mysterious ritual, a rite practised since Ancient times, unfolding by the light of torches to the sound of tambourines.
At the Exposition Universelle the table decoration enjoyed outstanding success. In the following years the figures were repeated numerous times in different sizes and single pieces are today to be found in museums in Paris, London, Vienna, Prague, Amsterdam etc.
A full set was presented by the French government to Nicholas II and Empress Alexandra Fyodorovna during their second visit to France in April 1901. On his return to Russia, Nicholas II ordered that they be given to the Imperial Hermitage.
J.V.

100
NÎMES VASE
Sèvres Porcelain Manufactory. *1886*
Decoration by Horace Bieuville, *1888*
Mark: in black *S 86*; decoration mark *1888*
Hard paste porcelain; decoration en pâtes colorées (in the pâte-sur-pâte technique), gilding
Height 150
Inv. No. ZF 23733
Provenance: 1896 presented to Nicholas II by the French Ministère de l'Education Publique on behalf of the French government and transferred to the Hermitage from the Hofmarshal's Department of the Winter Palace.
Literature: Kazakiewitsch 1997; Kazakevitch 2002; Kazakevich 2003, pp. 221-33; Rappe 2006, p. 15.

Today we use the term pâte-sur-pâte to describe items made in white porcelain mass against a coloured ground. In the 19th century, however, at the Sèvres Manufactory it was also used for a kind of decoration adorned with coloured masses or pâtes colorées that were fired at very high temperatures. During the last decades of the century pâte-sur-pâte was perfectly suited to the Art Nouveau style, one of the characteristic features of which was a borrowing of traditions from Oriental art. These combined most naturally with Sèvres and indeed pan-European porcelain traditions, in which Chinese and Japanese ceramics had always been the object of admiration and imitation.
J.V.

101
Vase
Royal Porcelain Manufactory, Copenhagen. *1897-1902*
Painter Gerhard Vilgelm Ernest Heilmann
Porcelain; underglaze painting
Height 28.2
Inv. No. ZF 25001
Provenance: 1937 transferred to the Hermitage via the State Museums Fund.
Literature: Leningrad 1974, No. 92.

Heilmann worked at Copenhagen's Royal Porcelain Manufactory for twelve years, from 1890 to 1902. A number of the pieces he painted were deliberately produced in very small runs, forming a treasury of Copenhagen's achievements in porcelain in the Art Nouveau style. This vase is just such a piece.
A line of running reindeer was to be one of his favourite motifs. Manifesting his inherent taste and invention, Heilmann managed to harmoniously combine apparently incompatible decorative elements. In other works, he combined his northern reindeer in a single composition with international elements such as flowering irises, a favourite Art Nouveau motif. The stylistic purity of this piece is only set off by the contrast with those earlier stylistic experiments, of considerable interest yet redolent of Eclecticism.
L.L.

102
Vase
Royal Porcelain Manufactory, Copenhagen. *1895*
Painter Carl Laurits Nicolaj Mortensen
Porcelain; underglaze painting
Height 46.5
Inv. No. ZF 26840
Provenance: 1895 acquired by Grand Duke Alexander Mikhaylovich; 1967 transferred to the Hermitage from the Regional Finance Department [Rayfinotdel], Leningrad.
Literature: Leningrad 1974, No. 83.

'Today our artist Carl Mortensen is travelling to St Petersburg, where he will be spending six months at the Imperial Porcelain Factory' wrote Philip Schou, director of Denmark's Royal Porcelain Manufactory, in his dairy on 10 September 1894 (cited in: St Petersburg, 2006, p. 72). Mortensen trained Russian painters in the use of Copenhagen's celebrated underglaze painting technique. Many of his works from the St Petersburg period found their way into the collections of the aristocracy in Russia's then capital. This vase with its image of an overgrown pond, so close in theme and manner of painting to the work of the French Impressionists, was purchased in 1895 by Grand Duke Alexander Mikhaylovich, grandson of Nicholas I.
L.L.

103
Figure of a Mermaid
Royal Porcelain Manufactory, Copenhagen. *1911*
Model by Christian Thomsen
Porcelain; underglaze painting
Height 25
Inv. No. ZF 25442
Provenance: 1947.
Literature: Leningrad 1974, No. 90; Liackhova 2006, pp. 108, 117.

Within the context of the national romantic mood that largely determined the nature of Copenhagen's version of Art Nouveau, the tales of Hans Christian Andersen were perceived as the cornerstone of a genuinely Danish literary tradition. It was with reason, therefore, that the figure of the Mermaid from Andersen's tale, produced in 1913 by the sculptor Edvard Eriksen, was to become the city's symbol. Two years before the appearance of that celebrated work, however, Christian Thomsen produced his own little Mermaid. He produced more than a hundred different models for various porcelain sculptures but it was his series of figures from Andersen's tales that was to transform him into a national figure.
L.L.

104
Mimosa Vase
Imperial Porcelain and Glass Manufactory, St Petersburg. *March – April 1917*
Porcelain; polychrome underglaze painting
22 x 17
Inv. No. ERF 7638
Provenance: 1962 acquired via the Hermitage Purchasing Commission.
Previously unpublished.

In the 1900s particular emphasis was placed on underglaze painting at the Imperial Porcelain Manufactory. Each year more than 200 porcelain vases were produced there bearing original painting designs, each model produced in two copies: one for presentation to the Imperial Court, the other for the Manufactory's Museum. Artists transferred onto the porcelain their own landscape studies made during trips around Russia. and sketches of flowers made in the Manufactory's hothouses.
E.Kh.

105
Red Datura Vase
Grigory Gorkov, Imperial Porcelain and Glass Manufactory, St Petersburg. *1914*
Porcelain; polychrome underglaze painting
43.8 x 19.8
Inv. No. ERF 8423
Provenance: 1985 acquired via the Hermitage Purchasing Commission.
Previously unpublished.

Grigory Gorkov worked at the Imperial Porcelain Manufactory from the start of the 20th century. He specialised in original underglaze painting, mainly depicting flowers as well as birds and animals.
E.Kh.

106
FAN
France. *1900s*
Horn, net, sequins, paste jewels, metal
Length 36
Inv. No. E 10103
Provenance: 1920 transferred to the Hermitage from the Vorontsov-Dashkov collection, Petrograd.
Literature: Leningrad 1970, No. 56 (not reproduced).
E.Ab.

107
FAN
Louis-Léon-Eugène Billotey, Duvelleroy Firm, Paris. *1900s*
Inscription on the back of the outer right rib: *Duvelleroy*; signed on the screen, top right: *Billotey*
Tortoiseshell, silk, gouache
Length 32.3
Inv. No. E 17611
Provenance: 1900 purchased for the Stieglitz Museum in Paris; 1933 transferred to the Hermitage from the 1st Branch of the Hermitage (formerly the Stieglitz Museum), Leningrad.
Previously unpublished.

Many celebrated artists worked for Paris' leading firm for the production of fans, Duvelleroy. Louis-Léon-Eugène Billotey (1883-1940) graduated from the Bernard Palissy school in Paris. He studied under Jules Lefebvre and Tony Robbert-Fleury and went on to exhibit regularly at the Paris Salon. Billotey frequently worked on commissions for Duvelleroy, for instance fan screens with flowers and insects in soft pastel tones. The Hermitage fan is a typical example of his art.
E.Ab.

108
BUCKLE BROOCH
Mikhail Perkhin, Firm of Carl Fabergé, St Petersburg. *Early 20th century*
Marks: St Petersburg, craftsman, fineness mark *56*
Gold, rose-faceted diamonds, pearls, enamel
7.2 x 3.5
Inv. No. E 17175
Provenance: 1951 transferred to the Hermitage from the State Museums Fund.
Literature: Leningrad 1989, No. 43.

Carl Fabergé (1846 -1920) was one of the most famous jewellers of the late 19th and early 20th centuries. He had numerous pupils and followers. From 1870 he was owner of the celebrated firm founded in 1842 by his father Gustav. The firm was to have a number of branches, first in Moscow (from 1887) and then in Odessa and London.
E.Ab.

109
SMALL SHELL-SHAPED BOX
Mikhail Perkhin, Firm of Carl Fabergé, St Petersburg. *Late 19th century*
Marks: St Petersburg, firm of Fabergé, craftsman, fineness mark *56*
Jade, gold, rose-faceted diamonds, rubies
6.3 x 6.1 x 3
Inv. No. E 17151
Provenance: 1951 transferred to the Hermitage from the State Museums Fund.
Literature: Lugano 1986, No. 122; Leningrad 1989, No. 50; Stockholm 1997, No. 84; USA 1998-2001, No. 212; Amsterdam 2004, No. 131.

Artists have been attracted by the form of shells for many centuries, imitating their forms in many different materials. Fabergé took his inspiration from the cultural heritage of the past and thus he too took up the motif. This piece was previously shown at the exhibition *Nicholas & Alexandra* in the Hermitage Amsterdam in 2004-5.
E.Ab.

110
BRACELET IN A CASE
Gustav Fabergé shop, St Petersburg. *Mid-19th century*
Inscription on the case: G.FABERGÉ. *Joaillier et Bijouterie. Grande Morskayi (...) se la Kirpitchny (...) Rouadz (...)* S.PETERSBOURG
Marks: St Petersburg, craftsman *FL*, fineness mark *56*
Gold, amethysts. Case: wood, leather, velvet, silk, paper, metal
Diameter 6
Inv. No. E 17759
Provenance: 1984acquired via the Hermitage Purchasing Commission.
Literature: Pforzheim 1995-96, pp. 208-9.

This gold bracelet has a most unusual central feature in which two twisting snakes intertwine and pass through four oval plaques to form a flower adorned with five amethysts.
The whole is still in its original case, provided when it was sold in the shop of Gustav Fabergé (1814-1893), father of the celebrated jeweller Carl. Gustav founded his jewellery workshop and shop at 16/18 Bolshaya Morskaya street in the centre of St Petersburg in 1842. There he sold not only the products of his own workshop but of other jewellers too, including works imported from abroad, each object placed in a special case.
E.Ab.

111
SMALL BOX
Firm of Carl Fabergé, St Petersburg. *Late 19th century*
Jade, gold, rose-faceted diamonds
2.8 x 7.1 x 5.2
Inv. No. E 17152
Provenance: 1951 transferred to the Hermitage from the State Museums Fund.
Literature: Lugano 1986, No. 128; Zurich 1989, No. 26; Stockholm 1997, No. 171; USA 1998-2001, No. 213.
E.Ab.

112
Cornflowers and Ears of Wheat
Firm of Carl Fabergé, St Petersburg. *Late 19th century*
Gold, rose-faceted diamonds, enamel, rock crystal
Height 19
Inv. No. E 13353
Provenance: 1922 transferred to the Hermitage from the former collection of the Princes Yusupov, Petrograd.
Literature: Leningrad 1974, No. 17; Helsinki 1980, No. 2; Munich 1986-87, No. 398; Zurich 1989, No. 166; St Petersburg-Paris-London 1993, No. 172; Lopato 2006, pp. 89-97.

The firm of Carl Fabergé produced a whole group of items consisting of flowers made of precious stones and set in rock crystal vases. These elegantly conceived objects are amazingly naturalistic. An imitation of nature was characteristic of art during the second half of the 19th century but in the products of Fabergé this was transformed into an almost literal copying of nature. Marina Lopato suggested that this 'photographic' reproduction should be seen as a whole new style (Lopato 2006, p. 89). There was a similar vase with cornflowers in the collection of the late Queen Elizabeth, the Queen Mother, in London.
E.Ab.

113
Small Fan-shaped Box
Mikhail Perkhin, Firm of Carl Fabergé, St Petersburg. *Late 19th century*
Marks: St Petersburg, firm of Fabergé, craftsman Mikhail Perkhin, fineness mark *72*
Rock crystal, gold, rose-faceted diamonds, enamel
Length 7.5
Inv. No. E 15729
Provenance: 1951 transferred to the Hermitage from the State Museums Fund.
Literature: Lopato 1984, No. 263, p. 49; Munich 1986-87, No. 507A; Leningrad 1989, No. 49; Zurich 1989, No. 8; Stockholm 1997, No. 84; USA 1998-2001, No. 215.

Fans were at the very height of their popularity at the turn of the 19th and 20th centuries. It is no surprise, therefore, that the firm of Carl Fabergé should produce this little box in the form of so very widespread an element of ladies' attire.
E.Ab.

114
Small Box
Mikhail Perkhin, Firm of Carl Fabergé, St Petersburg. *1890s*
Marks: St Petersburg, firm of Fabergé, craftsmen, fineness mark *56, N – 47449*
Gold, enamel, diamonds, rubies, sapphires; engraved, polished
2.8 x 2.3 x 2.2
Inv. No. E 307
Provenance: 1908 from the collection of Grand Duke Alexey Alexandrovich, St Petersburg.
Literature: Leningrad 1989, No. 52; St Petersburg-Paris-London 1993, No. 66; Stockholm 1997, No. 86; USA 1998-2001, No. 210

Originally the box was in the collection of Grand Duke Alexey Alexandrovich (1850-1908), fourth son of Tsar Alexander II and favourite brother of Alexander III. He was Commander in Chief of the Fleet and the Naval Office from 1881 to 1905, Adjutant-General and Admiral-General. The inventory of his collection includes this bonbonnière that cost 600 roubles made in the Indian style by Fabergé.
O.K.

115
Matchbox
Western Europe. *Late 19th century*
Inside a plaque with the inscription: *BAUGRAND*
Silver, enamel
1.4 x 6.4 x 3
Inv. No. E 13013
Provenance: 1924 transferred to the Hermitage from the former collection of Prince Alexander Sergeevich Dolgorukov, Leningrad.
Previously unpublished.
E.Ab.

116
Small Box with a Lady Drinking Coffee
Western Europe. *1900s*
Marks: illegible, *STERLING*, fineness mark *935*; stamped *103*
Silver, enamel
1.3 x 7.7 x 5.8
Inv. No. E 16652
Provenance: 1951 transferred to the Hermitage from the State Museums Fund.
Previously unpublished.
E.Ab.

117
Vodka Glass in the Form of an Elephant's Head
Firm of Carl Fabergé, St Petersburg. *Early 20th century*
Obsidian, rose-faceted diamonds
4.5 x 9.1 x 5.5
Inv. No. E 17154
Provenance: 1951 transferred to the Hermitage from the State Museums Fund.
Literature: Lugano 1986, No. 129; Munich 1986-87, No. 261; Leningrad 1989, No. 160; Zurich 1989, No. 160; Stockholm 1997, No. 162; USA 1998-2001, No. 211; Amsterdam 2004, No. 130.
E.Ab.

118
Cup
Konstantin Linke, Firm of Carl Edvard Bolin, Moscow. *1899-1906*
Inscription on the bottom: *Svoemu Totoshe ot Krestnogo* ('To my Totosha from your Godfather')
Marks: Moscow 1899-1906, firm of K. E. Bolin, craftsman Konstantin Linke
Silver, enamel
Height 7.4; diameter 6.7
Inv. No. E 9540
Provenance: 1922 transferred to the Hermitage via the State Museums Fund.
Literature: St Petersburg-Paris-Moscow 1992, No. 175; Moscow 2001, No. 224.

Carl Edvard Bolin's jewellery house was established in St Petersburg in 1845 and the Bolins became court jewellers and assay-

ers to the Cabinet of His Imperial Majesty. In 1852 the firm opened a shop in Moscow, where the range of goods available was aimed at a much wider circle of people: it included silver vessels and cutlery and various haberdashery items. It was the works produced by Bolin in Moscow that demonstrated most clearly the Art Nouveau style, this glass being a typical example.
E.Ab.

119
PORTE-CIGAR WITH A HERON
Western Europe. *Early 20th century*
Marks: fineness mark *935*
Inside an almost illegible inscription and the date: *July 1919*
Silver, enamel
8 x 5.2 x 0.8
Inv. No. E 17850
Provenance: 1987 acquired via the Hermitage Purchasing Commission.
Previously unpublished.

This composition reveals the influence of Japanese art.
E.Ab.

120
ORCHIDS IN A VASE
Paris. *Late 19th century*
Marks: Paris for 1847-1919
Gold, diamonds, enamel, jasper, rock crystal
Height 17.5
Inv. No. E 14892
Provenance: collection of Grand Duchess Maria Pavlovna, St Petersburg; 1919 transferred to the Hermitage from the former collection of Arkady Rudanovsky.
Literature: Leningrad 1974, No. 47; Lugano 1986, No. 154; Munich 1986-87, No. 629; St Petersburg-Paris-Moscow 1992, No. 28; USA 1998-2001, No. 219.

Table decorations in the form of little bouquets of flowers standing in rock crystal vases were extremely popular at the end of the 19th century. Celebrated firms of jewellers such as Fabergé and Cartier made them from semi-precious and precious stones combined with gold and enamel. Of all the many flowers employed, Art Nouveau artists had a particularly taste for orchids, the flowers of which were so often of most unusual form.
E.Ab.

121
BROOCH
St Petersburg (?). *Late 19th century*
Gold, silver, diamonds, sapphires, enamel
3.8 x 5.3
Inv. No. E 17841
Provenance: 1988 acquired via the Hermitage Purchasing Commission.
Literature: St Petersburg-Paris-Moscow 1992, No. 155; Pforzheim 1995-96, pp. 220-21.

Virtuoso in execution, made using the plique à jour technique (which allows light to fall through the enamel), this little butterfly brooch seems extremely naturalistic, in keeping with the dominant aesthetic of the second half of the 19th century.
E.Ab.

122
CIGAR BOX
Bapst & Falise, Paris. *1870s*
Inscription on the edge of the lid: *Bapst & Falise. Paris*
Marks: mark of Bapst & Falise
Wood, silver
20.1 x 12.9 x 5.5
Inv. No. E 17932
Provenance: 1988 acquired via the Hermitage Purchasing Commission.
Previously unpublished.
M.L.

123
PORTE-CIGAR
Tiffany & Co., New York. *Late 19th century*
Marks: stamped *TIFFANY & CO MAKERS STERLING SILVER AND OTHER METALS; ET*, fineness mark *870*
Silver, gold, lacquer, cotton
9.1 x 6.2 x 2.1; length of chain 17; length of cord 23
Inv. No. E 17334
Provenance: Pavlovsk Palace Museum; 1951 allocated to the Hermitage from the Central Stores for Museum Funds, Pushkin.
Literature: St Petersburg-Paris-Moscow 1992, No. 42; Edinburgh 2005, No. G51.

The firm of Charles Louis Tiffany (1812-1902) was founded in New York in 1837, initially under the name Tiffany & Young. It dealt in European items of applied and decorative art. In 1848, however, Tiffany set up his own jewellery workshop in which he employed American craftsmen. This soon flourished and in 1850 the firm opened a branch in Paris. From 1853 the company was called Tiffany & Co. By 1900 its clients included members of European royal families, presidents, millionaires and celebrities. It was thanks to Tiffany that Europeans began to take an interest in American jewellery. After the death of Charles Louis, the business was run by his son Louis Comfort Tiffany (1848-1933).
E.Ab.

124
SHOT GLASS
St Petersburg. *Late 19th century*
Gold, enamel
Height 4.7; diameter 4.2
Inv. No. E 17155
Provenance: 1951 transferred to the Hermitage from the State Museums Fund.
Literature: St Petersburg-Paris-Moscow 1992, No. 169.

Made using the plique à jour technique, this glass is striking not only because of its use of colour – the gold combined with red and green vegetable ornament – but because of the way it allows light to pass through the enamel. Set into the base is a Russian gold rouble of the year 1758.
E.Ab.

125
PENDANT WITH A BALL OF SNAKES
René-Jules Lalique, Paris. *1901*
Marks: Paris for 1847-1919, craftsman René-Jules Lalique
Gold, pearls, enamel
Height 11

Inv. No. E 15364
Provenance: 1902 purchased in Paris for the Stieglitz Museum for the Decorative and Applied Arts, St Petersburg; 1921 transferred to the Hermitage from the Stieglitz Museum.
Literature: London 2000, No. 19; Fabergé – Cartier 2003, No. 948; Yakovleva 2004, pp. 14-20.

Lalique was consistently seeking new subjects and forms even while he continued to perfect those already in use. At the Exposition Universelle in Paris in 1900 he showed a corsage brooch, *Snakes*. This pendant is a version on the motif.
E.Ab.

126
Fir-tree Pendant
René-Jules Lalique, Paris. *1900-1*
Marks: Paris for 1847-1919, craftsman René-Jules Lalique
Gold, enamel, glass
7.2 x 6.5
Inv. No. E 15363
Provenance: 1902 acquired in Paris for the Stieglitz Museum for the Decorative and Applied Arts, St Petersburg; 1921 transferred to the Hermitage from the Stieglitz Museum.
Literature: Fabergé – Cartier 2003, No. 947; Yakovleva 2004, pp. 14-20.

One of the three surviving designs for very similar items of jewellery bears the date 21 November 1900. The main composition remains unchanged, only the drawing of the trees in the distant altering (Yakovleva 2004, p. 17). The craftsman daringly brings together apparently incompatible materials, gold and glass.
E.Ab.

127
Toilet Box with Two Ladies Singing
Austria (?). *Late 19th – early 20th century*
Marks: *GAS*, *B5*, fineness mark *84*
Silver, enamel
2.1 x 6.6 x 4.3
Inv. No. E 17752
Provenance: 1984 acquired via the Hermitage Purchasing Commission.
Previously unpublished.

Although executed with great finesse, Austrian Art Nouveau items are marked by a somewhat coarse choice of colours and extreme linearity, as in this toilet box.
E.Ab.

128
Vase
Peterhof Lapidary Factory, St Petersburg
Mounted by Yuly Rapoport, firm of Carl Fabergé, St Petersburg. *1898*
Marks: St Petersburg before 1899, firm of Fabergé, craftsman Yuly Rapoport, fineness mark *88*
Smoky quartz. Mount: silver
Height 37
Inv. No. E 17576
Provenance: possibly presented to the Imperial Court in 1898; 1931 transferred to the Hermitage from the Winter Palace, Leningrad.
Literature: Leningrad 1974, No. 23; Lopato 1984, No. 263; Lugano 1986, No. 120; Munich 1986-87, No. 281; Leningrad 1989, No. 65; Zurich 1989, No. 33; St Petersburg-London-Paris 1993, No. 55; USA 1998-2001, No. 218; Fabergé 2000, No. 176; Amsterdam 2004, No. 134; Lopato 2006, p. 90.

Marina Lopato has suggested that it should be identified with the 'little vase of smoky topaz' (the name used for smoky quartz at the time) that was on 23 May 1898 presented to the Imperial Court' by the Director of the Peterhof Lapidary Factory. There is an archive document recording payment for the making of a setting and case for the vase at a cost of 275 roubles. The vase itself was priced at 1,880 roubles (Fabergé 2000, pp. 288-301). The high quality and complexity of the work permitted Lopato to suggest that the vase itself was carved by the renowned Robert Pestou, invited from Berlin by the Factory's director A. L. Gun.
E.Ab.

129
Shot Glass
René-Jules Lalique, Paris. *1902*
Inscription on the bottom: LALIQUE
Glass, silver
Height 16
Inv. No. E 17577
Provenance: 1902 acquired in Paris for the Stieglitz Museum for the Decorative and Applied Arts, St Petersburg; 1923 transferred to the Hermitage from the Stieglitz Museum.
Literature: Leningrad 1974, No. 65; Lugano 1986, No. 158; Munich 1986-87, No. 630; Fabergé – Cartier 2003, No. 952; Yakovleva 2004, pp. 14-20.

Lalique was passionately interested in working with glass and here he skilfully combined it with precious metals.
E.Ab.

130
Cane with a Dragonfly
René-Jules Lalique, Paris. *Early 20th century*
Marks: Paris for 1838-1919, craftsman René-Jules Lalique
Bamboo, silver, gold, steel, enamel
Length 92
Inv. No. E 17258
Provenance: belonged to Empress Alexandra Fyodorovna; Alexander Palace, Tsarskoe Selo; 1956 allocated to the Hermitage from the Central Stores for Museum Funds, Pushkin.
Literature: Edinburgh 2005, No. G05.

We know that Alexandra Fyodorovna purchased and commissioned a number of jewellery and other items from Lalique.
E.Ab.

131
Allegory of Peace
Lucien Falize, Paris. *1896*
Signed and dated on the cross-section of the base: *Falize orf.1896*
Inscription on the laurel wreath: *PAX PORTIBUS, A.S.M./NICOLAS II/EMPEREUR DE TOUTES LES RUSSES/LA VILLE DE PARIS*
[Bearer of peace. To H[is] M[ajesty] Nicholas II, Emperor of all the Russians, from the city of Paris]
Silver, casting, engraving, parcel-gilt

Height 60
Inv. No. E 17253
Provenance: probably 1896 presented to Nicholas II by the city of Paris; until 1941 Alexander Palace, Tsarskoe Selo (later Pushkin); 1956 allocated to the Hermitage from the Central Stores for Museum Funds, Pushkin.
Literature: Leningrad 1974, No. 67; St Petersburg 1994, No. 321.

Lucien Falize portrayed Minerva as an allegory of Peace. His treatment reveals the influence of both Salon art and Art Nouveau. The inscription reveals that the figure was a gift to Nicholas II from the city of Paris, probably on the occasion of his coronation in 1896.
M.L.

132
MIRROR IN THE FORM OF A FAN
Firm of Alphonse Giroux – Veuve Ferdinand Duvinage, Paris. *1877-82*
Signed: *ALPH GIROUX PARIS, FD Bté* [Ferdinand Duvinage Breveté]
Different varieties of wood, ivory, brass
55 x 31
Inv. No. Epr 6583
Provenance: 1931 Alexander Palace, Tsarskoe Selo.
Literature: Geyko 2006, pp. 104, 105.

This early mirror is recorded as being in the apartments of Maria Fyodorovna in an inventory made of her property there in 1882. With its original mosaic decoration, it was produced at the celebrated Paris firm of Alphonse Giroux which in 1867 passed into the hands of Ferdinand Duvinage and Harinkouck and then was continued by Duvinage alone and lastly – from 1874 to 1882 – by his widow (whose name is never given except as 'widow of Ferdinand Duvinage'). It was during this last period in the firm's history, marked by a search for new artistic devices, that the Hermitage's mirror was produced. In 1877 the widow of Ferdinand Duvinage received a patent for the invention of a new kind of mosaic intended for application to applied art and furniture. Over the next five years the firm produced a very great variety of such items adorned in this characteristic technique. Today we know of a cabinet in the Musée d'Orsay in Paris as well as dishes, tables and smaller items.
The closest analogy for the Hermitage mirror is another mirror, sold at auction at Sotheby's in London on 27 May 1994.
A.G.

133
PENDANT LAMP WITH TWO DRAGONFLIES
Eugène and Désiré Muller, Nancy. *1910s*
Bronze, glass
Diameter 60
Inv. No. Epr 7600
Provenance: transferred to the Hermitage from the Winter Palace.
Previously unpublished.

The bronze parts of this lamp – in the form of dragonflies – are extremely characteristic of the decoration found on lamps and chandeliers by craftsmen of the School of Nancy. The Muller brothers created several versions of this lamp.
A.G.

134
CHANDELIER
Eugène Soleau, Paris. *1903*
Bronze, matt glass
Upper part height 42, diameter 17; lower part height 55, diameter 74
Inv. No. Epr 7116
Provenance: 1978 acquired via the Hermitage Purchasing Commission.
Previously unpublished.

135-136
PAIR OF WALL LAMPS
Eugène Soleau, Paris. *1903*
Marks: craftsman Eugène Soleau
Bronze, matt glass
73 x 31; 76 x 30
Inv. No. Epr 7117, Epr 7118
Provenance: 1978 acquired via the Hermitage Purchasing Commission.
Previously unpublished

Eugène Soleau is a well known but little studied maker of items in decorative bronze and of lamps. His name first appears in connection with the Exposition Universelle of 1889 at which he received a silver medal for works designed by Joseph Chéret, brother of the celebrated poster painter Jules Chéret. In the 1890s Soleau was an active participant in international exhibitions in Chicago, Brussels, St Petersburg and Moscow. This chandelier with its waterlilies was presented to the public at the Paris Salon of 1903. Such was the model's success that Soleau was to repeat it on many occasions, sometimes on a much larger scale.
A.G.

137
EVENING DRESS (BODICE AND SKIRT)
OF GREEN SATIN AND BLACK CHIFFON
Workshop of Nadezhda Lamanova, Moscow. *1910s*
On the corsage ribbon the printed mark of the workshop:
N. Lamanova
Silk, metal threads, tassels, embroidery
Back of bodice 38; length of skirt 161
Inv. No. Ert 16063 a,b
Provenance: 1971 acquired from the collection of Valentina Karakhan via the Hermitage Purchasing Commission.
Literature: Korshunova 2002, p. 34.

Made in Neo-Classical style in the Moscow workshop founded in 1895 by one of the most celebrated of all Russian dress designers, Nadezhda Lamanova (1861-1941). In 1902-3 Lamanova was to be a successful participant – along with famous French designers such as Paul Poiret, Callot Soeurs and others – in the First International Exhibition of Historical and Modern Costume held in the Tauride Palace in St Petersburg. From 1904 she was permitted to use the title Supplier to the Court. After the Revolution in 1917, Lamanova played an active role in establishing a Soviet school of dress design. In 1925 she and the Russian sculptor Vera Mukhina received a Grand Prix at the Exposition Universelle in Paris for their joint costume designs making use of elements of traditional Russian folk attire. From the start of the century until her death in 1941 Lamanova worked extensively in the theatre.
T.K.

138

Tapestry: The Adoration of the Magi

William Morris & Co., Merton Abbey, Surrey. *1902*

Cartoon by Edward Burne-Jones. *1890*

Woven into the upper border: *THE 'ADORATION' DESIGNED BY SIR E. BVRNE-JONES AND EXECVTED BY MORRIS AND COMPANY AT MERTON ABBEY IN SVRREY ENGLAND.*

Wool

255 x 379

Inv. No. T 15431

Provenance: until 1917 collection of Sergey Shchukin, Moscow; 1949 transferred from the Hermitage to the Museum of New Western Art, Moscow.

Literature: Leningrad 1974, No. 269; Hermitage English Art 1979, Nos. 350-52; Paris 1989, pp. 40-41; St Petersburg 1996, No. 770.

In 1887 Edward Burne-Jones produced a watercolour sketch from which William Morris and John Dirl created the cartoon for this tapestry, introducing changes to the colour combinations and adding in flowers and background details. The first copy of the tapestry was woven in 1890 for the Chapel of Exeter College in Oxford. Similar tapestries are today to be found at Eton College, in the Art Gallery of South Australia in Adelaide and in the Museum für Kunst und Gewerbe in Hamburg. Along with other tapestries woven at Merton Abbey, *The Adoration of the Magi* represents the earliest attempt to revive an art form that had declined considerably in the 19th century until it had become largely a form of repetitive reproduction. Burne-Jones' design was repeated ten times between 1890 and 1907. This, the sixth repetition, dates from 1902.

N.B.

139-142

Tapestries from the Series The Seasons

Gobelins Manufactory, Paris. *1910-14*

Cartoons by Jules Chéret

Wool, silk, eight warp threads per 1 cm

Provenance: 1914 gift of French President Raymond Poincaré; 1924 transferred to the Hermitage from the Winter Palace.

Literature (for the whole series): Kuhl 1905-6; Guiffrey 1911, No. 252; Birukova 1974, Nos. 46-49; Leningrad 1974, Nos. 270-73; St Petersburg 1994, Nos. 333-36; London 1998, No. 303.

The series consists of four tapestries which were complemented by furniture upholstery covers.

139

L'Hiver. Les Houx [Winter. Holly]

1911-13

Woven by Ch. Thuaire, L. Claude

Woven bottom right by the border: *Chéret 1910*; along the border to right the mark of the manufactory, the date *1911-1913* and the weavers' signatures: *Ch. Thuaire, L. Claude*

Stitched to the back is a label with the mark: *Manufacture Nationale des Gobelins. No 625. D'après M.J. Chéret. Les Houx (replique)*

270 x 170

Inv. No. T 15595

140.

Le Printemps. Les Roses [Spring. Roses]

1911-13

Woven by Chevalier, Cuneo

Woven bottom right by the border: *Chéret*; along the border to right the mark of the manufactory, the date *1911-1913* and the weavers' signatures: *Chevalier, Cuneo*

Stitched to the back is a label with the mark: *Manufacture Nationale des Gobelins. No 637. Les Roses (replique) D'après le modèle M.J. Chéret*

280 x 176

Inv. No. T 15592

141

L'Eté. Les Blés [Summer. Ears of Wheat]

1911-12

Woven by H. Gauzy, G. Gagnot, E. Deluzenu

Woven bottom right by the border: *Chéret*; along the border to right the mark of the manufactory, the date *1911-1912* and the weavers' signatures: *H. Gauzy, G. Gagnot, E. Deluzenu*

Stitched to the back is a label with the mark: *Manufacture Nationale des Gobelins. No 621. Les Blés (replique) D'après M.J. Chéret*

278 x 172

Inv. No. T 15593

142

L'Automne. Les Pampres [Autumn. Vines]

1912-14

Woven by H. Bouchet, Gonnet, Claude, F. Laurent

Woven bottom right by the border: *Chéret*; along the border to right the mark of the manufactory, the date *1912-1914* and the weavers' signatures: *H. Bouchet, Gonnet, Claude, F. Laurent*

Stitched to the back is a label with the mark: *Manufacture Nationale des Gobelins. No 657. Les Pampres (replique). D'après M.J. Chéret*

275 x 170

Inv. No. T 15594

N.B.

143

Georges Becker

Ceremonial Greeting of Nicholas II in Paris. 1896-97

Oil on canvas

180 x 200

Inv. No. ERZh-II-545

Provenance: 1955 transferred to the Hermitage from the Museum of the Revolution, Leningrad.

Literature: Edinburgh 2005, No. E12.

Nicholas II and Alexandra Fyodorovna, together with their little daughter Grand Duchess Olga Nikolaevna, arrived in France on 5 October (23 September in Russia) 1896. The Russian sovereign's visit to France was of great importance in reinforcing the Russo-French alliance concluded in 1892. This was the first official visit to republican France by a Russian monarch.

In this painting we see the ceremonial greeting accorded the Russian Tsar in Paris. Standing beside Nicholas II before the richly adorned station as he looks on this parade by French troops is the French president, Felix Faure. Nicholas is wearing the insignia of the French Légion d'honneur while Faure clearly wears the blue sash of the Russian Order of St Andrew the First-called.

S.P.

THE MELTZER FURNITURE MANUFACTORY

The F. Meltzer furniture manufactory was founded by Friedrich Johann (known in Russia as Fyodor Andreevich) Meltzer (1831-1922), a native of Prussia. With his brother Adam and father-in-law N. Stange, Meltzer was joint owner in the 1860s of a large lamp and furniture enterprise in St Petersburg. In 1884 the brothers divided their affairs, Adam Andreevich heading his father-in-law's company, and Fyodor Andreevich taking the firm F. Meltzer & Co., which moved to a new address. The Meltzers saw their furniture manufactory as one of the oldest in St Petersburg, since it was founded in the 1840s by A. Tur. By the late 19th century it was one of the country's largest furniture producers, sending its products to many towns around Russia and showing them at numerous Russian and foreign exhibitions. In 1892 Meltzer took Russian citizenship and in 1894 left the business, passing on control to his wife Sofia Khristianovna Meltzer (1837-1915) and their two sons, Fyodor and Roman. They had a shop on Nevsky Prospekt. In 1906 Sofia left the business, followed by Fyodor in 1916, leaving Roman in sole control.

From the late 1880s Roman Fyodorovich (Robert Friedrich) Meltzer (1860-1943), an architect who in 1888 graduated from the Academy of Arts, was in charge of artistic affairs at F. Meltzer & Co. The manufactory had a large library with an immense collection of books on art history, architecture and various applied arts, as well as the catalogues of leading European manufactories. Among the company's regular clients were members of the imperial family. In 1894-96, for instance, the Meltzers were involved in redesigning and furnishing the apartments in the Winter Palace being decorated for the newly married sovereign and his wife, going on to create interiors for rooms in the New Palace at Alexandria (1895) and the Cottage (for the Dowager Empress Maria Fyodorovna, 1896; both Peterhof), the Alexander Palace at Tsarskoe Selo (1895), the Livadia Palace near Yalta (1910-11) and many more. Other clients included wealthy bankers and merchants, businessmen, actors and artists. Today there are dozens of surviving designs bearing the stamp of the Meltzer company and several albums or catalogues with photographs (most of these now in the Hermitage collection) providing convincing evidence that by the end of the 1910s the company was putting out both stylised (i.e. Historicist) furniture and highly fashionable and up to date pieces in the spirit of Art Nouveau and Neo-Classicism. In the autumn of 1918 Roman Meltzer left for Germany via Finland and Sweden, opening up his own furniture workshop there. From 1921 he lived in New York, receiving a diploma from the University of New York State and establishing his own company design buildings and interiors.

N.G.

144

DESIGN FOR A SOFA WITH HIGH BACK, IN A MOUNT

F. Meltzer, St Petersburg. *Late 19th century*

Pencil, watercolour

23.7 x 27.7

Inv. No. ERMb-III-1331

Provenance: transferred from the Winter Palace.

Previously unpublished.

145

DESIGN FOR TWO TABLES

F. Meltzer, St Petersburg. *Late 19th century*

Pencil, watercolour

18 x 15; 18 x 15

Inv. No. ERMb-III-1350

Provenance: transferred from the Winter Palace.

Previously unpublished.

146

CHAIR WITH ROUNDED BACK

F. Meltzer, St Petersburg. *Early 20th century*

Mahogany, velvet upholstery with waterlilies

81 x 55 x 45

Inv. No. Epr 3866

Provenance: Alexandria Palace, Peterhof; 1933 transferred to the Hermitage.

Literature: Leningrad 1974, p. 67.

T.R.

147

CHAIR WITH A HIGH BACK

F. Meltzer, St Petersburg. *Early 20th century*

Mahogany, velvet upholstery with stylised bluebells

121 x 52 x 50

Inv. No. Epr 3869

Provenance: Alexandria Palace, Peterhof; 1933 transferred to the Hermitage.

Literature: Leningrad 1974, p. 67.

T.R.

148

CABINET CUPBOARD WITH COLUMNS ALONG THE SIDES AND A WATERCOLOUR INSET WITH A JAPANESE WOMAN

Master Cleuler, L'Escalier de Cristal, Paris. *1894*

Bronze by master Peste

To a design by E. Lièvre

On the door the signature: *Escalier de Cristal*

On the watercolour the signature: *G.Clairin*

Palisander, bronze, watercolour on paper

205 x 115 x 66

Inv. No. E 7536

Provenance: 1894 made for Grand Duke Vladimir, kept for some time in the Anichkov Palace, St Petersburg; after 1917 transferred to the Hermitage from the Winter Palace.

Literature: Rappe 1991, pp. 120-27; Rappe 2006, p. 18.

The French house of L'Escalier de Cristal provided goods to the ruling Russian Romanov family. This cabinet is an example of the Japanising trend in furniture design of the 1870s to 1890s. In outline it recalls a pagoda, the bronze work is in oriental style and the watercolour by G. Clairin shows a Japanese woman wearing a kimono and holding a fan. A close analogy for this cabinet is another such piece in the Musée d'Orsay, Paris, with a watercolour inset by the artist J.-B. Detaille to a design by J.-B. Lièvre. Philippe Thiébaut considers that the cabinet in the Musée d'Orsay was the original version, designed by J.-B. Lièvre. That design, he suggests, was acquired by L'Escalier de Cristal in 1894 and six similar cabinets were then made, one of which was sold to Grand Duke Vladimir.

T.R.

149
Armchair
F. Meltzer, St Petersburg. *1907-1910s*
Designed by Ivan Fomin
Mahogany; carving; block-printed chintz
68 x 60 x 60
Inv. No. ERMb 1748
Provenance: 1984 gift of P. I. Kostrov.
Literature: Leningrad 1986; Guseva 2006, pp. 64-65.

This armchair represents a repetition of forms created by the architect Ivan Fomin in 1907-8 for the St Petersburg apartment of the Pomer family. Fomin revealed his great skill in stylisation, successfully combing elements of both Art Nouveau and Neo-Classicism in a single item. The clearly legible 'Classical' silhouettes are enriched with decoration in the form of acorns, spirals and garlands. The brightly coloured chintz upholstery has a waterlily motif characteristic of Art Nouveau that introduces freshness and sense of colour to the whole. Ivan Fomin, celebrated for his architectural designs of the turn of the 19th and 20th centuries, was no less talented – and successful – as a designer. He showed his work at the Exhibition of Architecture and Artistic Industry in the New Style that was held in Moscow in 1902-3. Combining different materials – wood, metal and ceramics – in original fashion, his works stood alongside pieces by the great names of European Art Nouveau such as Olbrich and Mackintosh. From the 1900s Fomin collaborated with the Meltzer brothers, creating designs for furniture in the spirit of Art Nouveau and Neo-Classicism.
N.G.

150
Stand
F. Meltzer, St Petersburg. *Late 19th century*
Structure of coniferous woods, mahogany veneer
Height 126, base 26 x 26
Inv. No. Epr 7114
Provenance: transferred from the Winter Palace.
Previously unpublished.

Part of one of a number of sets of furniture that adorned the private apartments of Nicholas II in the Winter Palace, refurnished in 1894-96 in the wake of his marriage to the Princess of Hesse-Darmstadt (Empress Alexandra Fyodorovna). The work was entrusted to St Petersburg's leading furniture companies, a considerable proportion being carried out by the firm of Fyodor Meltzer.
T.S.

151
Armchair: Yoke, Axe and Mittens
Russia. *Late 19th century*
Designed by Vasily Shutov
Oak; carved
97 x 52 x 58
Inv. No. ERMb 420
Provenance: 1941 transferred to the Hermitage from the State Museum for the Ethnography of Peoples of the USSR, Leningrad.
Literature: Sokolova 1973, No. 190.

Vasily Shutov was a St Petersburg craftsman, owner of a furniture workshop and teacher at the Baron Stieglitz Central School of Technical Drawing. He first produced an armchair along these lines, in the Russian style, in 1871. His repetitions of the design, with all kinds of variations in the details, were produced in Russia right into the 1910s.
N.G.

152
Marquetry Table with Carved Dragonfly Legs
Manufactory of Emile Gallé, Nancy. *c. 1900*
Signed in the lower right corner of the tabletop: *Gallé*
Marks: court manufacturer N. I. Shmidt
Label: *M. Gorchakov. Fontanka 18, N 72*
Pearwood, marquetry of different kinds of wood including mahogany, thuya and maple
76 x 74 x 49
Inv. No. E 1226
Provenance: 1923 transferred to the Hermitage from the former collection of the Princes Gorchakov, Petrograd.
Literature: Leningrad 1974, 267; St Petersburg 1999, pp. 108-9.

In an essay Gallé described his furniture with dragonflies thus: 'Nous avons essayé cependant d'ajouter à toute la ménagerie chimérique du mobilier quelques images réelles, et "la frissonnante libellule" immobilisée un instant, a prêté ses ailes à la statique des consoles' [We sought meanwhile to add to this chimerical menagerie on the furniture certain real images, and 'the trembling dragonfly' immobilised for a moment lent wings to the static nature of the consoles (E. Gallé, 'Le Mobilier contemporain orné d'après la nature', Revue des Arts décoratifs, November – December 1900; reprinted in *Ecrits pour l'Art*, Marseille, 1980, p. 263).
It is thought that Gallé introduced this type of table with dragonfly legs in 1894, going on to repeat it on numerous occasions. There is a letter to a friend from the owner of a shop in Strasbourg, in which he describes tables on dragonfly legs on sale in his shop, noting that they had sold six of them in just fifteen days. Two kinds of this table are known, on three and on four legs. The Hermitage table bears the mark of Gallé and of N.I. Shmidt (Schmidt), a supplier to the imperial court. Presumably the table was purchased in France by Shmidt for sale in Russia.
T.R.

153
Table with Marquetry Top: Flore de Lorraine
Manufactory of Emile Gallé, Nancy. *October 1893*
Designed by Emile Gallé and L Hestaux
Signed in the bottom right corner: *Emile Gallé dec.f.t.oct.1893*
Inscriptions: *Flore de Lorraine. Gardez les coeurs qu'avez gagnés* and numerous inscriptions over the whole surface giving the names of plants, towns and provinces
Walnut, marquetry of different kinds of wood including pearwood, thuya, mahogany and maple; engraved, pokerwork, glass inlay, metal chasing
207 x 97 x 77
Inv. No. E 3867
Provenance: 1893 acquired from the Gallé Manufactory, Nancy.
Literature: Vachon s.a., pp. 172-80; Champier 1893/94; Champier 1896; Leningrad 1974, No. 268; Sorez 1898, p. 345, Rappe 1991, pp. 18-24; St Petersburg 1999, pp. 112-117; Rappe 2006, pp. 16-17; Japan 2006-7, No. 31.

Gallé's workshop produced this table in just 20 days in October 1893. It is crammed with symbolism dictated by its purpose as a gift to the Russian people from three provinces of Lorraine. Along the left edge of the table are the names of towns and settlements in Lorraine, the main towns of the three regions, Meuse, Meurthe et Moselle and Epinal, yet the names do not stand out, seeming rather to be interwoven into the floral ornament that adorns the table top. Even the flowers and trees are not chance illustrations for they are all plants linked with Lorraine, either serving as symbols of towns (perhaps forming part of their coats-of-arms) or being native to the region. Elongated forms and an emphatically asymmetrical approach dominate in their depiction. Most of the floral design is in the right side of the table; nearer to the centre, on the spot on which the accompanying Gold Book of Lorraine (see cat. 155) was to lie, are the arms of Lorraine. Thus the table itself can be read like a book, albeit only by the well-informed! Using the language of flowers – not always comprehensible at first sight – it relates the sad story of the province of Lorraine, which had been passed helplessly from the control of one country to another in recent centuries.
Emile Gallé's design for this table can be seen in the Gold Book of Lorraine (cat. 155, drawing 31). Some 5,760 francs were spent on creating the table, making it the most expensive of all the numerous gifts presented to Alexander II via the visiting Russian sailors by the province of Lorraine.
T.R.

154
SHEET OF PAPER WITH CRAFTSMEN'S SIGNATURES
Nancy. *1893*
Pen and pencil on paper
50 x 35
Inv. No. ONP 16
Provenance: discovered inside the table *Flore de Lorraine* (cat. 153).
Literature: St Petersburg 1999, p. 116.

During restoration of the body of the table this sheet of paper was discovered. It was not a total surprise, however, as its existence had been indicated in the literature. On a simple piece of paper the names of all the craftsmen involved in making the table are fitted into a frame of 'broken heart' flowers. There are 23 names in all, among them master joiners, marquetry specialists, sculptors, bronzeworkers and modellers. Their signatures – which cannot always be deciphered – are accompanied by a description of their job and where they lived and by the touching text: 'Emile Gallé et les ouvriers et collaborateurs ont enfermé ce page dans la table offert par la Lorraine au Peuple Russe, et qu'ils ont confectionnée dans un sentiment de fraternité et de patriotique espérance; ils espèrent que leur ouvrage de bois et de bronze sera moins durable que l'amitié et la grandeur des deux Peuples, la Russie et la France' [Emile Gallé and his workers and colleagues have enclosed this page in the table presented by Lorraine to the Russian People and which they have created in a sentiment of fraternity and patriotic hope; they hope that their work in wood and bronze shall be less long-lived than the friendship and greatness of the two Peoples, Russia and France.'
T.R.

155
LA LIVRE D'OR DE LORRAINE
(THE GOLD BOOK OF LORRAINE)
Nancy. *1893*
Album with the stamped title *LA LORRAINE A LA RUSSIE 1893*
Containing 84 drawings, five prints, 1,713 signatures of the mayors of towns and communes, 520 signatures of the heads of various societies and representatives of the press
Binding adorned with allegorical images, the arms and Cross of Lorraine, silver corners, a buckle and two stands
Binder René Wiener
Artists Emil Victor Prouvé, Camille Martin
Silversmith S. Ronga
Inscriptions on the binding: on the front cover *Victor Prouvé*; on the back cover *Pax* and *Camille Martin*
Inside the front cover, below: *René Wiener relieur. Mosaiqueur. Nancy*
Inscriptions on the silver fittings: in the corners *S. Ronga* and on all the details the assay mark of France for 1878 to 1910
Yellow morocco leather, tinted in places; stamped; chased silver, red velvet
67.3 x 59.5 x 22
Inv. No. OR 13529/a
Provenance: 1893, from Nancy.
Literature: Rappe 1991, pp. 18-24.

According to the concept of this gift from Lorraine to the Russian Emperor, Gallé's marquetry table (cat. 153) was to serve but as a pedestal for the main 'message', this Golden Book of Lorraine. The message is carried in an emotional but restrained voice, filled with hope that it will meet with understanding and assistance from France's powerful ally. That voice can be heard in the various texts, in the 17,013 signatures of mayors of towns and communes, in the 520 signatures of the heads of societies and representatives of the press. Then come 84 drawings interspersed with several lithographs and etchings.
N.P.

The drawings in the Gold Book of Lorraine have their own numbers.

Drawings in the Gold Book of Lorraine, Inv. Nos. OR 13529-13612

1
E. Auguin. 1893
Dedication text
Pen and ink; *63.5 x 46.5*

Text of the address: 'La Livres d'Or de la Lorraine, vers la Néva, vers Moscou, vers l'Oural, vers la Mer Caspienne, vers l'Asie lointaine, partout où Flotte de Drapeau Russe, porter le Salut Fraternel d'un peuple ami. Dis bien que sur cette terre éminemment Française il n'y a pas une Commune qui ne soit pénétrée du même sentiment. Aucun de nous n'oublie que, l'année dernière, dans une Circonstance solennelle, Nancy, notre vieille Capitale, a reçu la visite du Grand-Duc Constantin. Ce Souvenir reste gravé au fond de nos coeurs. Nos hommages se sont partagés, ce jour-là, entre le Représentant de Sa Majesté l'Empéreur de Russie et le Président de la République Française. Cronstadt, Nancy, Toulon, trois dates mémorables dans notre histoire, trois anneaux d'une même chaîne, gages définitifs d'amitié et de confiance entre deux Généreuses Nations! Nous connaissons les devoirs que nous imposent de si Grands Témoignages de Sympathie; notre Race de Patriotes et de Soldats saura les remplir jusqu'au bout avec fidélité.
A. Mézières de l'Académie française.'

2
Emil Victor Prouvé
Allegorical Female Figures
Ink wash; *55 x 39*

Text of the address: 'Les Fidèles Lorraines sont heureux de célébrer l'amitié qui lie les deux Grandes Nations Européennes pour l'œuvre de paix et de justice. Unis dans un même sentiment de fierté et d'allégresse patriotiques ils saluent avec émotions l'arrivée d'une escadre Russe dans la Méditerranée. Les dix sept cent treize Communes les cinq cent vingt Sociétés et la Presse de Lorraine ont signé sur ce Livre d'Or, et envoient à la noble, à la vaillante Russie, l'affirmation unanime de leur confiante, loyale et fraternelle affection.
Vive la Russie!
Vive la France!'

3
Camille Martin
Thistle with the Title *Artistes Lorrains*
Pen and ink, ink wash; *64 x 46.5*

4
Jean Paul Aubé
Study of a Seated Model for a Figure of Strength on the Monument to Gambetta
Pencil; *31.2 x 22.5*

5
Auburtin
Allegorical Figure of a Seated Woman with a Sword on her Knees
Pen and ink, white heightening; *37 x 22*

6
Albert Barbier
Road with Boulders in the Forest of Fontainbleau
Ink wash; *36.5 x 26.5*

7
Frédéric Auguste Bartholdi
The Statue of Liberty in New York
Watercolour; *14 x 23*

8
Léon Barillot
Two Cows
Pen and ink; *18 x 27*

9
Léonie de Bazelaire
Mountainous Landscape in les Vosges
Sepia, watercolour; *24 x 18*

10
Albert Bettanier
Despair (The Soldier's Return After a Defeat)
Pencil; *42 x 50.5*

11
H. Blain
Study for a Male Head (Portrait of Maurice Blaise)
Charcoal, grey wash; *24 x 18*

12
J.-A. Carl
Army Trumpeter
Pen and ink, ink wash; *33 x 24.5*

13
André Chabellard
The Fisherman
Pen and ink; *32 x 25*

14
A. E. Charbonnier
Place de Liverdun
Pen and ink; *24 x 31.5*

15
Emile Chepfer
French Solder Holding a Horse's Bridle
Watercolour; *37 x 26.5*

16
Paul Emile Colin
Our Lady of the Snows
Watercolour; *23.5 x 16*

17
Marie Lucie Cornélius
Street and Cathedral Tower in Strasbourg
Watercolour; *37 x 27*

18
L. Curel
Two Parrots
Watercolour; *18.5 x 13*

19
Jules Daubeil
Street in Tunis
Watercolour; *32 x 23*

20
Auguste Daum
Cup with the Inscription *'Les fideles [sic] Lorrains...'*
Pencil; *19.5 x 14*

21
Paul Descelles
Children Eating
Graphite pencil, pen and ink, scraping out; *22.5 x 30*

22
R. de Dombasle
Village at Twilight (Sunset)
Watercolour; *31 x 21.5*

23
J. Duflot
Group of Soldiers with Banners
Pen and ink; *32 x 24*

24
Léon Ehrmann
Female Head
Red chalk; *35 x 27*

25
J. Elardin
Silver Cup In Commemoration of Azov with the Words *Pamiat-Azowa*
Pen and ink, blue pencil; *29.5 x 44*

26
A. Faillot
Stream
Watercolour: *25 x 15.5*

27
Eugène Feyen
Girl Carrying Crabs
Pencil: *22 x 14.5*

28
L. Flot
Two Children in Sailor Costume
Watercolour; *30 x 23*

29
Emile Friant
Girl of Lorraine
Black chalk; *46.3 x 39.8*

30
François-Louis Français
Autumn Landscape. River Bank
Ink wash and white heightening; *28.5 x 22*

31
Emile Gallé
Examples of the Flora of Lorraine. Preparatory drawing for part of a marquetry table
Black chalk and charcoal; *50 x 32*

32
Henry Ganier-Tanconville
Soldier Wearing the Uniform of the Preobrazhensky Regiment
Watercolour; *37 x 27*

33
E. Gœpfert
Cows at Pasture in a Meadow
Watercolour; *34 x 24*

34
G. Hennequin
Study of a Soldier with a Dog
Pencil; *17.7 x 14*

35
G. Hennequin
Hunting Trophies and a Dog's Head
Pencil; *13 x 24*

36
Louis Hestaux
Thistle with a View of a Monastery Behind
Pen and ink, watercolour; *37 x 25*

37
Charles Jacquot
Drawing for Two Versions of the Sculpture *Mother and Child*
Black chalk, charcoal; *37 x 29*

38
Joseph Jacquot
View of Strasbourg Cathedral Framed by Flowers and Birds, with an Anchor and Broken Shield Below
Pen and ink, watercolour; *42 x 28.2*

39
Monogrammist AR
Design for a Faience Dinner Service Presented by the Keller and Guérin Ceramics Manufactory to Admiral Avellan
Watercolour; *38.5 x 27.5*

40
Anonymous Artist
Two Porcelain Vases Offered to Admiral Avellan by the Ceramics Manufactory at Saint-Clément
Watercolour; *37.5 x 28*

41
Albert Larteau
Soldier
Black chalk; *27 x 17*

42
Alphonse Legros
Four Groups of Infantry and Cavalry Divisions of Lorraine
Pen and ink; *37 x 26.5*

43
L. Leher
View of a Tower with Part of a Bridge in Front of the Fortress Gates at Verdun
Pen and ink, wash; *38 x 27*

44
Hector Leroux
An Artist in a Classical Chiton in Front of a Fresco
Pen and ink; *29.5 x 20*

45
Henri Léopold Lévy
Three Women with Children
Pen and ink, ink wash, white heightening; *24 x 33.5*

46
Paul Licourt
Landscape with a Ditch and Wooden Posts at Brousil-Sivry
Pencil; *21 x 16.5*

47
Paul Licourt
Landscape with Trees and Bushes
Pencil; *14 x 23.5*

48
Edmond Lombard
Landscape with Women in a Vineyard
Watercolour; *26 x 20.5*

49
Camille Martin
Design for a Vase with Thistles
Pen and ink, ink wash; *32 x 44*

50
Hélène Maréchal
Autumn Landscape
Watercolour; *24 x 33.5*

51
Charles de Dombasle Meixmoron
View of a Lake
Watercolour; *30 x 23.5*

52
Alphonse Monchablon
Allegory in Honour of the Franco-Russian Alliance
Watercolour; *21 x 30*

53
Jan Monchablon
Studies of a Male and a Female Figure
Black chalk and white heightening on grey paper; *36 x 27*

54
Edouard Moyse
Study of a Seated Cleric with a Book
Charcoal, white heightening and red chalk on grey paper; *35 x 23*

55
Léon Parent
View of the Town of Etain with its Arms
Watercolour on grey paper; *20 x 29*

56
Jules Julien Paquin
Rest by the Shore of a Lake
Watercolour; *36 x 26*

57
Charles Peccatte
Morning in les Vosges
Black chalk, stumping; *36.5 x 28.5*

58
Edmond Marie Petitjean
View of the Porte de Bourgogne in Moret
Pen and ink; *23 x 32*

59
Paul Pierre
View of the Basilica of St Nicholas
Watercolour; *36.5 x 27*

60
M. de Ravinel
Landscape with a Lake
Watercolour; *37 x 27*

61
Félix Regamey
Figure of a Boy in a Sailor Suit and a Caricature Head
Watercolour on yellow paper; *19.5 x 15*

62
Félix Regamey
Caricature
Watercolour; *18 x 14*

63
Bernard Louis Borione
Old Man with his Grandson Watching a Swan
Pen and ink, watercolour; *15.5 x 11*

64
Kauffman
Sunken Boat with an Old Mariner Above
Pen and ink; *16 x 10.5*

65
Félix Regamey
Figure of a Boy, with a Medallion Above Containing a Profile Portrait of an Elderly Lady
Watercolour; *16 x 11*

66
Félix Regamey
Boy Seated on a Pouffe
Watercolour on yellowish paper; *16 x 11*

67
Félix Regamey
Boy in a Beret
Watercolour on yellowish paper; *16 x 11*

68
Félix Regamey
Boy Standing by a Table
Watercolour on yellowish paper; *16 x 11*

69
J. Reinhart
Winter Landscape
Charcoal, white heightening; *36 x 28*

70
A. Renaudin
Nasturtiums
Watercolour; *37 x 25*

71
Henri Rovet
Head of a Girl
Lead pencil on prepared paper; *37 x 27*

72
Henri-Paul Royer
Peasant Woman of Lorraine
Black chalk; *37 x 27*

73
Olga Saladin
Nasturtiums
Watercolour on yellowish paper; *44.5 x 30*

74
Gaston-Gilbert-Daniel Save
Joan of Arc's Vision
Pen and ink, wash, watercolour, white heightening; *32 x 24*

75
Jules Seltz
Portrait of a Lady
Lead pencil; *36.5 x 26.5*

76
G. Serrier
A Street in the Town of Langeac
Black chalk on brown paper; *32.5 x 26*

77
Jules Tridémy
View of the Town of Etain
Pencil on brown paper; *25.5 x 34*

78
Henri Thirïot
French Soldier with a Rifle
Watercolour; *32.5 x 23*

79
A. Véry
Drawing of a Statue of a Blacksmith
Watercolour on grey paper; *35.2 x 25.5*

80
H. Vierling
Interior with a Woman Wearing National Costume Seated in an Armchair
Watercolour; *30 x 22.5*

81
Jules Voirin
Cavalryman with a Banner
Watercolour; *37 x 27.5*

82
P. Waidmann
Old Church in a Semi-circle of Flowers
Pen and ink, ink wash; *36.5 x 26.5*

83
Georges Weiss
Tailor Seated by a Window
Pen and ink; *19 x 15*

84
E. Wittmann
Rue Saint-Georges, Nancy
Watercolour; *26 x 21*

Bibliography

Aarhus 1990
Kunstskatte fra Zarenes hof 1860-1917, exh. cat., Aarhus Kunstmuseums, 1990

Amsterdam 2004
Nicholas and Alexandra, exh. cat., Hermitage Amsterdam, 2004

Anisimova 2001
E. Anisimova, 'Vazy raboty Emilya Galle iz lichnykh pokoev Nikolaya II i Aleksandry Fyodorovny v Zimnem dvortse' [Vases by Emile Gallé from the Private Apartments of Nicholas II and Alexandra Fyodorovna in the Winter Palace], *Gosudarstvennyy muzey-zapovednik 'Tsarskoe Selo'. Sud'by muzeynykh kollektsiy. Materialy VII Tsarskosel'skoy nauchnoy konferentsiy* [Tsarskoe Selo State Museum Reserve. The Fates of Museum Collections. Materials from the VII Tsarskoe Selo Scholarly Conference], St Petersburg, 2001, pp. 202-8

Anisimova 2006
E. Anisimova, 'Evropeyskoe khudozhestvennoe steklo epokhi moderna' [European artistic glass of the age of Art Nouveau era], in the anthology: *Na rubezhe vekov... Iskusstvo epokhi Moderna* [At the Turn of the Centuries... Art from the age of Art Nouveau], Hermitage Museum, St Petersburg, 2006, pp. 71-87

Arwas 1987
V. Arwas, *Glas vom Jugendstil zur Art Deco*, Stuttgart, 1987

Babin 1994
A. A. Babin et al, *Great Art Treasures of the Hermitage Museum*, St Petersburg London, 1994, vol. II

Bacri 1993
C. Bacri, *Daum. Masters of French Decorative Glass*, London, 1993

Barovier Mentasti 1982
Rosa Barovier Mentasti, *Il vetro veneziano, Milan*, 1982

Bernstamm 1913
Serge Bernstamm, *Léopold Bernstamm. Sa vie – Son œuvre*, Paris, 1913

Birukova 1974
N. Birukova, *Les tapisseries françaises de la fin du XVe au XXe siècle dans les collections de l'Ermitage*, Leningrad, 1974

Brunet, Préaud 1978
M. Brunet, T. Préaud, *Sèvres. Des origines à nos jours*, Fribourg (Switzerland), 1978

Catalogue 1904
Katalog muzeya Imperatorskogo Obshchestva Pooshchreniya Khudozhestv [Catalogue of the Museum of the Imperial Society for the Encouragement of the Arts], St Petersburg, 1904

Champier 1893/94
V. Champier, 'Les cadeaux offerts à l'escadre russe', *Revue des arts décoratifs*, vol. 14, Paris, 1893/94, pp. 129-35

Champier 1896
V. Champier, 'Souhaits d'artistes à propos de la Réception des Souverains russes', *Revue des arts décoratifs*, 1896, No. 16

Corning 1989
Russian Glass of the 17th – 20th Centuries, exh. cat., Corning Museum of Glass, New York, 1989

Duncan 1984
Alastair Duncan, G. de Bartha, *Glass by Gallé*, London, 1984

Edinburgh 2005
Nicholas and Alexandra. The Last Tsar and Tsarina, National Museum of Scotland, Edinburgh, 2005

Fabergé 2000
Fabergé: Imperial Craftsman and his World, by Dr Géza von Habsburg with contributions by Alexander von Solodkoff, Dr Robert Bianchi, London-New York, 2000

Fabergé – Cartier 2003
Fabergé – Cartier. Rivalen am Zarenhof, Munich, 2003

Garner 1990
Philippe Garner, *Emile Gallé*, London-New York, 1990

Geyko 2006
A. Geyko, 'Problema vostochnogo vozdeystviya na khudozhestvennuyu kul'turu Frantsii vtoroy poloviny XIX – nachala XX v.' [The Question of Oriental Influence on French Artistic Culture in the Second Half of the 19th and Early 20th Century], in the anthology: *Na rubezhe vekov... Iskusstvo epokhi Moderna* [At the Turn of the Centuries... Art of the Age of Art Nouveau], Hermitage Museum, St Petersburg, 2006, pp. 99-106

Guiffrey 1911
Jules Guiffrey, 'Les Gobelins', *Le Figaro illustré*, March 1911

Guseva 2006
Natalya Guseva, 'Russkaya mebel' v stile modern' [Russian Furniture in Art Nouveau Style], in the anthology: *Na rubezhe vekov... Iskusstvo epokhi Moderna* [At the Turn of the Centuries... Art of the Age of Art Nouveau], Hermitage Museum, St Petersburg, 2006, pp. 47-70

Helsinki 1980
Carl Fabergé and his Contemporaries, exh. cat., The Museum of Applied Arts, Helsinki, 1980

Hermitage English Art 1979
The Hermitage. English Art Sixteenth to Nineteenth Century. Paintings, Sculpture, Prints and Drawings, Minor Arts, compiled and edited by Larissa Dukelskaya, Leningrad, 1979

Hilschenz-Mlynek 1985
Helga Hilschenz-Mlynek, H. Ricke, *Glas:* Bd. 1, *Frankreich, Die Sammlung Hentrich im Kunstmuseum Düsseldorf. Historismus, Jugendstil, Art Deco*, Düsseldorf-Munich, 1985

HISTORICAL ARCHIVE
RGIA (*Russkiy Gosudarstvennyy Istoricheskiy Arkhiv*, Russian Historical State Archive)

HODGE 1999
J. Hodge, *Lalique*, San Diego (CA), 1999

IVANOVA 1983
Elena N. Ivanova, 'Ob osobennostyakhh stekla masterov shkoly Nansi na materiale sobraniy Ermitazha' [On the Specific Features of Glass by Craftsmen of the School of Nancy on the Basis of Material in the Hermitage Collections], *Gosudarstvennyy Ermitazh. Prikladnoe iskusstvo Zapadnoy Evropy i Rossii. Sbornik nauchnykh trudov* [The State Hermitage. Applied Art of Western Europe and Russia. Anthology of Scholarly Papers], Leningrad, 1983, pp. 128–37

JAPAN 2006–7
Emile Gallé et les frères Daum dans la collection des derniers tsars russes, Takamatsu City Museum of Art, Kagawa; Bunkamura Museum of Art, Tokyo; Iwaki City Art Museum, Fukushima; Iwate Museum of Art, 2006 (in Japanese with some French)

KAZAKEVICH 2003
N. I. Kazakevich, *Zapadnoevropeyskiy farfor v Ermitazhe. Istoriya sobraniya* [Western European Porcelain in the Hermitage. The History of the Collection], St Petersburg, 2003

KAZAKEVITCH 2002
N. Kazakevitch [Kazakevich], 'Le vase de Nîmes, cadeau de la France au tsar Nicolas II', *Estampille / L'Objet d'art*, No. 370, June 2002, pp. 85–86

KAZAKIEWITSCH 1997
N. Kazakiewitsch [Kazakevich], 'Zur Geschichte der Porzellangalerie der Ermitage', *Keramos*, 1997, No. 158, pp. 63–76

KORSHUNOVA 2002
T. T. Korshunova, *Russkiy model'er Nadezhda Lamanova. 1861–1941* [The Russian Designer Nadezhda Lamanova. 1861–1941], exh. cat., Hermitage Museum, St Petersburg, 2002

KUHL 1905/6
M. Kuhl, 'Les tapisseries de Chéret', *L'Art et Les Artistes*, 1905/6, II

LENINGRAD 1967
Khudozhestvennoe steklo, exh. cat., Hermitage Museum, Leningrad, 1967–68

LENINGRAD 1970
Zapadnoevropeyskie veera XVIII–XIX vv. iz sobraniya Gosudarstvennogo Ermitazha [Western European Fans of the 18th–19th Centuries from the State Hermitage Collection], exh. cat., Hermitage Museum, Leningrad, 1970

LENINGRAD 1974
Prikladnoe iskusstvo kontsa XIX – nachala XX veka [Applied Art of the Late 19th to Early 20th Century], exh. cat., Hermitage Museum, Leningrad, 1974

LENINGRAD 1977
Novye postupleniya Ermitazha. 1966–1967 [New Acquisitions by the Hermitage. 1966–1967], exh. cat., Hermitage Museum, Leningrad, 1977

LENINGRAD 1979
Pamyatniki kul'tury i iskusstva priobretennye Ermitazhem v 1978–1979 godakh [Cultural and Artistic Monuments Acquired by the Hermitag ein 1978–79], exh. cat., Hermitage Museum, Leningrad, 1979

LENINGRAD 1983
Pamyatniki kul'tury i iskusstva priobretennye Ermitazhem v 1981–1982 godakh [Cultural and Artistic Monuments Acquired by the Hermitage in 1981–82], exh. cat., Hermitage Museum, Leningrad, 1983

LENINGRAD 1984
Pamyatniki kul'tury i iskusstva priobretennye Ermitazhem v 1983–1984 godakh [Cultural and Artistic Monuments Acquired by the Hermitage in 1983–84], exh. cat., Hermitage Museum, Leningrad, 1984

LENINGRAD 1985
Prikladnoe iskusstvo Italii v sobranii Ermitazha [Italian Applied Art in the Hermitage Collection], exh. cat., Hermitage Museum, Leningrad, 1985

LENINGRAD 1986
Khudozhestvennoe ubranstvo russkogo inter'era XIX veka. Ocherk-putevoditel' [Artistic Furniture in the Russian 19th-century Interior. An Essay Guide], Leningrad, 1986

LENINGRAD 1989
Velikiy Faberzhe. Iskusstvo yuvelirov pridvornoy firmy [Great Fabergé. The Art of the Court Firm's Jewellers], catalogue of the first exhibition in the USSR, Elagin Island Palace Museum, Leningrad, 1989

LEONARD 2000
Agathon Leonard. Jeu de l'Echarpe, exh. cat., Bröhan-Museum, Berlin, 2000

LIACKHOVA 2006
Lydia V. Liackhova, 'Skul'ptor Khristian Tomsen: traditsii i novatsii v khudozhestvennoy praktike kopengagenskoy Korolevskoyo farforovoy manufaktury' [The Sculptor Christian Thomsen: Traditions and Innovation in Artistic Practice at the Copenhagen Royal Porcelain Manufactory], in the anthology: *Na rubezhe vekov... Iskusstvo epokhi Moderna* [At the Turn of the Centuries... Art of the Age of Art Nouveau], Hermitage Museum, St Petersburg, 2006, pp. 107–17

Librovich 1913
S. F. Librovich, 'Skul'ptor Bernshtam i ego syn' [The Sculptor Bernstamm and his Son], *Vestník literatury* [Literary Herald], 1913, No. 12, pp. 309-15

London 2000
Art Nouveau. 1890-1914, exh. cat., Victoria and Albert Museum, London, 2000

Lopato 1984
Marina Lopato, 'Fresh light on Fabergé', *Apollo*, No. 263, January 1984

Lopato 2006
Marina N. Lopato, 'Faberzhe i modern' [Fabergé and Art Nouveau], in the anthology: *Na rubezhe vekov... Iskusstvo epokhi Moderna* [At the Turn of the Centuries... Art of the Age of Art Nouveau], Hermitage Museum, St Petersburg, 2006, pp. 89-97

Lugano 1986
Ori e argenti dall'Ermitage, exh. cat., Collection Thyssen-Bornemisza, Villa Favorita, Lugano, 1986

Minsk 1989
Zapadnoevropeyskoe príkladnoe iskusstvo XI-XX vekov iz fondov Gosudarstvennogo Ermitazha [Western European Applied Art of the XI to XX Centuries from the Stores of the State Hermitage], exh. cat. (travelling exhibition), Minsk, 1989

Moscow 2001
Bolín v Rossií. Prídvornyy yuvelír kontsa XIX – nachala XX vekov [Bolin in Russia. A Court Jeweller in the Late 19th and Early 20th Century], exh. cat., Moscow Kremlin Museums, Moscow, 2001

Munich 1986-87
Fabergé, Juwelier der Zaren, exh. cat., Kunsthalle der Hypokulturstiftung, Munich, 1986-87

Nancy 1999
L'Ecole de Nancy, 1889-1909. Art nouveau et industries d'art, exh. cat., Galeries Poirel, Nancy, Paris, 1999

Nicholas & Alexandra 1998
Nicolas and Alexandra. The Last Imperial Family of Tsarist Russia. From the State Hermitage Museum and The State Archive of the Russian Federation, London, 1998

Paris 1985-86
Gallé, exh. cat., compiled and edited by F.-Th. Charpentier and Ph. Thiébaut, Musée du Luxembourg, Paris, 1985-86; Paris, 1985

Paris 1989
Tapisseries, Avec la participation exceptionelle du Musée de l'Ermitage, Yves Mikaeloeff, Paris, 1989

Petry s.a.
Claude Petry, *Daum dans les Musées de Nancy*, Nancy, s.a.

Pforzheim 1995-96
Zarengold: 100 kostbarkeiten der Goldschmiedekunst aus der Staatlichen Eremitage St.Petersburg. Die Gilde der ausländischen Meister, exh. cat., Schmuckmuseum Pforzheim, 1995-96; Stuttgart, 1995

Rappe 1983
T. Rappe, 'Novoe o frantsuzskoy firme Eskal'ye de Kristal' [New Information About the French Firm L'Escalier de Cristal', in the anthology: *Zapadnoevropeyskoe i russkoe iskusstvo* [Western European and Russian Art], pp. 120-27

Rappe 1991
T. V. Rappe, 'Pamyatniki russko-frantsuzskikh svyazey poslednego desyatiletiya XIX veka' [Monuments of Russo-French Relations in the Last Decade of the 19th Century], *Soobshcheniya Gosudarstvennogo Ermitazha* [Proceedings of the State Hermitage], issue LV, 1991

Rappe 2006
T. V. Rappe, 'Istoriya formirovaniya kollektsii evropeyskogo moderna v Ermitazhe' [History of the Formation of the Hermitage Collection of European Art Nouveau], in the anthology: *Na rubezhe vekov... Iskusstvo epokhi moderna* [At the Turn of the Centuries. Art of the Age of Art Nouveau], Hermitage Museum, St Petersburg, 2006

Ricke, Schmitt 2004
Helmut Ricke, Eva Schmitt, *Art Nouveau Glass. The Gerda Koepff Collection*, Munich-Berlin-London-New York, 2004

St Petersburg 1994
Nikolay i Aleksandra. Dvor posledníkh russkíkh imperatorov. Konets XIX – nachalo XX v. [Nicholas and Alexandra. The Court of the Last Russian Emperors. Late 19th – Early 20th Century], exh. cat., Hermitage Museum, St Petersburg, 1994

St Petersburg 1996
Istorizm v Rossií. Stil' i epokha v dekoratívnom iskusstve. 1820-e – 1890-e gody [Historicism in Russia. Style and Era in the Decorative Arts. 1820s-1890s], exh. cat., Hermitage Museum, St Petersburg, 1996

St Petersburg 1997
Novye postuplenie. Pamyatníki kul'tury i iskusstva, priobretennye Ermitazhem v 1992-1996 godakh [New Acquisitions. Cultural and Artistic Monuments Acquired by the Hermitage in 1992-96], exh. cat., Hermitage Museum, St Petersburg, 1997

St Petersburg 1999
Emil' Galle i Brat'ya Dom. "Lotaringskie Orkhidei..." [Emile Gallé and the Brothers Daum. "Lotharingian Orchids"], exh. cat., Hermitage Museum, St Petersburg, 1999

St Petersburg 2004
Imperatorskiy Steklyannyy zavod. 1777-1917 [The Imperial Glass Manufactory. 1777-1917], exh. cat., Hermitage Museum, St Petersburg, 2004

ST PETERSBURG 2005
Vena i Budapesht na rubezhe vekov. 1870-1920-e gg. [Vienna and Budapest at the Turn of the Centuries. 1870s-1920s], exh. cat., Hermitage Museum, St Petersburg, 2005

ST PETERSBURG-MOSCOW-STOCKHOLM 2000
Dragotsennosti i serebro. V. A. Bolin – 200 let [Jewels and Silver. V. A. Bolin – 200], Hermitage Museum, St Petersburg; Armoury Museum, Moscow; Nationalmuseum, Stockholm, 2000

ST PETERSBURG-PARIS-LONDON 1993
Géza von Habsburg, Marina Lopato, *Fabergé: Imperial Jeweller,* exh. cat., Hermitage, St Petersburg; Fabergé Arts Foundation, Paris; London, 1993

ST PETERSBURG-PARIS-MOSCOW 1992
The Fabulous Epoch of Fabergé, Exhibition at the Catherine Palace in Tsarskoe Selo, St Petersburg-Paris-Moscow, 1992

SCHIZUOKA 2005
'Life with Flowers'. Masterpieces from the State Hermitage Museum, exh. cat., Prefectural Museum of Art, Schizuoka, 2005 (in Japanese)

SEVERYUKHIN 1993
D. Ya. Severyukhin, 'Lyubimyy skul'ptor gosudarya' [The Sovereign's Favourite Sculptor], *Nevskiy arkhiv. Istoriko-kraevedcheskiy sbornik* [Nevsky Archive. A Historical and Local Historical Archive], St Petersburg, 1993, pp. 246-59

SHELKOVNIKOV 1962
B. A. Shelkovnikov, *Khudozhestvennoe steklo* [Artistic Glass], Leningrad, 1962

SHELKOVNIKOV 1967
B. A. Shelkovnikov, 'Russian Glass in the Second Half of the Nineteenth Century', *Journal of Glass Studies,* IX, New York, 1967

SOKOLOVA 1973
T. M. Sokolova, K. A. Orlova, Russkaya mebel' v Gosudarstvennom Ermitazhe [Russian Furniture in the State Hermitage], Leningrad, 1973

SOREZ 1898
Zh. Sorez, 'Podarok gorodov Lotaringii Aleksandru III' [A Gift from the Towns of Lotharingia to Alexander III, 1898, Nos. 1-2

SPEYER 1994
Der Zarenschatz der Romanov. Meisterwerke aus der Eremitage St. Petersburg, exh. cat., Historisches Museum der Pfalz, Speyer, 1994

STIEGLITZ MUSEUM 1994
Muzey barona Shtiglitsa. Proshloe i nastoyashchee [The Museum of Baron Stieglitz. Past and Present], St Petersburg, 1994

STOCKHOLM 1997
Carl Fabergé. Goldsmith to the Tsar, exh. cat., Nationalmuseum, Stockholm, 1997

LE TACON 1998
F. le Tacon, *L'Oeuvre de verre d'Emile Gallé,* Paris, 1998

TEZI, ROTENSTERN 1909
A. Tezi, P. I. Rotenstern, 'V masterskoy skul'ptora Bernshtama' [In the Studio of the Sculpture Bernstamm], *V mire iskusstv* [In the World of the Arts], 1909, No. 19, p. 8-10

TOKYO-KOBE-GUNMA 2003
Sèvres Porcelain from The Hermitage Museum, exh. cat., Mitsukoshi Gallery in Main Store, Nihombashi, Tokyo; Daimaru Museum Kobe; Museum of Modern Art, Gunma, 2003

USA 1998-2001
Nicholas and Alexandra: The Last Imperial Family of Tsarist Russia, Wilmington, Delaware; Mobile, Alabama; San Diego, California; 1998-2001

VACHON S.A.
M. Vachon, *Les Marins Russes en France,* Paris, s.a.

VILENSKY 2006
J. Vilensky, '"Tanets s sharfami" v Ermitazhe' ['The Dance with Scarves' in the Hermitage], in the anthology: *Na rubezhe vekov... Iskusstvo epokhi Moderna* [At the Turn of the Centuries... Art of the Age of Art Nouveau], Hermitage Museum, St Petersburg, 2006, pp. 129-36

YAKOVLEVA 2004
L. A. Yakovleva, 'Rene-Zhyul' Lalik i ego proizvedeniya v Ermitazhe' [René-Jules Lalique and his Works in the Hermitage], *Soobshcheniya Gosudarstvennogo Ermitazha* [Reports of the State Hermitage], LXI, St Petersburg, 2004

ZURICH 1989
Carl Fabergé. Kostbarkeiten russischer Goldschmiedekunst der Jahrhundertwende, exh. cat., Museum Bellerive, Zurich, 1989

FURTHER RECOMMENDED READING:

Ian Bennett, *Eastern Europe, Phaidon encyclopaedia of Decorative Arts 1890-1940,* Oxford, 1978

William Brumfield, 'The Decorative Arts in Russian architecture: 1900-1907', *The Journal of Decorative and Propaganda Arts,* Summer 1987

Wendy Salmond, *Moscow modern,* Art Nouveau Catalogue, 1890-1914, V&A publications, London, 2000

Colophon

Editors
Vincent Boele (editor-in-chief)
Arnoud Bijl

Coördination
Heleen van Ketwich Verschuur

Authors
Elena Anisimova
Natalya Guseva
Frans Leidelmeijer
Marina Lopato
Tamara Rappe

Authors of the catalogue
Ekaterina Abramova (E.Ab.)
Elena Anisimova (E.A.)
Nina Biryukova (N.B.)
Anna Geyko (A.G.)
Natalya Guseva (N.G.)
Elena Ivanova (E.I.)
Ekaterina Khmelnitskaya (E.Kh.)
Tamara Korshunova (T.K.)
Olga Kostyuk (O.K.)
Lydia Liackhova (L.L.)
Marina Lopato (M.L.)
Tamara Malinina (T.M.)
Nadezhda Petrusevich (N.P.)
Sergey Plotnikov (S.P.)
Tamara Rappe (T.R.)
Tatyana Semyonova (T.S.)
Evelina Tarasova (E.T.)
Jan Vilensky (J.V.)

Photography
Yuri Molodkovets
Konstantin Sinyavsky
Svetlana Suetova

Translations
Arnoud Bijl (*ru-nl*)
Michele Hendricks (*nl-en*)
Catherine Phillips (*ru-en*)

Graphic Design
Artgrafica, Amsterdam

DTP
Zeeman & Beemster, Amsterdam

Print
Waanders Drukkers, Zwolle

Catalogue for the exhibition *Art Nouveau under the last Tsars*, from 13 October 2007 till 5 May 2008, organised by the State Hermitage Museum in St Petersburg and the Hermitage Amsterdam.

ISBN 978-0-85331-987-0

Published by
Lund Humphries
Gower House
Croft Road
Aldershot
Hampshire GU11 3HR
United Kingdom

and

Lund Humphries
Suite 420
101 Cherry Street
Burlington
VT 05401-4405
USA

Lund Humphries is part of Ashgate Publishing

www.lundhumphries.com

British Library Cataloguing-in-Publication Data
A catalogue record for this book is available from the British Library

Library of Congress Control Number:
2007936900

COLOPHON *of the exhibition*
ART NOUVEAU UNDER THE LAST TSARS

Exhibition Committee

STATE HERMITAGE MUSEUM, ST PETERSBURG

PROFESSOR DR. MIKHAIL PIOTROVSKY
Director

PROFESSOR DR. GEORGE VILINBAKHOV
Deputy director

DR. VLADIMIR MATVEEV
Deputy director

DR. TAMARA RAPPE
Head of the Department of West European Decorative Art

HERMITAGE AMSTERDAM

ERNST W. VEEN
Director

CATHELIJNE BROERS
Deputy director

FRANS VAN DER AVERT
Head of Communication, Education & Marketing

PIETER VAN EMPELEN
Project director Hermitage phase II

MARLIES KLEITERP
Head of Exhibitions

Concept of the Exhibition

TAMARA RAPPE
Head of the Department of West European Decorative Art

ELENA ANISIMOVA
Curator of the Department of West European Decorative Art

VINCENT BOELE
Curator of Exhibitions, Hermitage Amsterdam

ARNOUD BIJL
Assistant Exhibitions, Hermitage Amsterdam

Coördination St Petersburg

SVETLANA PHILIPPOVA
Representative State Hermitage Museum
SWETLANA DATSENKO
Representative Hermitage Amsterdam

Special advisor to Hermitage Amsterdam

FRANS LEIDELMEIJER
Specialist 20th Century Decorative Art

Restoration & Conservation

The restoration of the exhibition items was prepared in the Conservation laboratories of the Department of Scientific Restoration of the State Hermitage Museum by

TATYANA BARANOVA

Exhibition Design

KINKORN, TILBURG

Light

JOOST DE BEIJ, ZALTBOMMEL

Graphic Design

ARTGRAFICA, AMSTERDAM

Packing & Transport

KHEPRI LTD, ST PETERSBURG

JAN KORTMANN ART PACKERS & SHIPPERS, AMSTERDAM

With thanks to

FILMMUSEUM AMSTERDAM

BETTY MAN

HERMITAGE AMSTERDAM

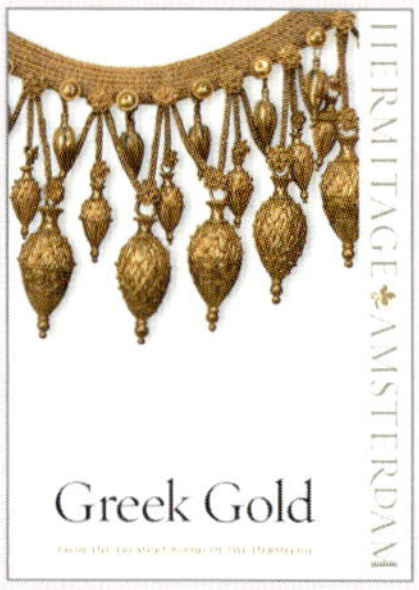

GREEK GOLD
ISBN 978-0-85331-924-5

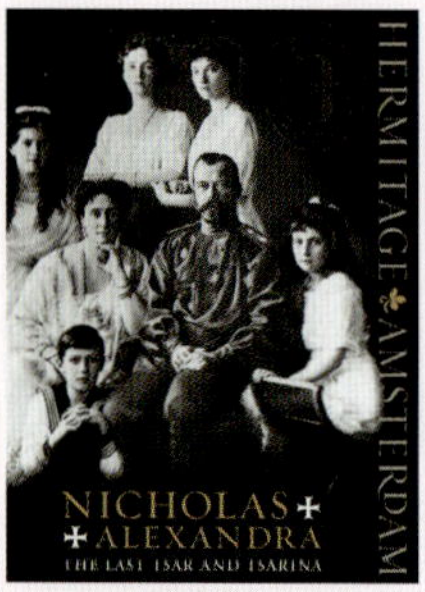

NICHOLAS & ALEXANDRA
ISBN 978-0-85331-925-2

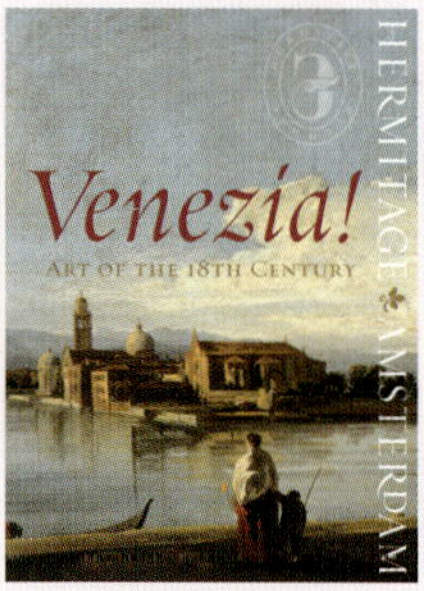

VENEZIA!
ISBN 978-0-85331-927-6

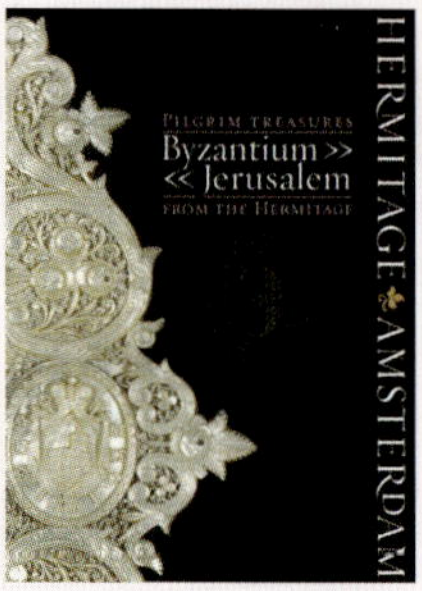

BYZANTIUM-JERUSALEM
ISBN 978-0-85331-939-9

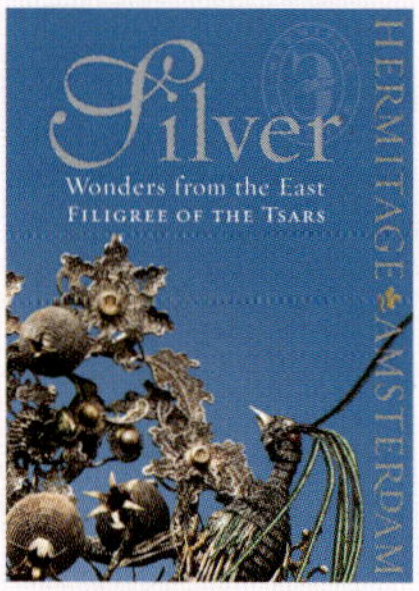

SILVER
ISBN 978-0-85331-948-1

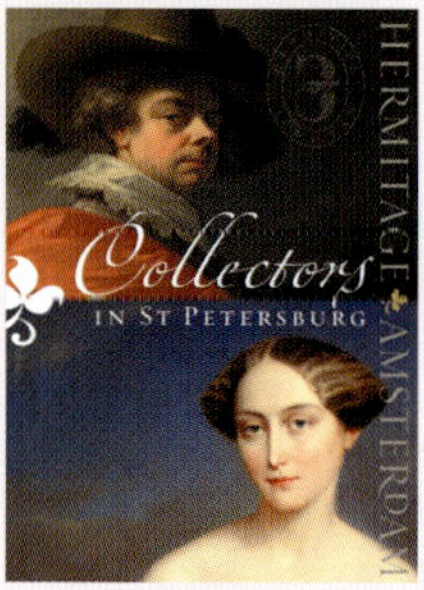

COLLECTORS
ISBN 978-0-85331-960-3

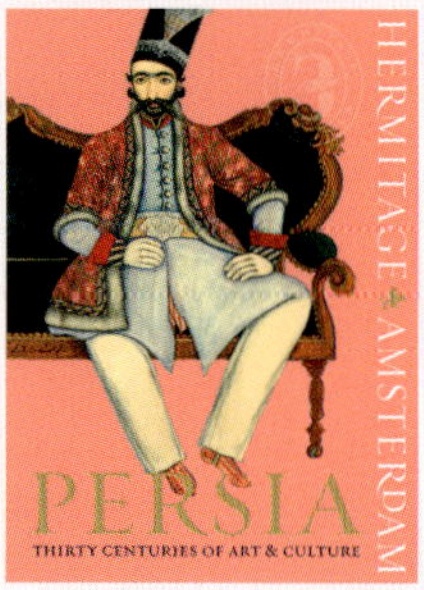

PERSIA
ISBN 978-0-85331-973-3

HERMITAGE AMSTERDAM
NIEUWE HERENGRACHT 14
AMSTERDAM

P.O. BOX 11675
1001 GR AMSTERDAM

TELEPHONE: 020 - 530 87 55
INFORMATIONNBR.: 020 - 530 87 51
FAX: 020 - 530 87 50
INFO@HERMITAGE.NL

Information about Lund Humphries
can be found on
WWW.LUNDHUMPHRIES.COM

Information about Hermitage Amsterdam
can be found on
WWW.HERMITAGE.NL

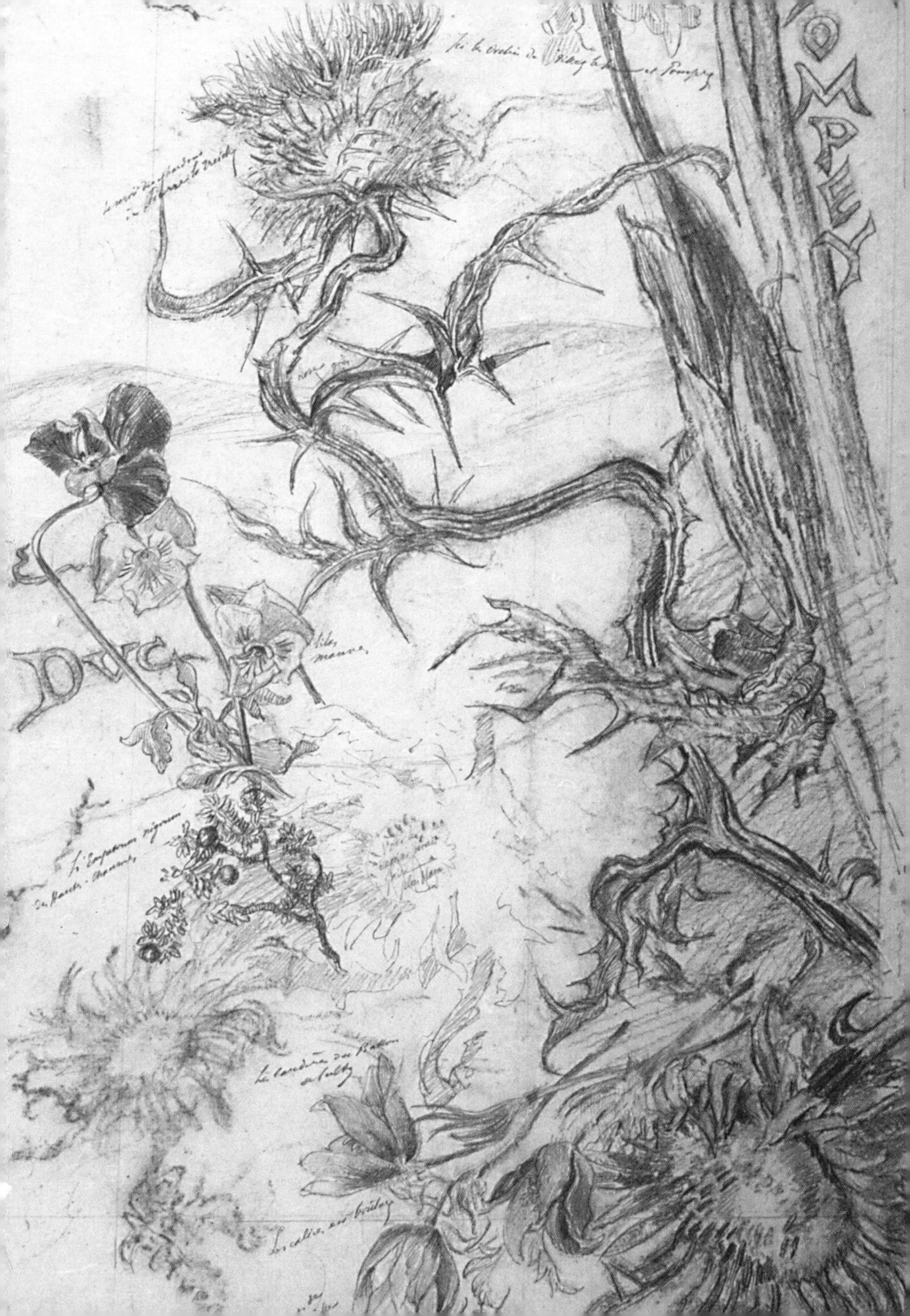

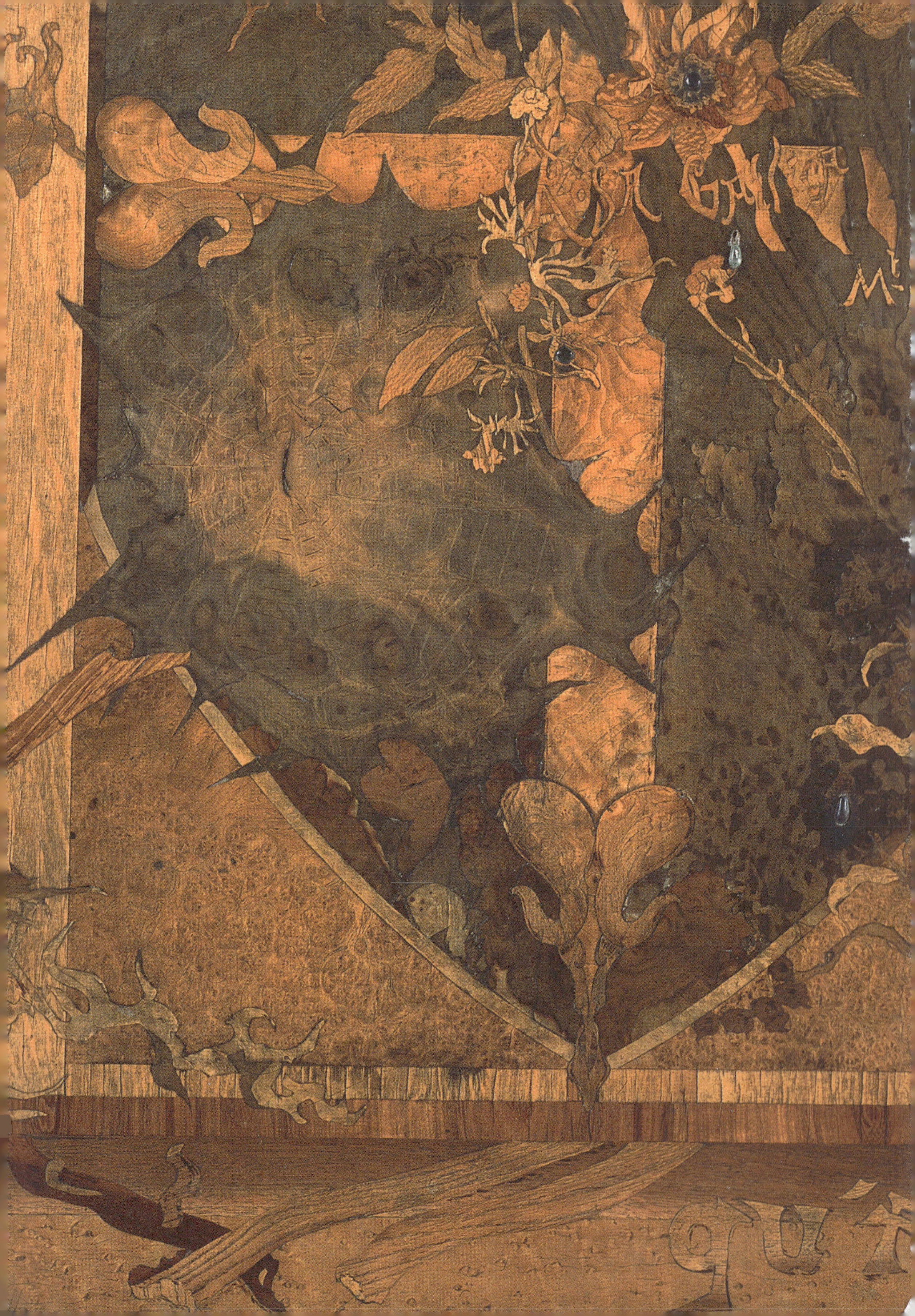